KILGORE **RANGERETTES**

1 **HORSE PERFORMANCE** 1989

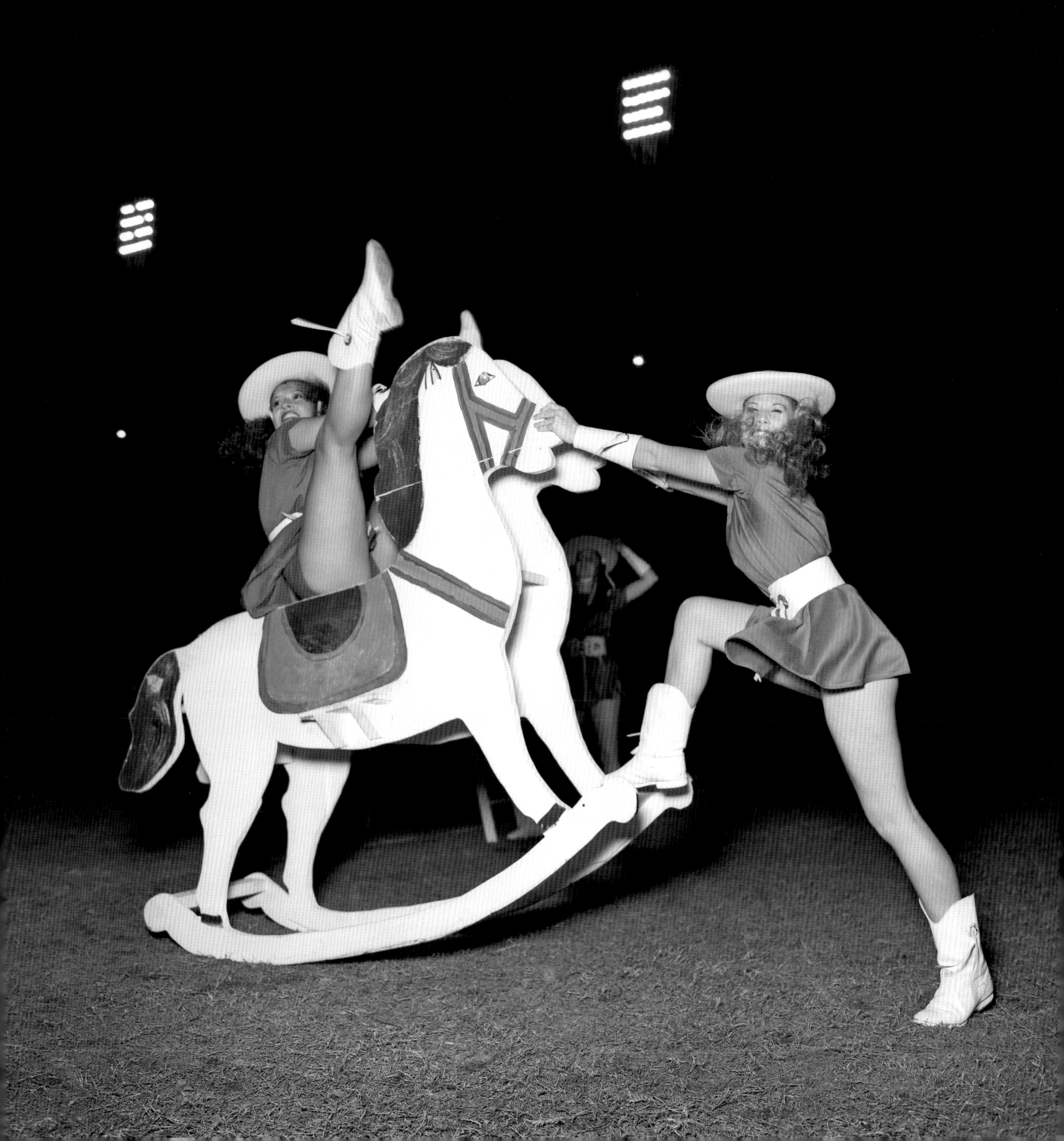

KILG
RANGE

PHOTOGRAPHS BY **O. RUFUS LOVETT** FOREWORD BY **ELLIOTT ERWIT**

ORE

RETTES

NTRODUCTION BY **KATY VINE** UNIVERSITY OF TEXAS PRESS, AUSTIN

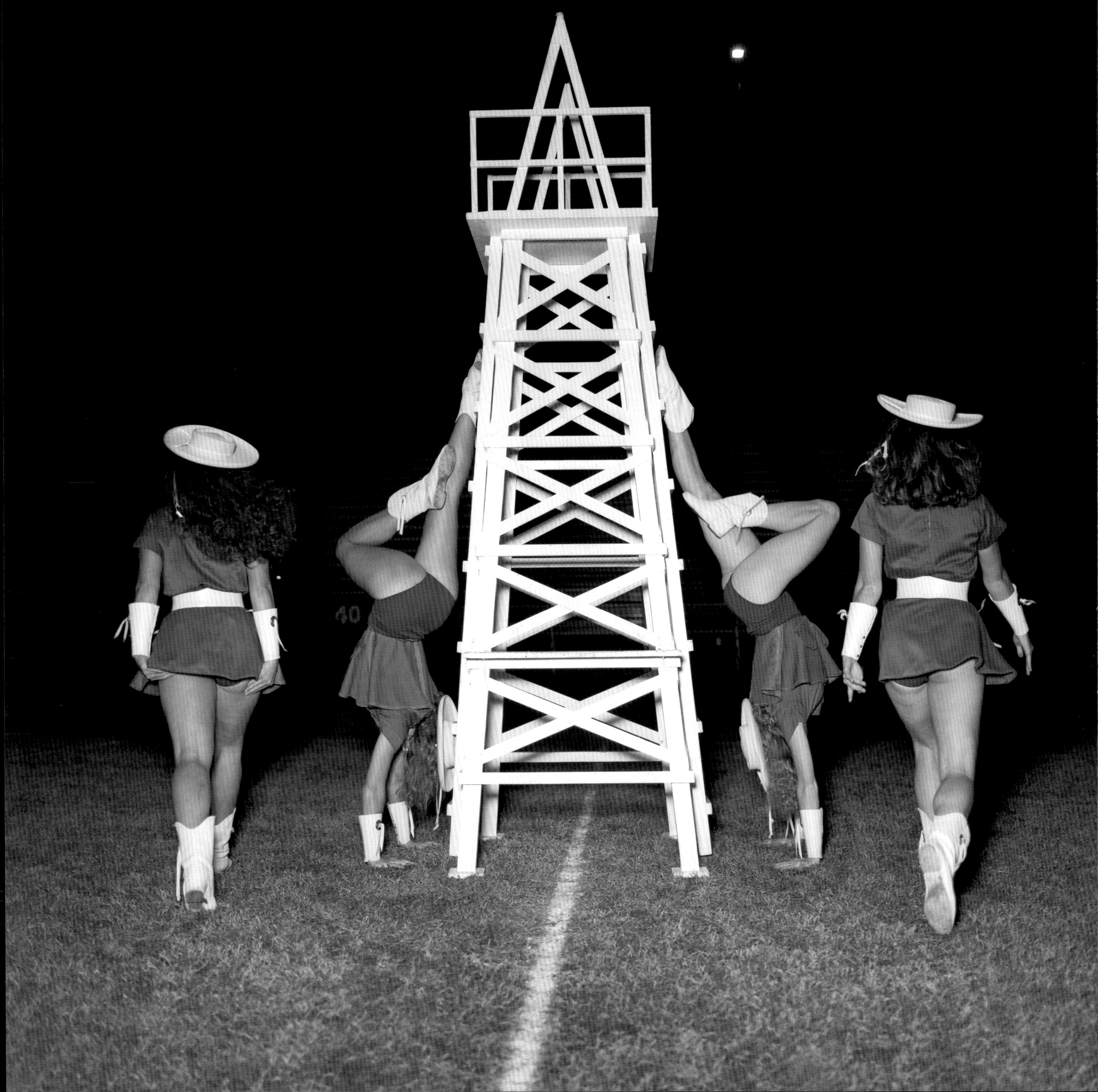

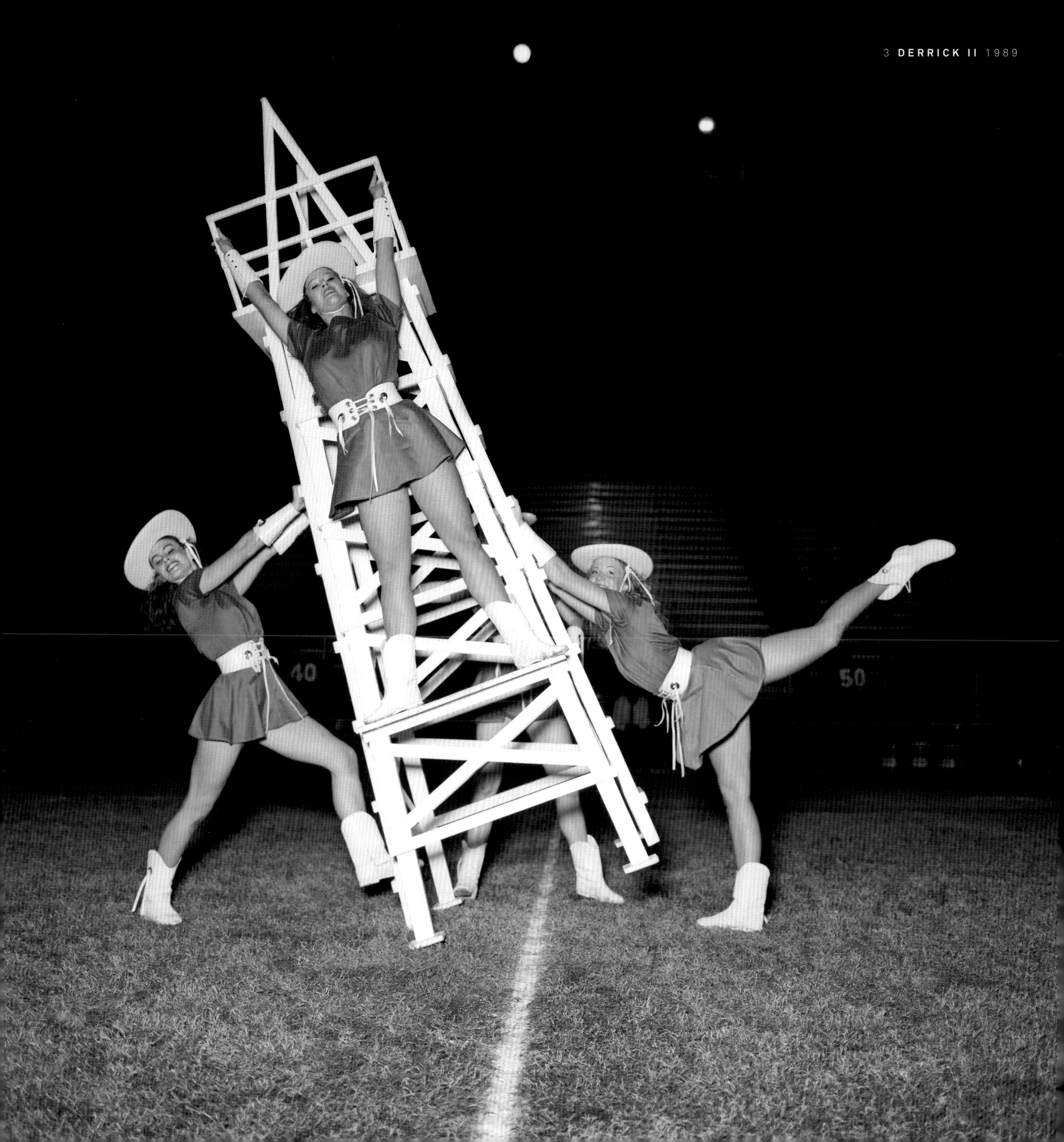
40
50

NUMBER THIRTEEN

CLIFTON AND SHIRLEY CALDWELL TEXAS HERITAGE SERIES

Publication of this work was made possible in part by Clifton and Shirley Caldwell, Richard and Martha Rorschach, and a challenge grant from the National Endowment for the Humanities.

Printed in China
First edition, 2008

♾ The paper used in this book meets the minimum requirements of
ANSI/NISO Z39.48-1992 (R1997) (Permanence of Paper).

Library of Congress Cataloging-in-Publication Data
Lovett, O. Rufus, 1952–
Kilgore Rangerettes / photographs by O. Rufus Lovett ; foreword by Elliott Erwitt ;
introduction by Katy Vine. — 1st ed.
p. cm. — (Clifton and Shirley Caldwell Texas heritage series ; no. 13)
ISBN 978-0-292-71673-5 (cloth : alk. paper)
1. Kilgore College. Rangerettes—Pictorial works.
2. Marching drills—Texas—Pictorial works.
3. Cheerleading—Texas—Pictorial works.
4. Dancers—Texas—Pictorial works.
5. Dance photography. I. Vine, Katy. II. Title.
GV1797.L887 2008
791.6409764'189—dc22
2008001832

Book and jacket design by DJ Stout and Julie Savasky, Pentagram, Austin

FOR OUR PARENTS

LAU KEN
SHUM KING SHEUNG

OPAL RUFUS LOVETT
OPAL DOLORES LOVETT

BEAUTY KNOWS NO PAIN

ELLIOTT ERWITT

In 1963, soon after the assassination of President Kennedy, European publishers developed a keen interest in Texas. I was assigned to produce a photo-essay on the subject for *Paris Match,* which at the time was the most important French picture magazine—as *Life* magazine once was in the United States. These were the golden days of picture magazines, before television came along and killed the craft of the thoughtful extended photo-essay.

My brief was to travel the state and just take pictures. They wanted me to shoot anything Texan, capturing images that would somehow describe the place and its atmosphere, and perhaps present a contrast with the stereotypical and mythical image portrayed in Western shoot-'em-up movies, with cowboys wearing big hats and toting six-shooters.

My travels took me far and wide, from Dallas to Corpus Christi to Odessa to Amarillo to Houston and onward. I met ordinary people (only a few wearing six-shooters), and some extraordinary ones. Among the latter were the legendary Ima Hogg and Oveta Culp Hobby. I was Mrs. Hobby's houseguest; at her kind invitation, I slept in the General George Marshall room of her beautiful home. It was Mrs. Hobby—the powerful Texan who was the head of the WACs during World War II and also publisher of the major Texas newspaper, the *Houston Post*—who helped me formulate an itinerary, and who turned me on to the town of Kilgore and the wonders of the Rangerettes.

My first visit to Kilgore was in 1963, when the former boomtown, once famous for its oil wells, was still a visual wonder, replete with spent oil derricks left standing as monuments to a past time. This was my first introduction to the Rangerettes, the extraordinary precision dance team that was founded by the incomparable Gussie Nell Davis almost seventy years ago, and whose modest competitors, the Apache Belles of Tyler Junior College, were just a few miles "down the road." (Everything in Texas is just a few miles down the road, whether 50 or 500 miles away.) On that visit I took still photographs of the current Rangerettes corps, and thought then that the subject was alluring enough to merit more than a few snaps in a foreign magazine. It would make a wonderful subject for an extended book on the tough process of how young hopefuls earn their stripes.

The visit made a deep impression on me that persisted for years, and I vowed to return and examine the subject in greater depth. I won't say that the Rangerette revelation was a turning point in my photographic life, but it came close. I was captured by the enthusiasm, energy, and discipline of these attractive young women, who went about their training with incredible discipline, competing for a spot on the line in which they would perform during the halftimes of important football games.

I went back to Kilgore, as I had promised myself I would, just before Christmas in 1971—in time to see the oil derricks festooned with blinking lights and decorations. I had decided to make a documentary based on the Rangerette slogan "beauty knows no pain." My film was completed in 1972 and has had wide distribution, including a national broadcast on the CBS program *60 Minutes* in 1973. But, happily, we now have an up-to-date volume by the very fine photographer O. Rufus Lovett, who has profoundly lived and recorded the Rangerette experience. That wonderfully crafted book is now in your hands.

I suspect that modernity or fashion has not now changed, nor will it ever change, the way of life of the Rangerettes. Some Rangerette graduates have had daughters, and perhaps by now even granddaughters and great-granddaughters, follow in their high-stepping footsteps. The tradition will continue. When a great tradition is deeply rooted and special, it endures, and no one dares mess with it.

September 2007

4 **MARIE I** 1989

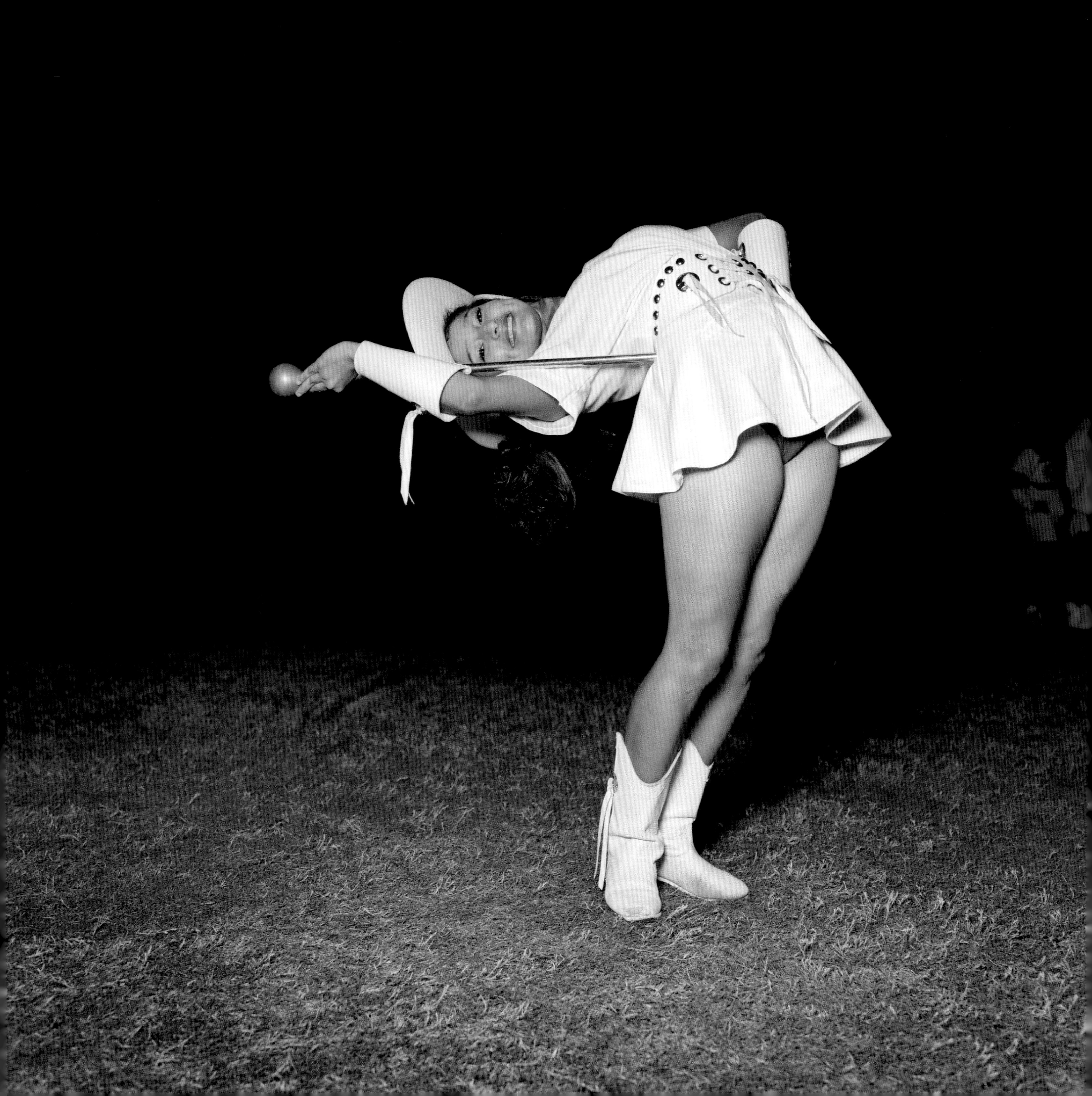

5 **MARIE II** 1989

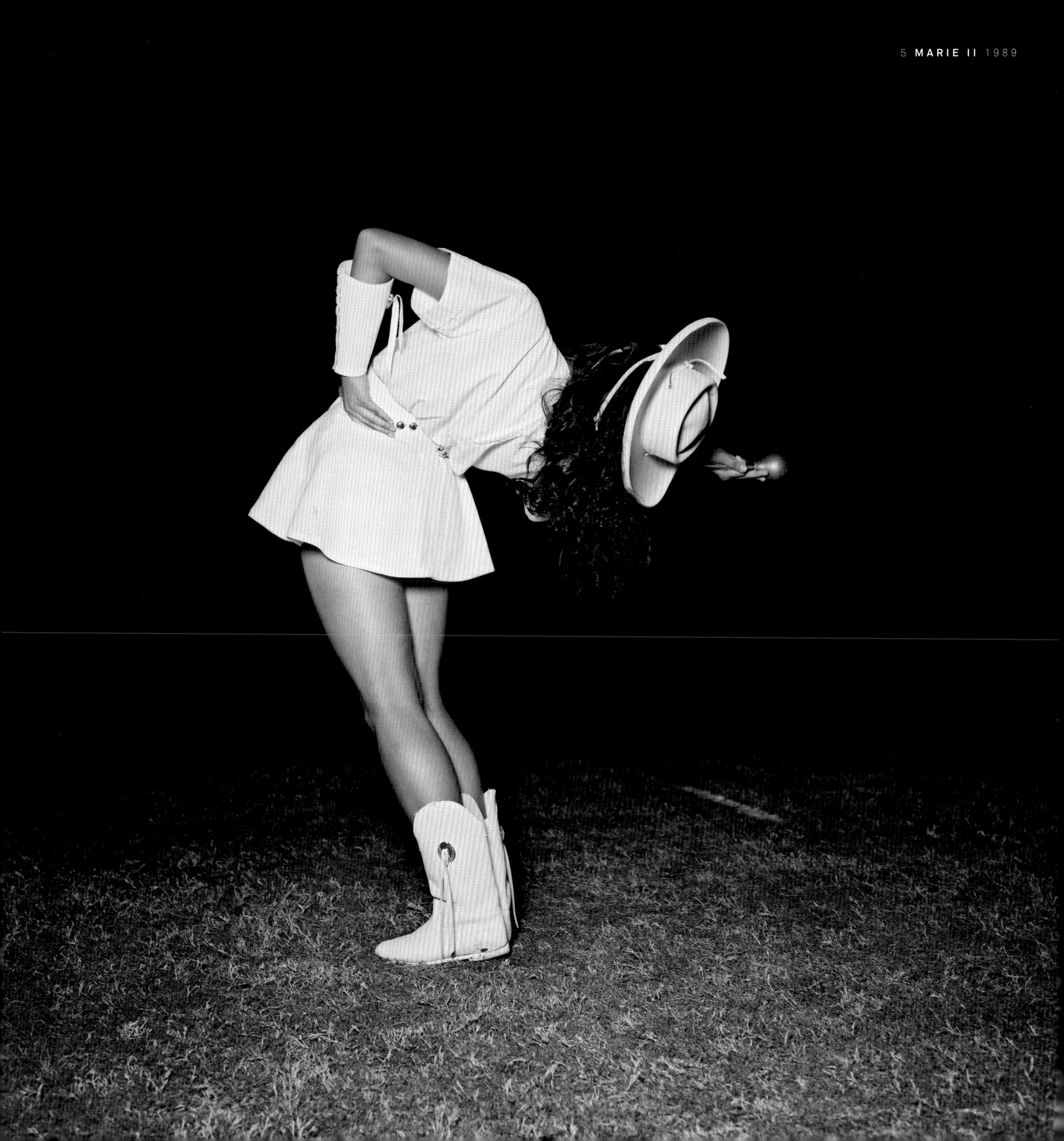

INTRODUCTION
KATY VINE

The kick is the trademark. Performed from Hong Kong to the local Brookshire Brothers grocery store, the girls' kick looks effortless, as if some unseen puppeteer were tugging their smooth, perfectly straight legs into the air with marionette strings. But the kick is not effortless. Girls have bloodied their own noses with the kick.

O. Rufus introduced me to Rangerette culture in 2004. Having been dispatched by *Texas Monthly* to write about the summer tryouts, I went behind what one local called "the pine curtain" of East Texas to this town of roughly 12,000, where girls dream big just as the oil wildcatters before them did. Here, stunningly fresh-faced beauties can have a pure drill team existence, like a dance tour of duty. One Kilgore College staffer attempted to prepare me for the spectacle. Watching the Rangerettes perform to the school's fight song, she said, was an experience so powerful "it will make your hair stand on end."

But my imagination didn't do the team justice. When Rufus called me after my first day with the girls on campus, he wasn't surprised to find me speechless. They looked like a handful of candies. During the weeks I visited, they color-coordinated their daily wardrobe in a way that allowed for individual interpretation—stripes, polka dots, solids—while maintaining unity across the squad. They are determined to show enthusiasm for everything. Primarily, they show enthusiasm for the Rangerettes themselves. They sing to each other, dance with each other, laugh loudly, and stomp on the ground to show how much fun they're having. The group lives together in a $3.75-million-dollar dorm, leaving each other only on weekends, when they drive back to their hometowns since there is little entertainment in Kilgore. There is no mall, as anyone in town will quickly point out; shopping at the Super Wal-Mart is considered the sole leisure activity, besides seeing a movie at the four-screen theater.

The group's devotion has sprouted legends. While they love their current director, Dana Blair, like a mother, and respect her predecessor, Deana Bolton Covin, they reserve their worship for Gussie Nell Davis, who formed the Rangerettes—the world's very first drill team—in 1940, and is therefore idolized around campus in the form of T-shirts, photos, even a bronze bust. Stories abound about the demands of this petite drill sergeant in four-inch heels. Once, when a Rangerette fainted on the field, Ms. Davis stomped up to her and yelled, "I have no time for this! Get up!" She expected the girls to be polished and flawless, by God, and not just in performances. They would learn manners. They would say, "Yes ma'am, thank you, ma'am," and they would open doors for others. Beyond mere drill team perfection, ideal womanhood was the goal. "By the time I was through with [my girls], they were scared to death to act like heathens," Ms. Davis once said.

Some might find the institution antiquated—an ambitious, aggressively anachronistic fixture in a town not recently known for audacity. And yet nearly one hundred "hopefuls" flock to Kilgore each year to attempt to become one of the thirty-some girls selected for the freshman squad. Since the team is all about positivity, they call these tryouts "pre-training." Those who are chosen will be an extension to the elite line of ambassadors who uphold the group's values. Grace, beauty, charm, discipline, optimism, endurance, and precision under pressure have guided many Rangerettes through hard times, said one former member, "even if it was difficult to understand that not everybody strives for perfection." So if their dedication seems a little fanatical, it must be remembered that the Rangerettes are not just about the kick. Not hardly.

One need not look very hard to find their principles at work. After a week with the Rangerettes, you wouldn't be fazed to hear one of them say, "I had the opportunity to jump-split onto the thirty-degree pavement in the parade!" I watched girls strut through dance performances with such confidence you could hardly tell that one had mono, or that another had just thrown up in the middle of the routine. If their code "beauty knows no pain" leaves you scratching your head, they'll give you another saying: "You can't understand it from the outside, and you can't explain it from the inside." No doubt this mysterious slogan has lured many a young girl. One hopeful told me, "They've got all kinds of secrets, like I don't think freshmen are allowed to wear colored hair clips. See that one? She's wearing a colored hair clip, but she's a sophomore. There's other stuff—I don't know what. That's why you want to get in."

Having existed for almost seventy years, the Rangerettes inevitably have experienced a little change. The modern All-American girl is no fuddy-duddy—anyway, many young women couldn't pick the wholesome icon Sandra Dee out of a lineup, let alone former Rangerette Alice Lon, the Champagne Lady whom Lawrence Welk fired for showing her knees. Who is considered All-American these days? Reese Witherspoon, Julia Roberts, and Sandra Bullock fit the bill, the girls told me, debating a little about Britney Spears before knocking her off the list. Each new generation's interpretation of the girl next door leaves some traditionalists puzzled. One former Rangerette from way back told me, "I think Gussie Nell was more of a drill team instructor and Mrs. Bolton remained in that spirit. Now they've modernized it to where they're shaking—well, I don't care for modern dance."

Now, about the skirts. They know. Despite the cheesecake appeal, however, men aren't the ideal audience for the Rangerettes. The most appreciative audience is that tough group of critics: those who have worn the boots, the hat, the skirt. They may have become accountants, physicians' assistants, schoolteachers, attorneys. They may have become Dallas Cowboys Cheerleaders or drill team instructors, spreading the word about the Rangerettes like missionaries so that girls can grow up not able to remember a time when they didn't know about the organization. Most former members say that being part of the Rangerettes was the best experience of their lives. And, really, after looking at these photos, would you doubt them?

October 2007

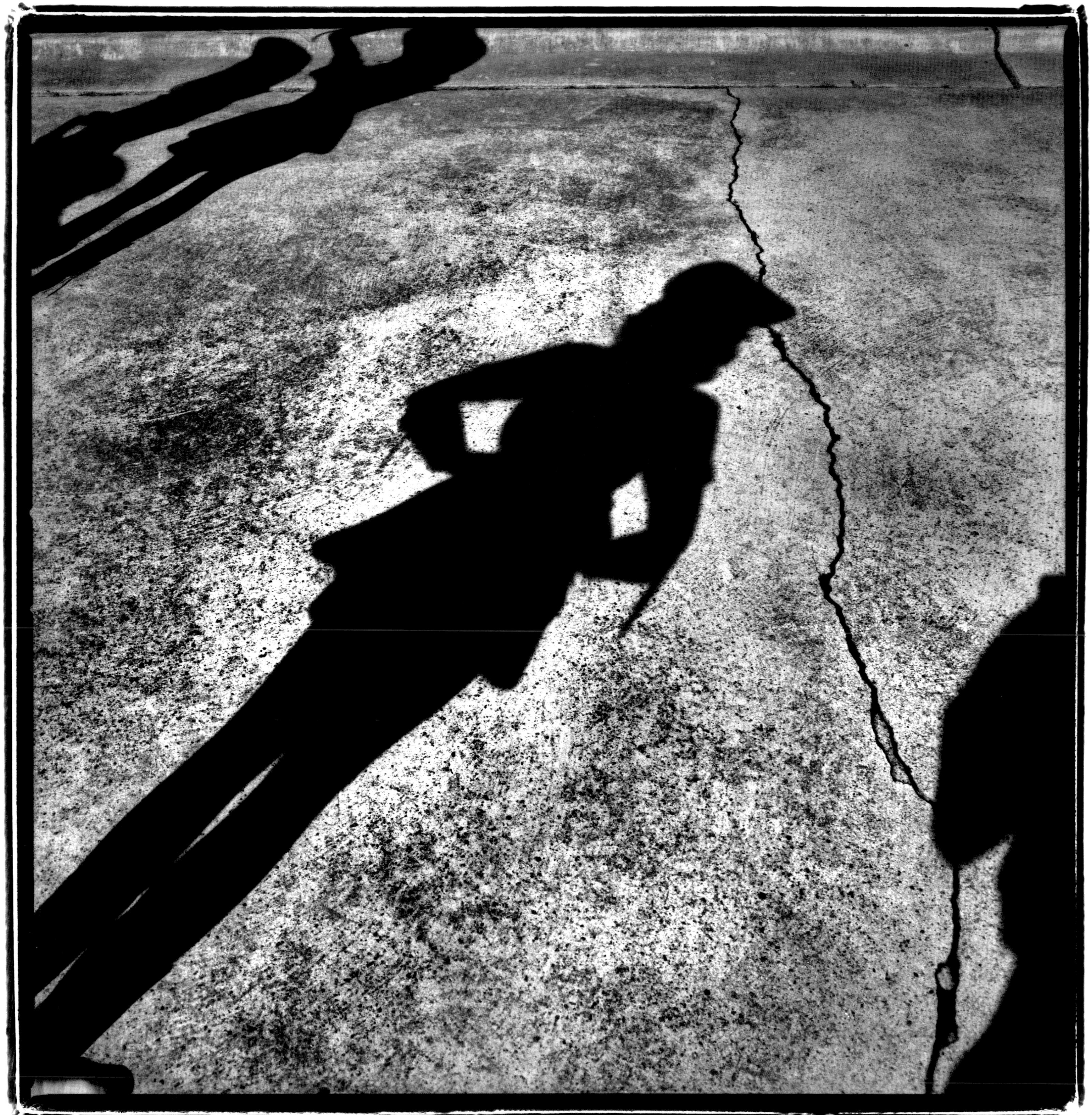

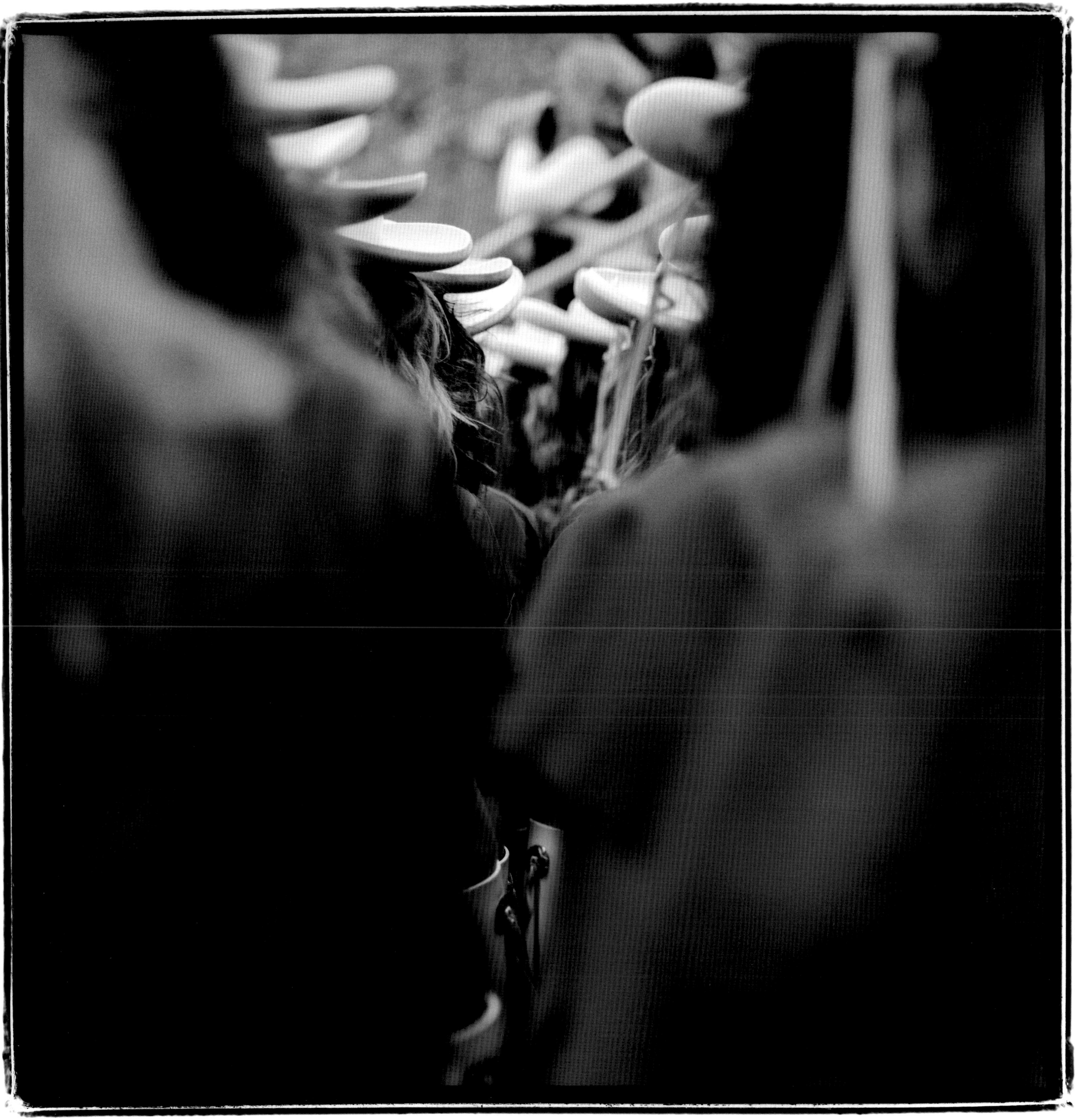

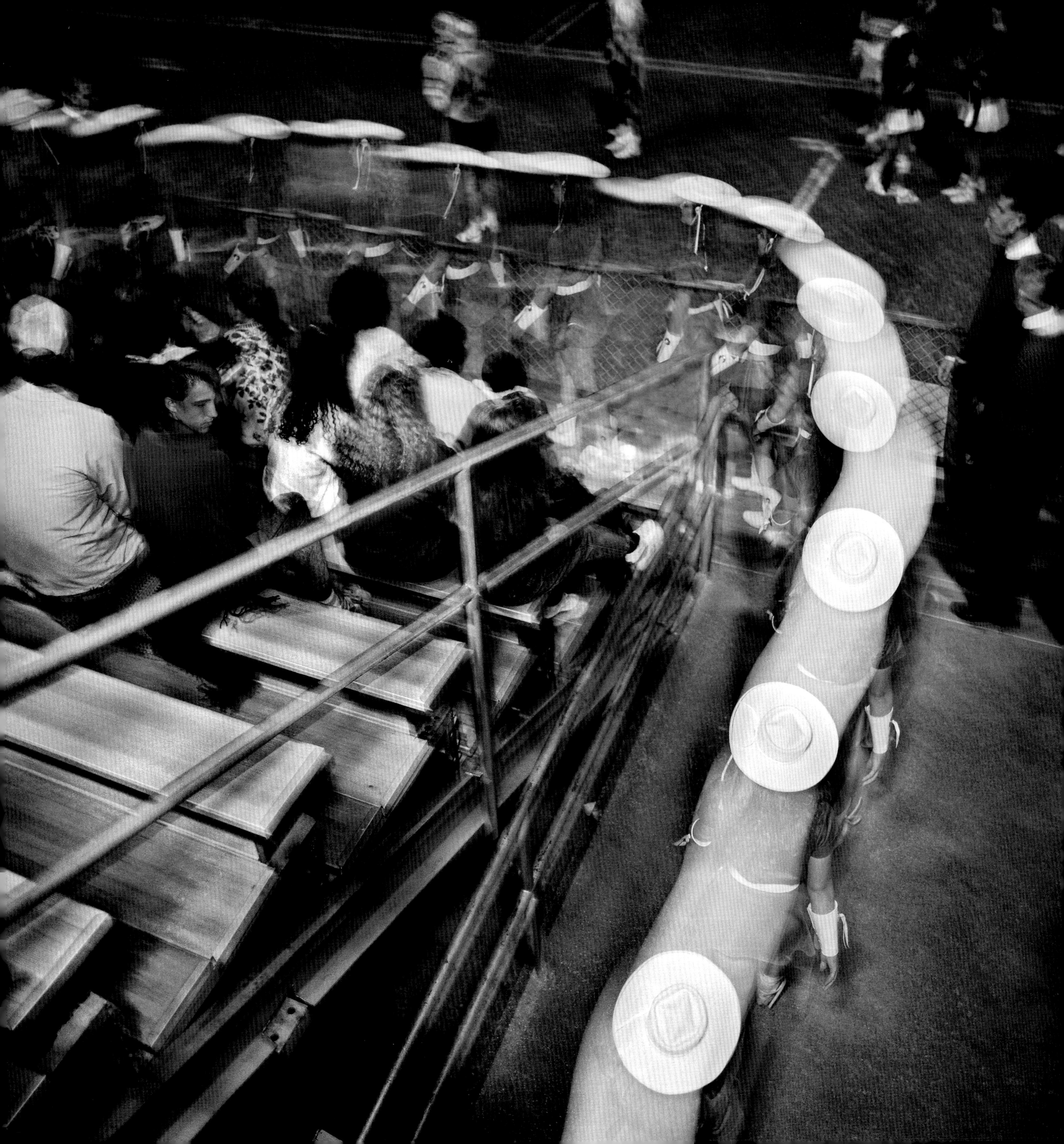

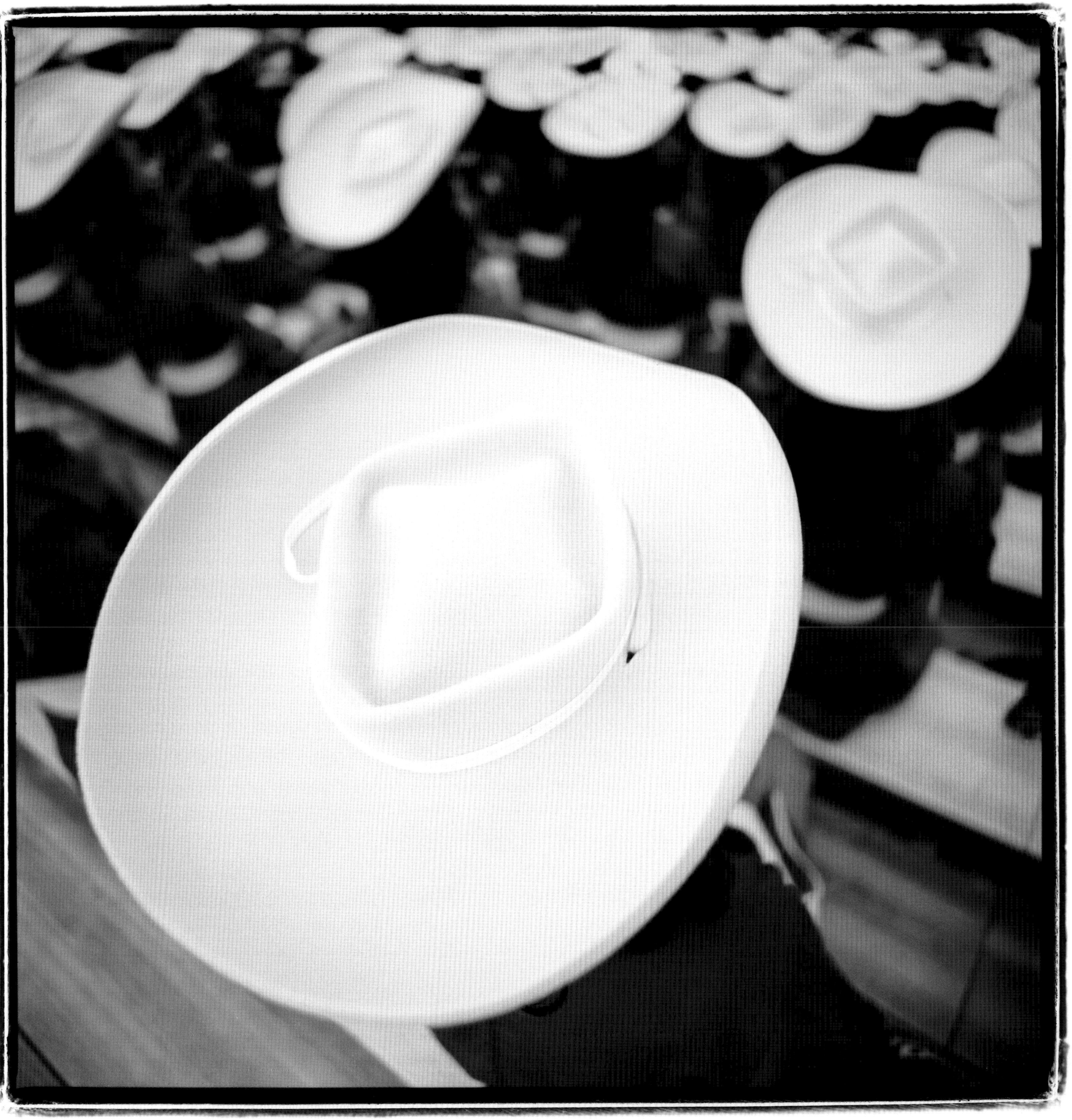

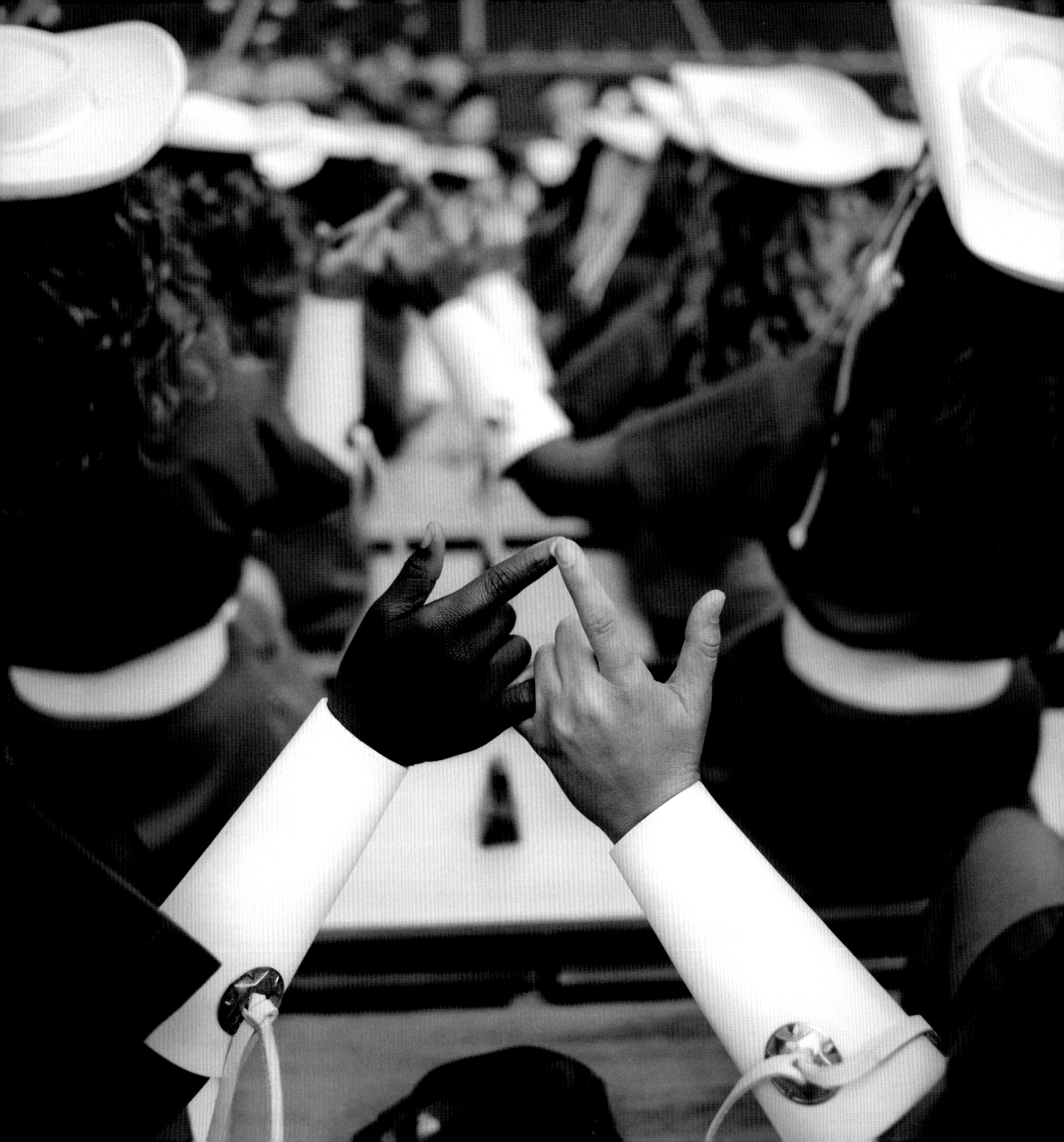

10 HANDS 2006

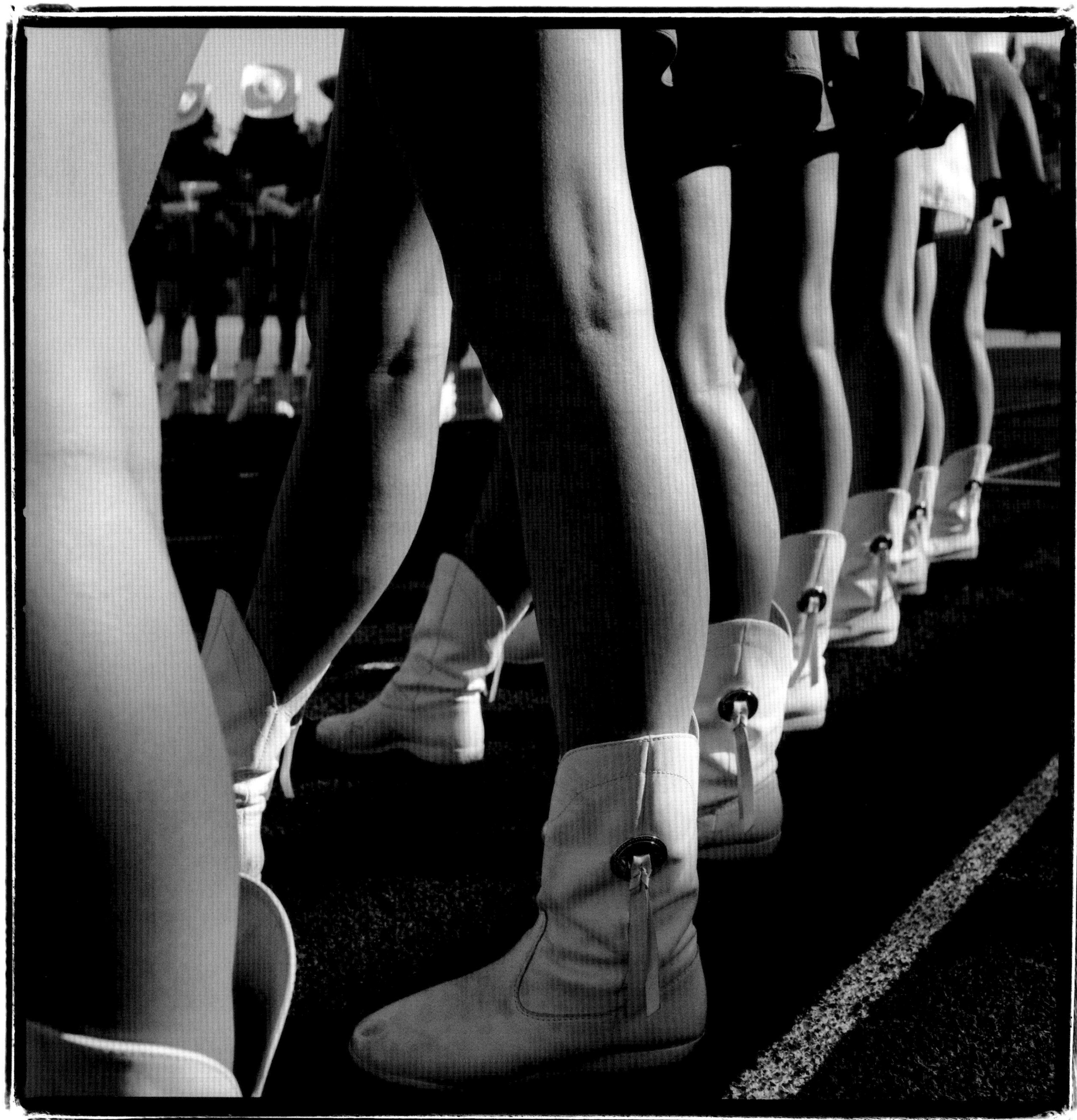

11 **PRAYER LEGS** 2005

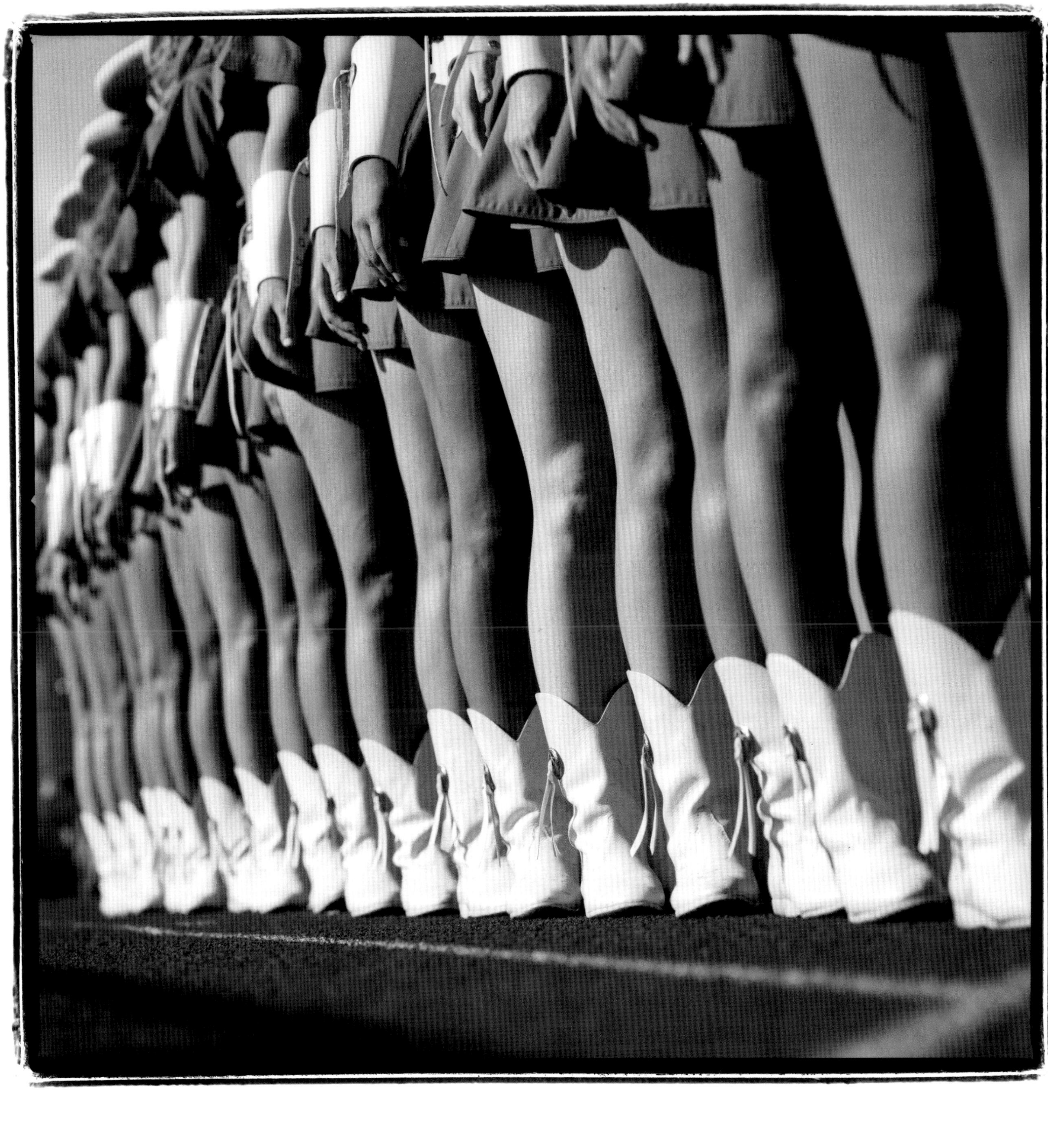

12 **LEGS, BOOTS, GAUNTLETS** 2006

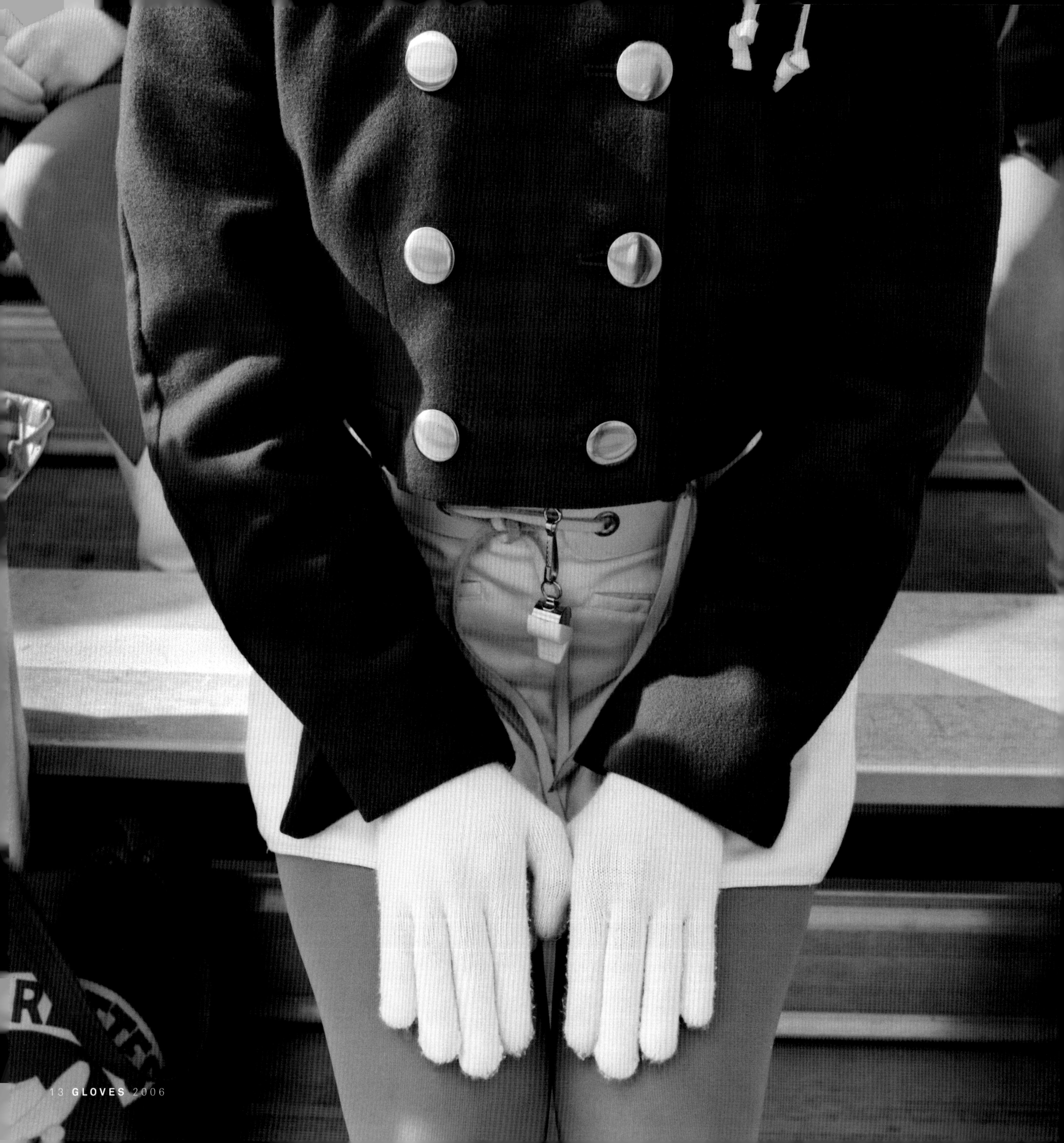

13 **GLOVES** 2006

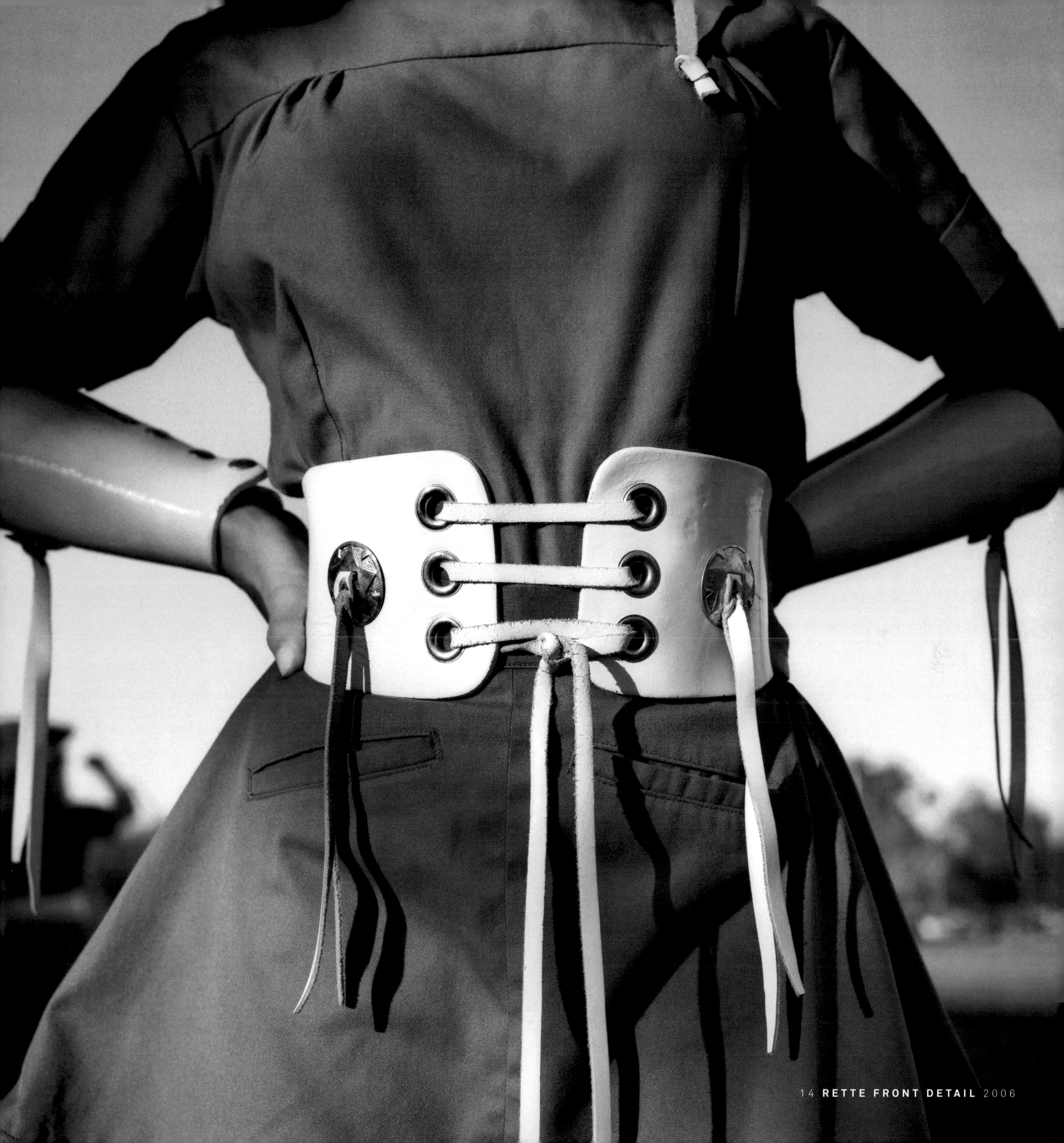

14 **RETTE FRONT DETAIL** 2006

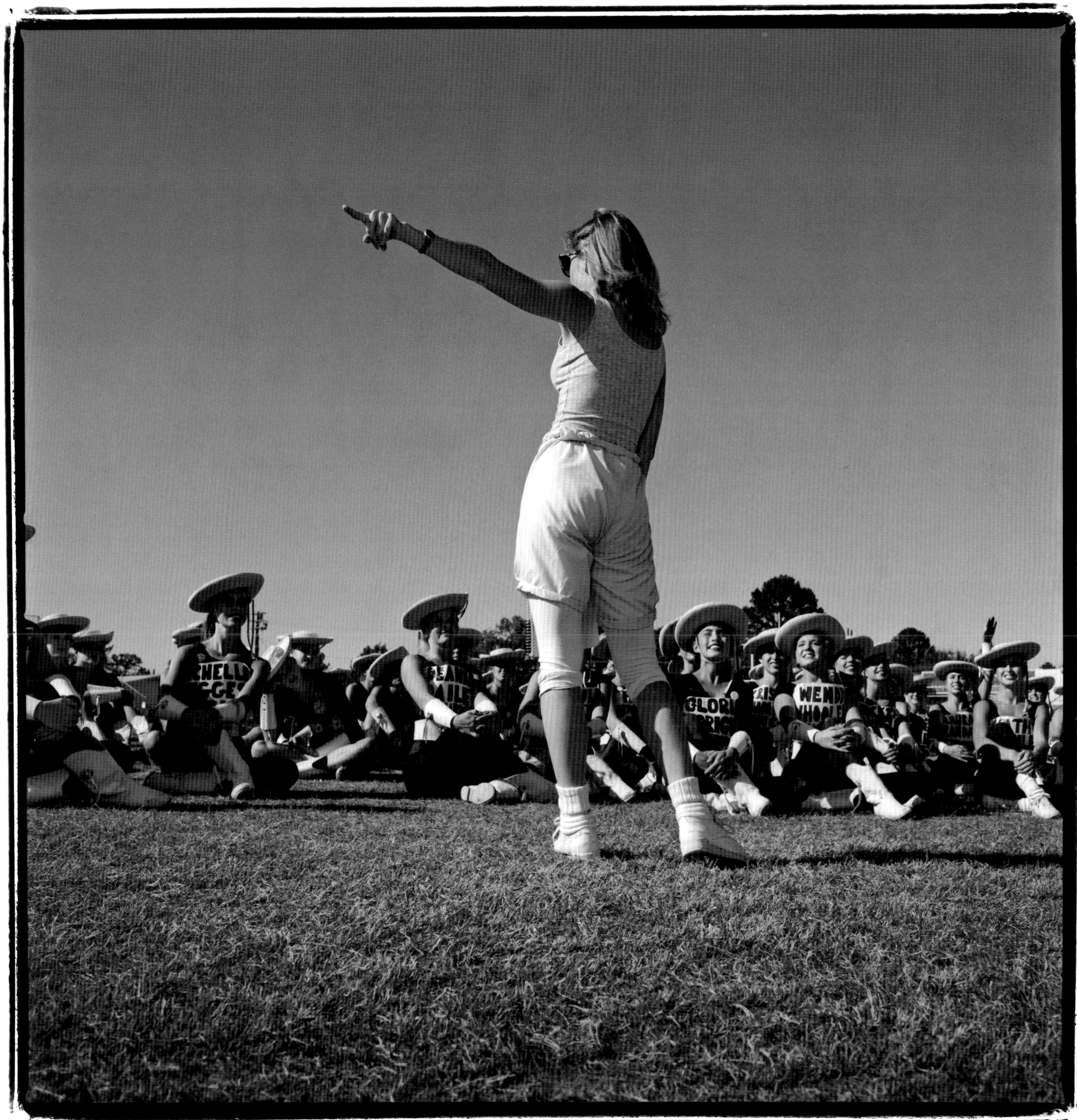
WENDY

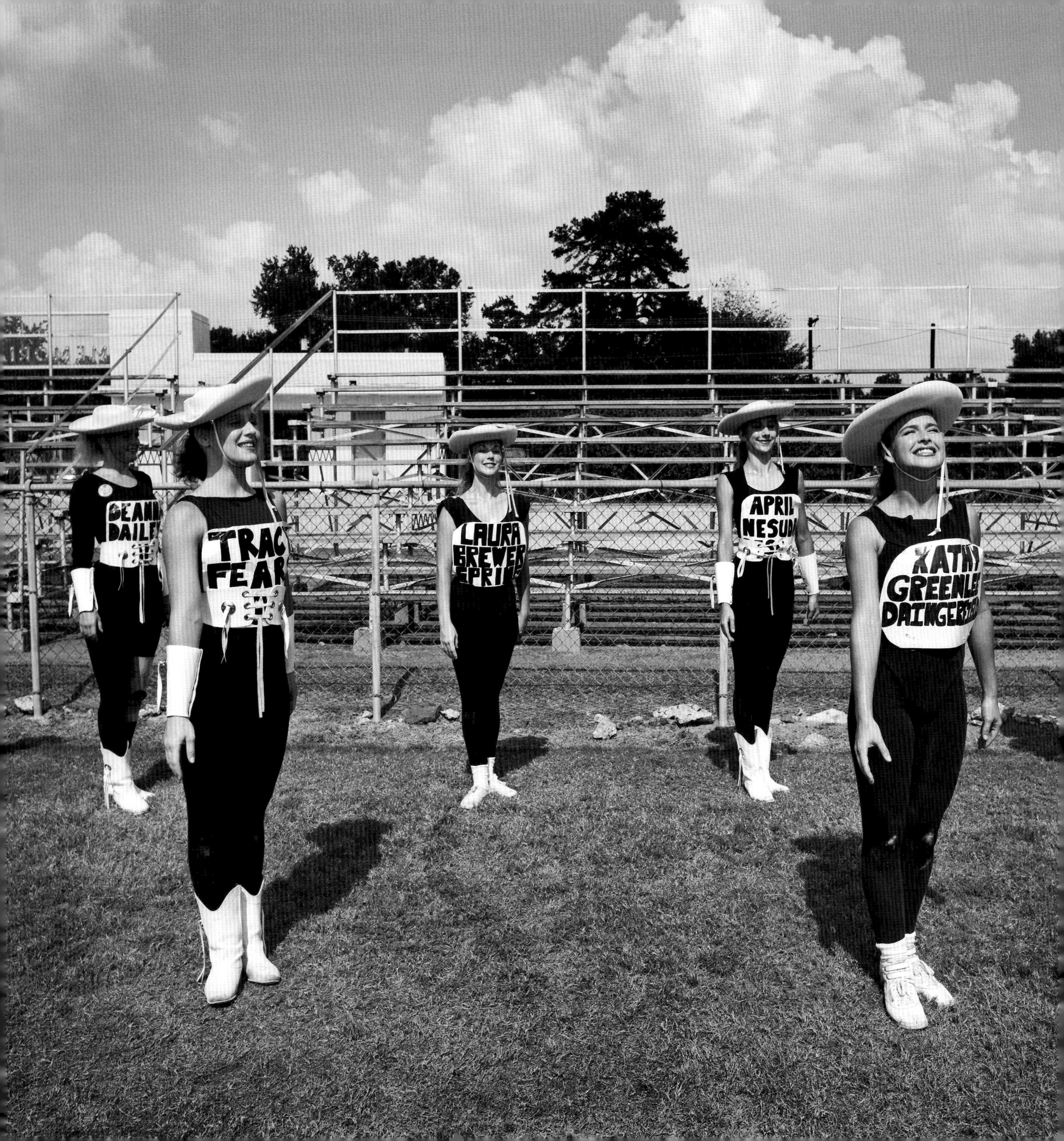
TRAC
FEAR
LAURA
BREWER
APRIL
KATHY

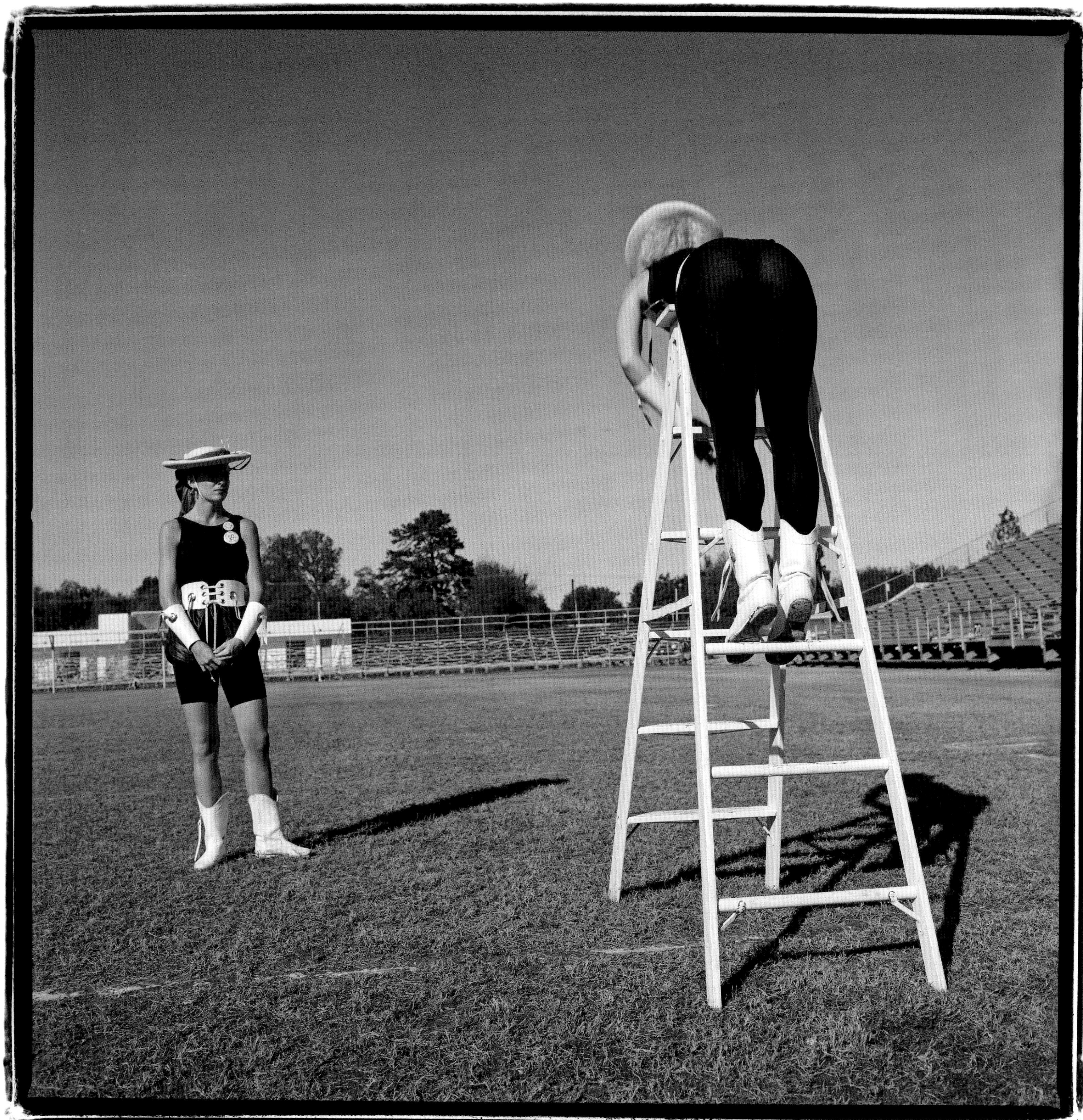

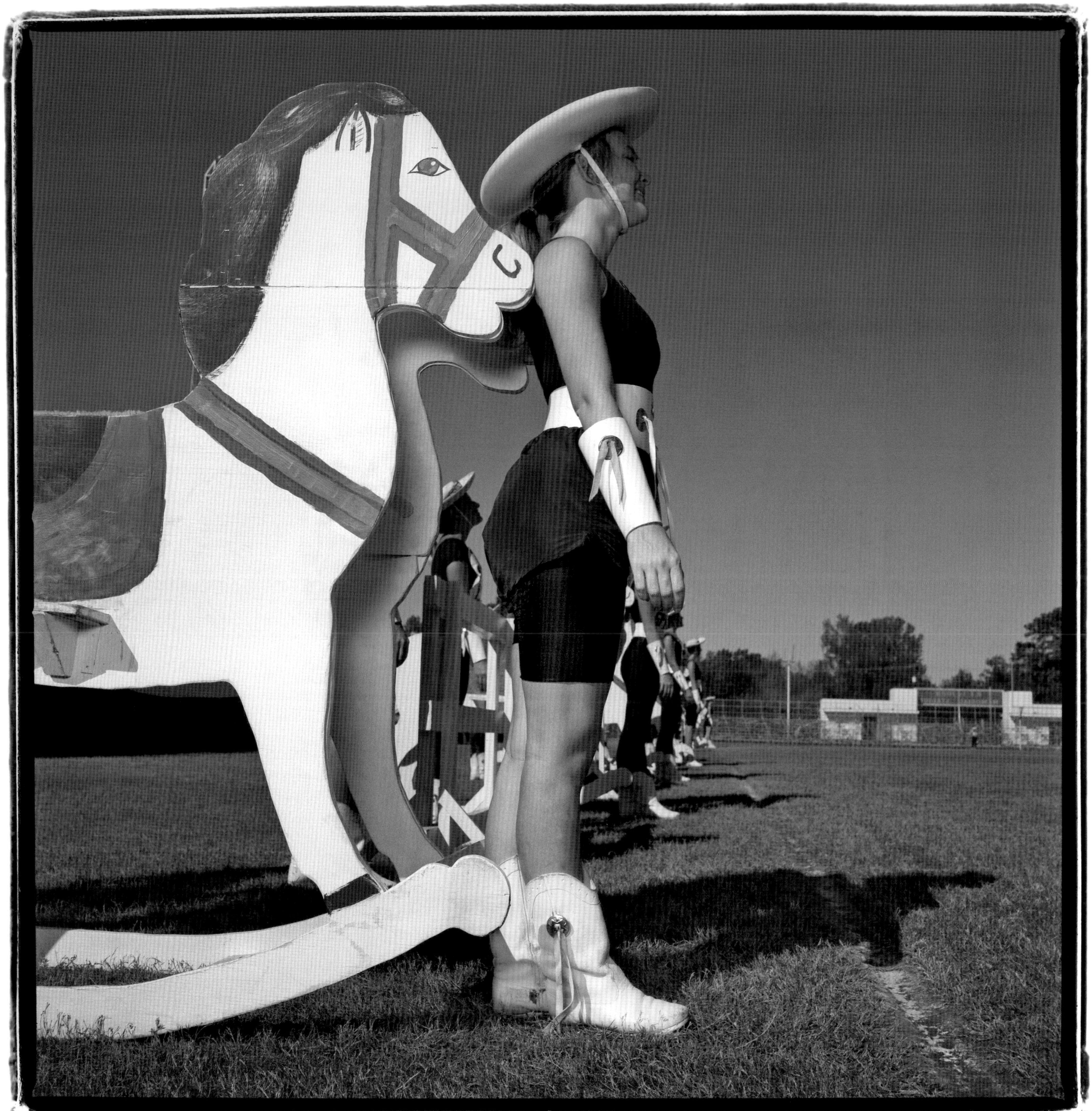

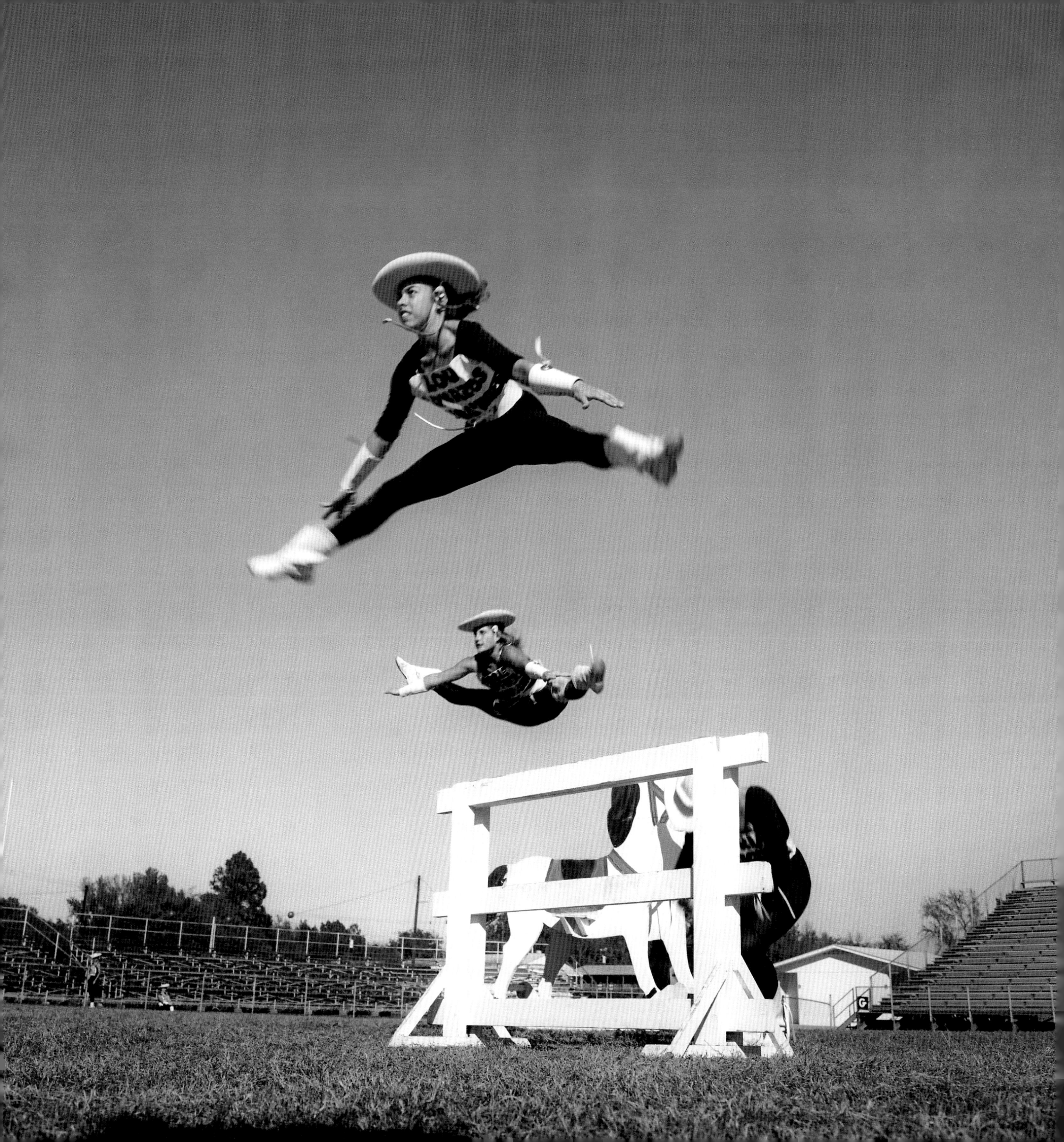

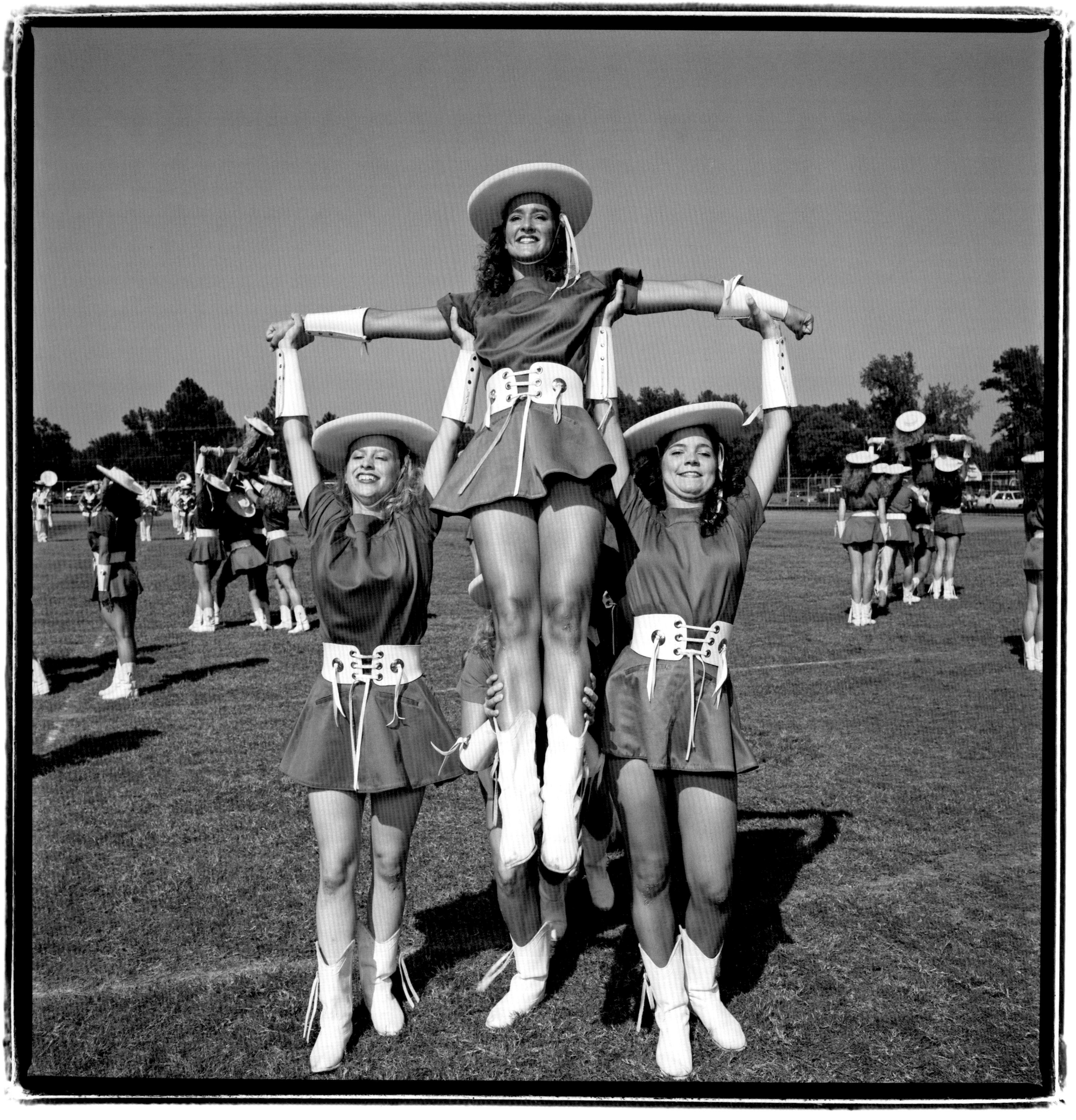

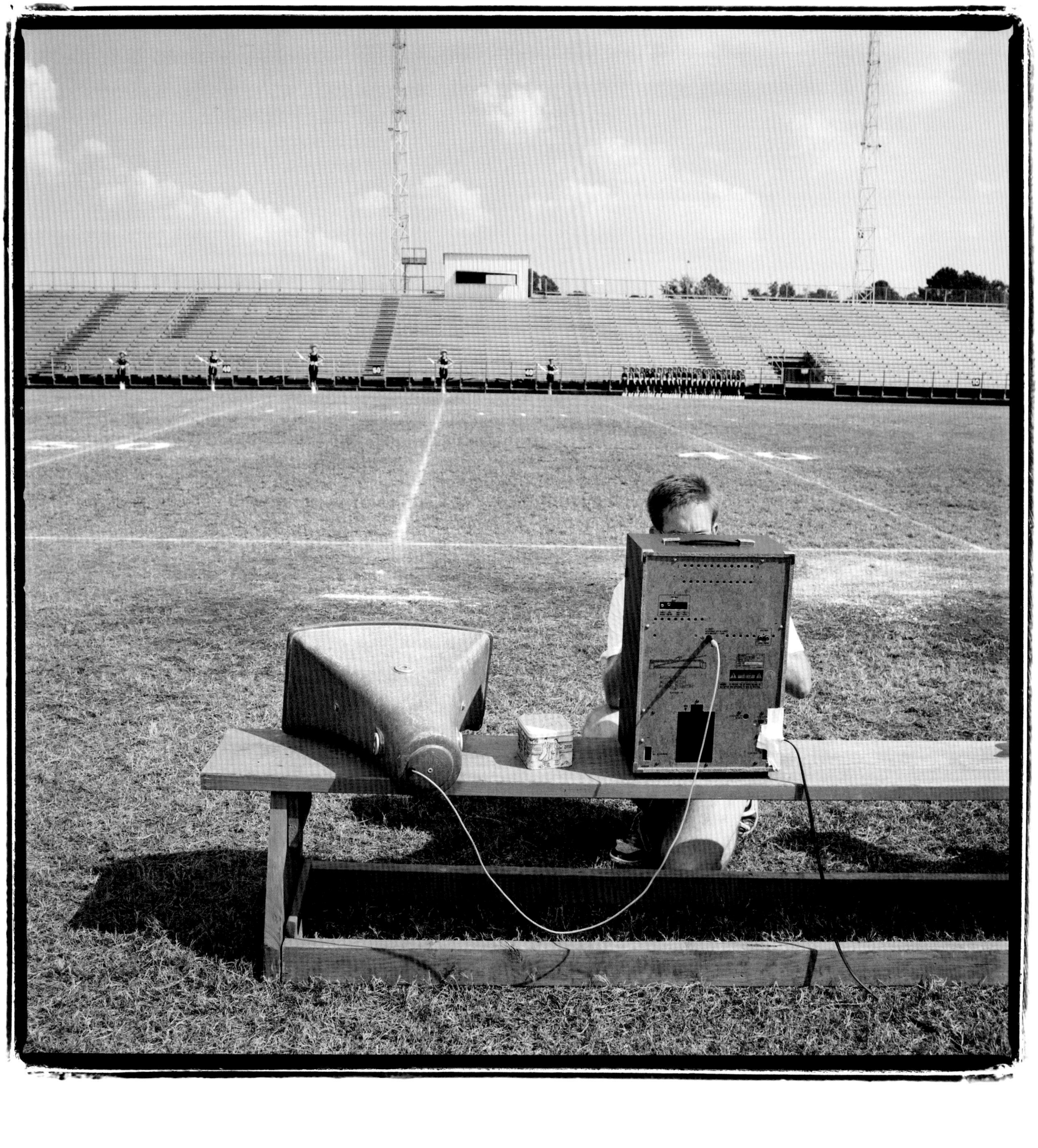

21 **RETTE MANAGER** 1989

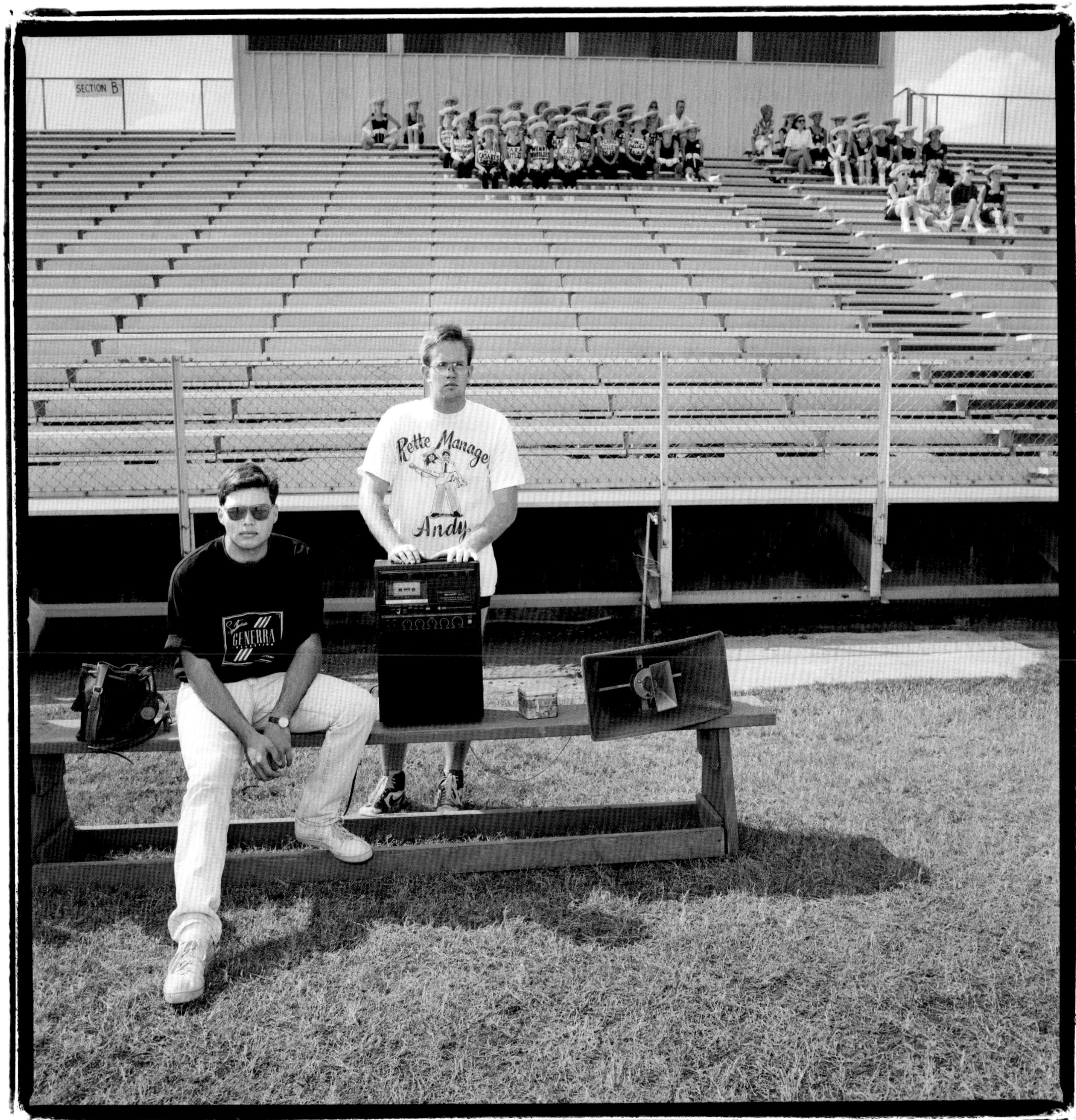
SECTION B
Rette Managers
Andy
GENERRA

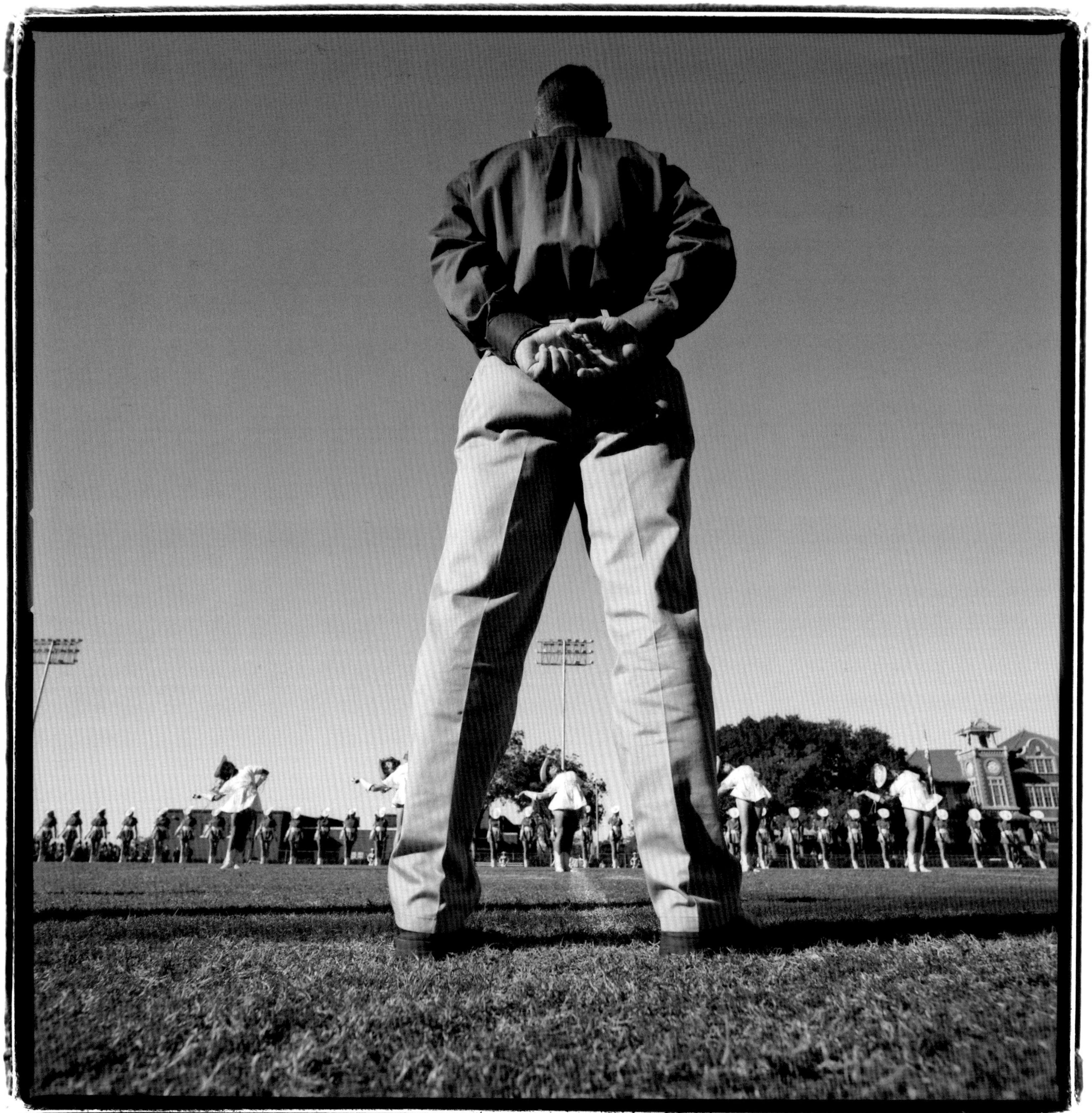

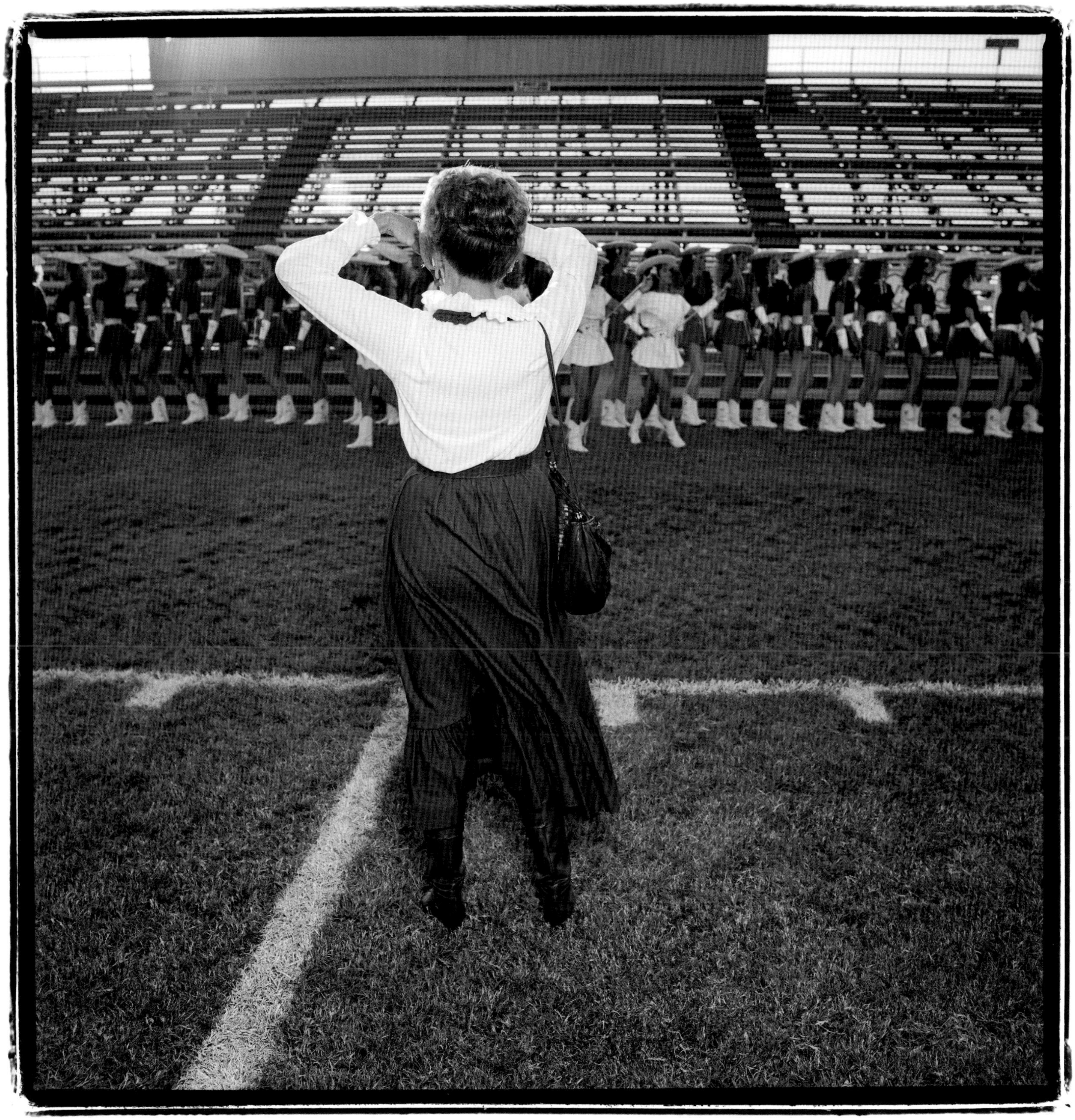

24 **DEANA'S INSTRUCTION** 1989

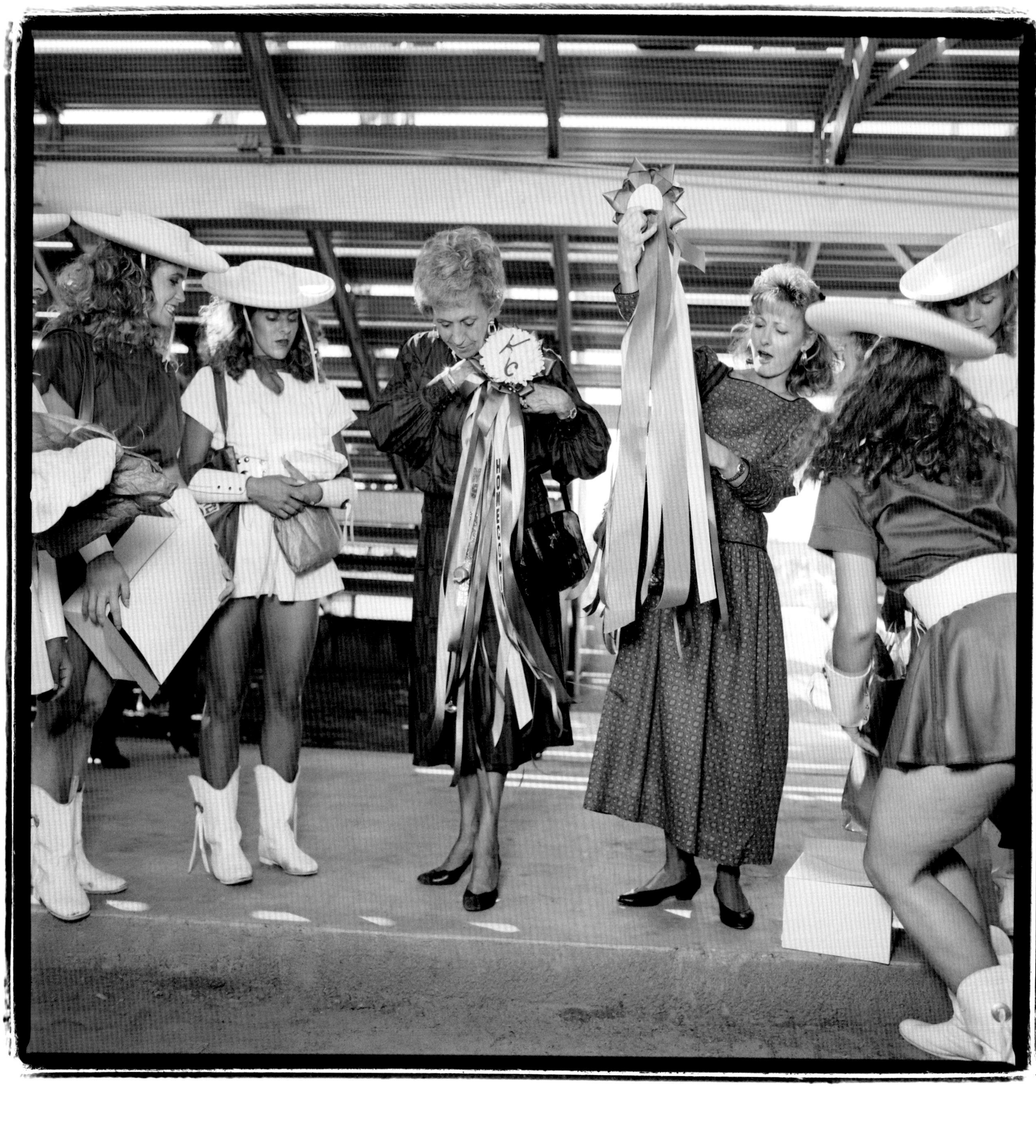

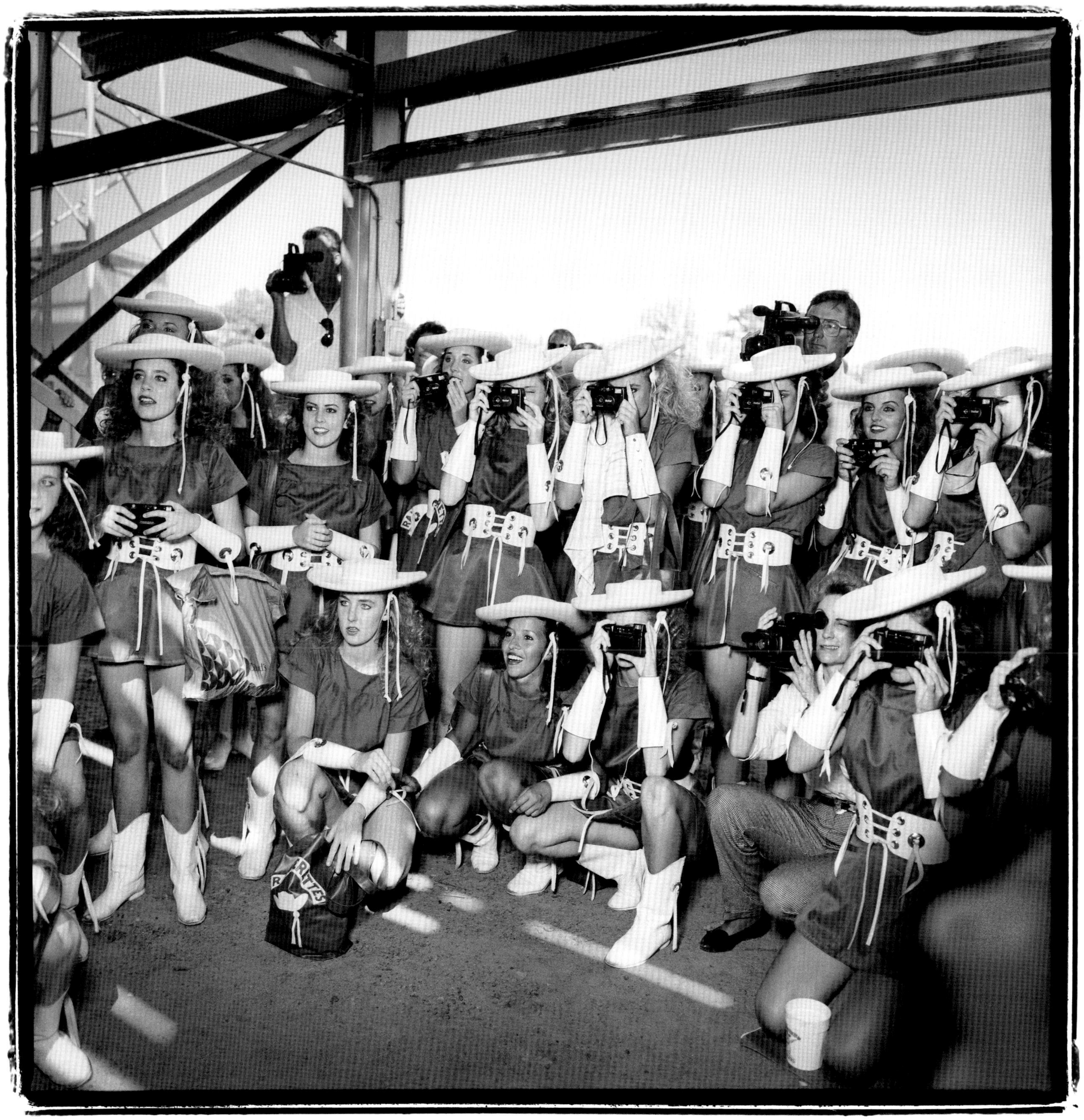

26 **DEANA'S DIPTYCH II** 1989

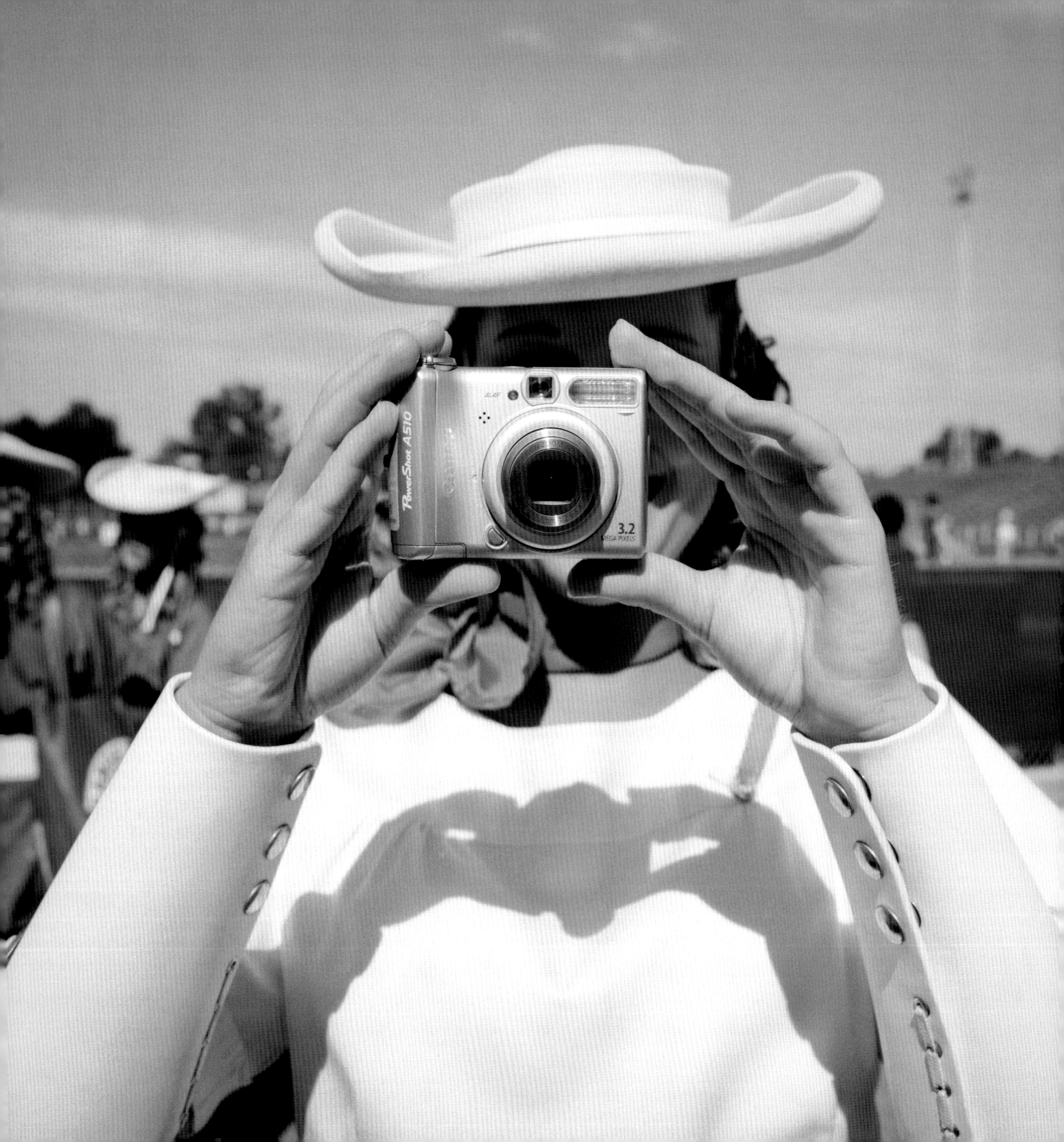
PowerShot A510
3.2
MEGA PIXELS

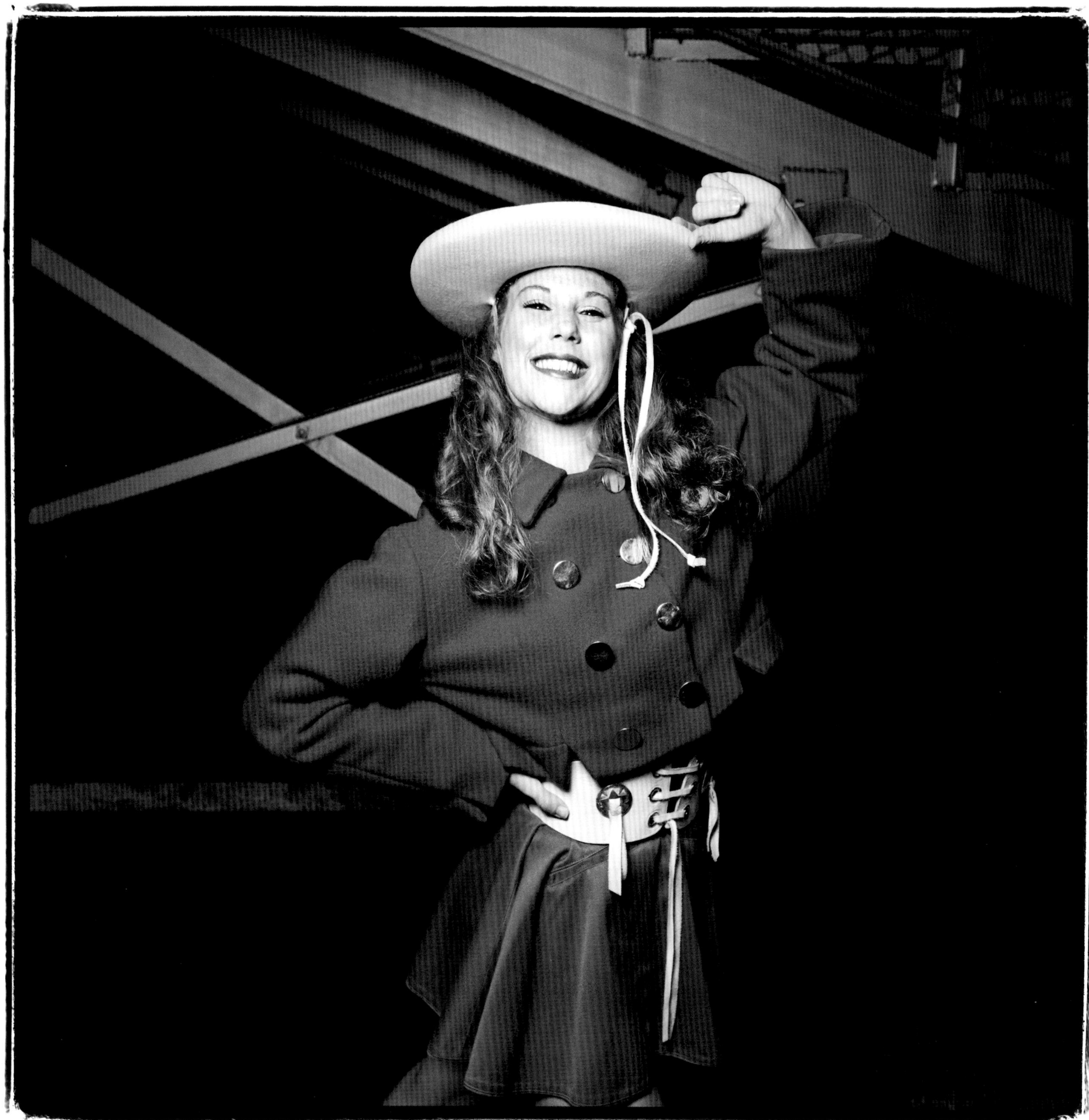

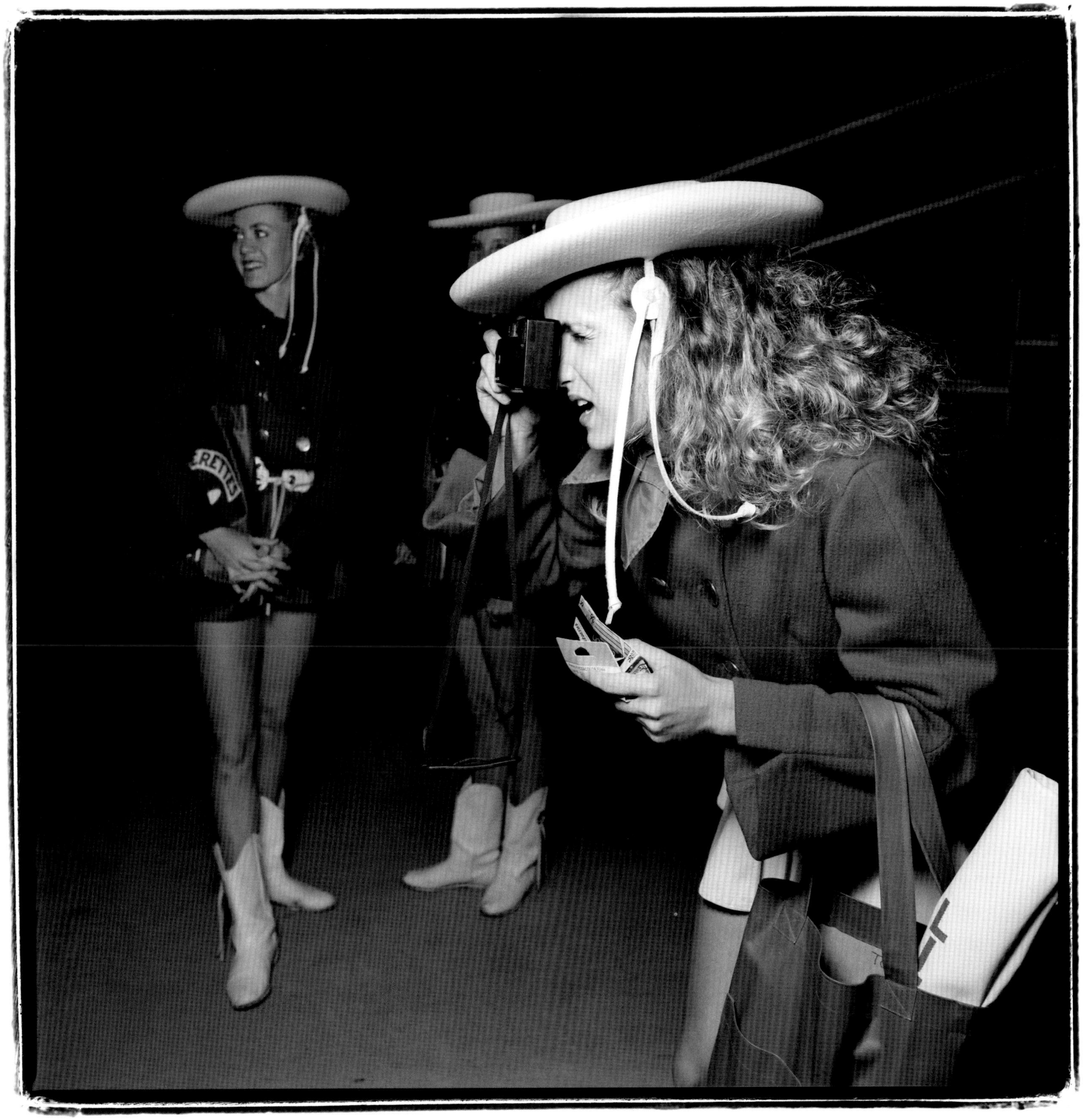

29 **RETTE PHOTOGRAPHER** 1989

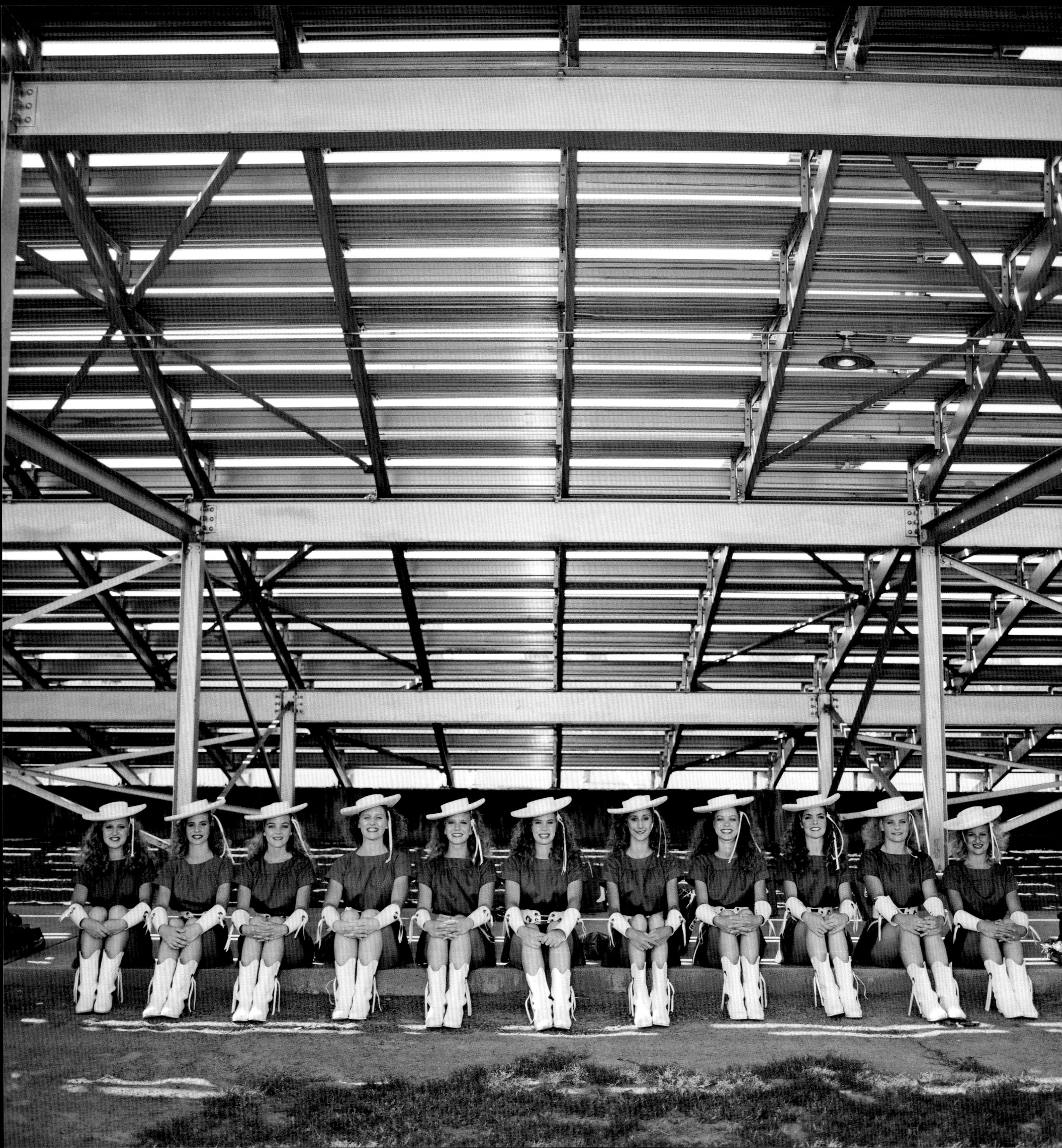

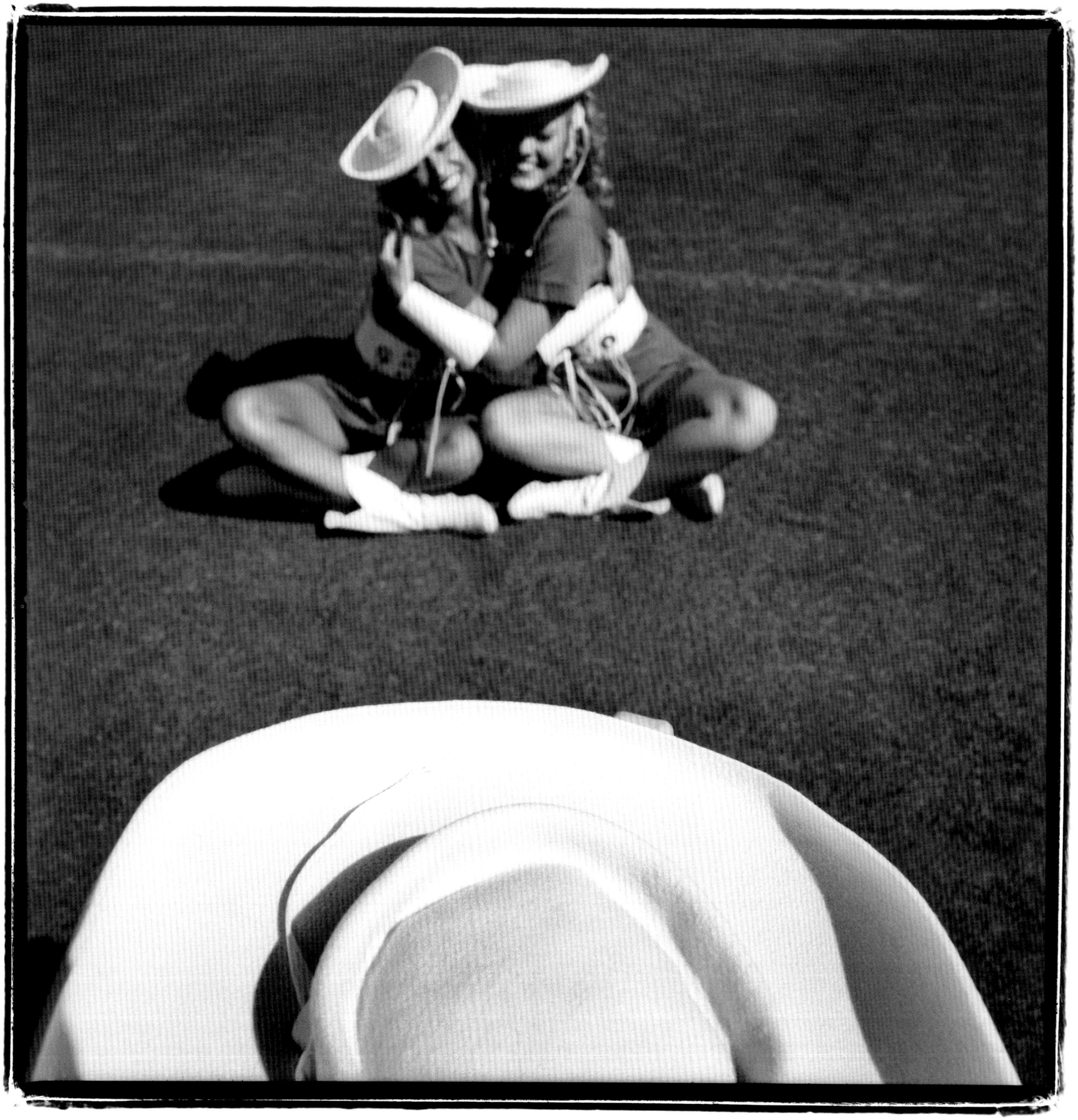

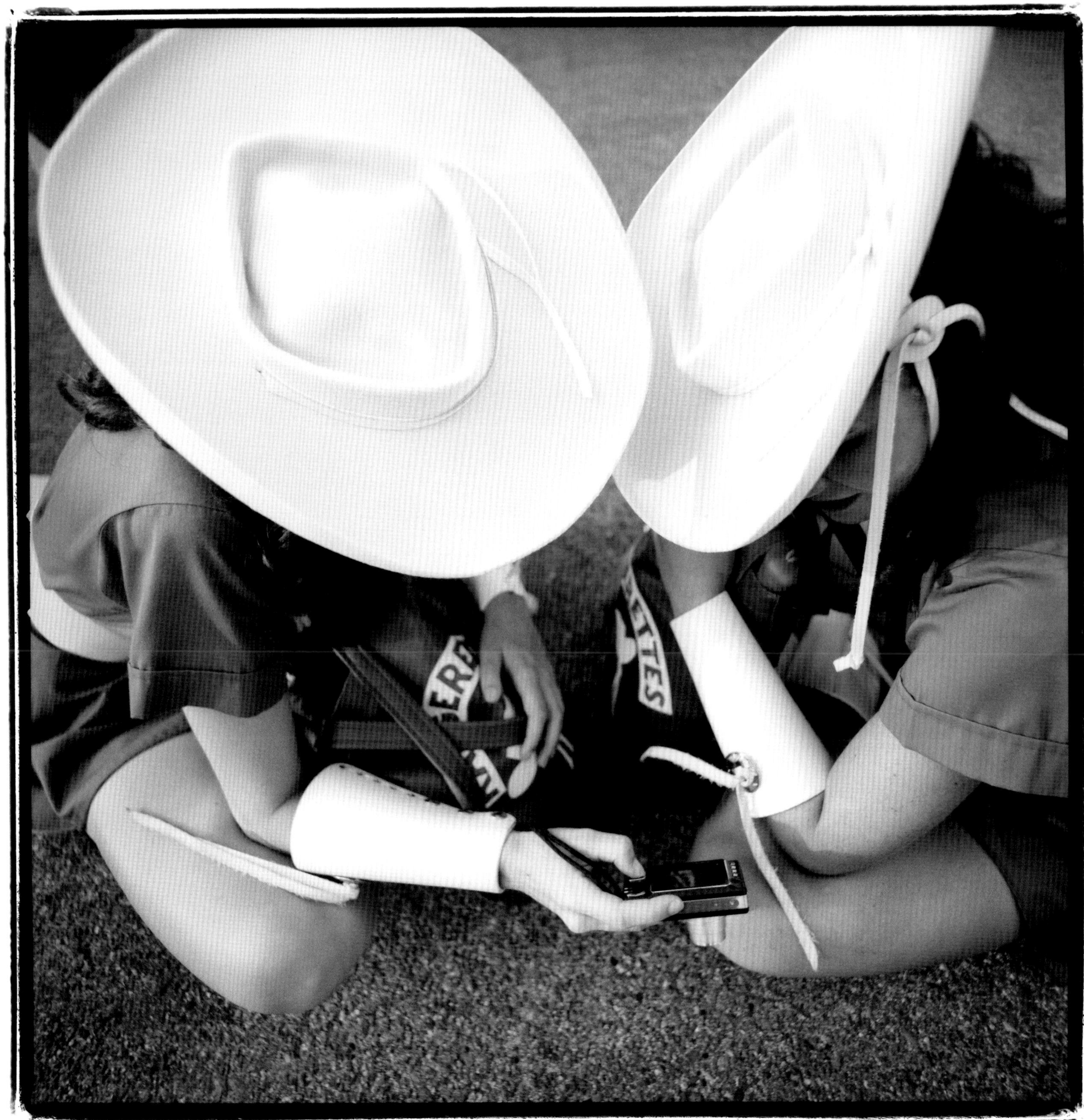

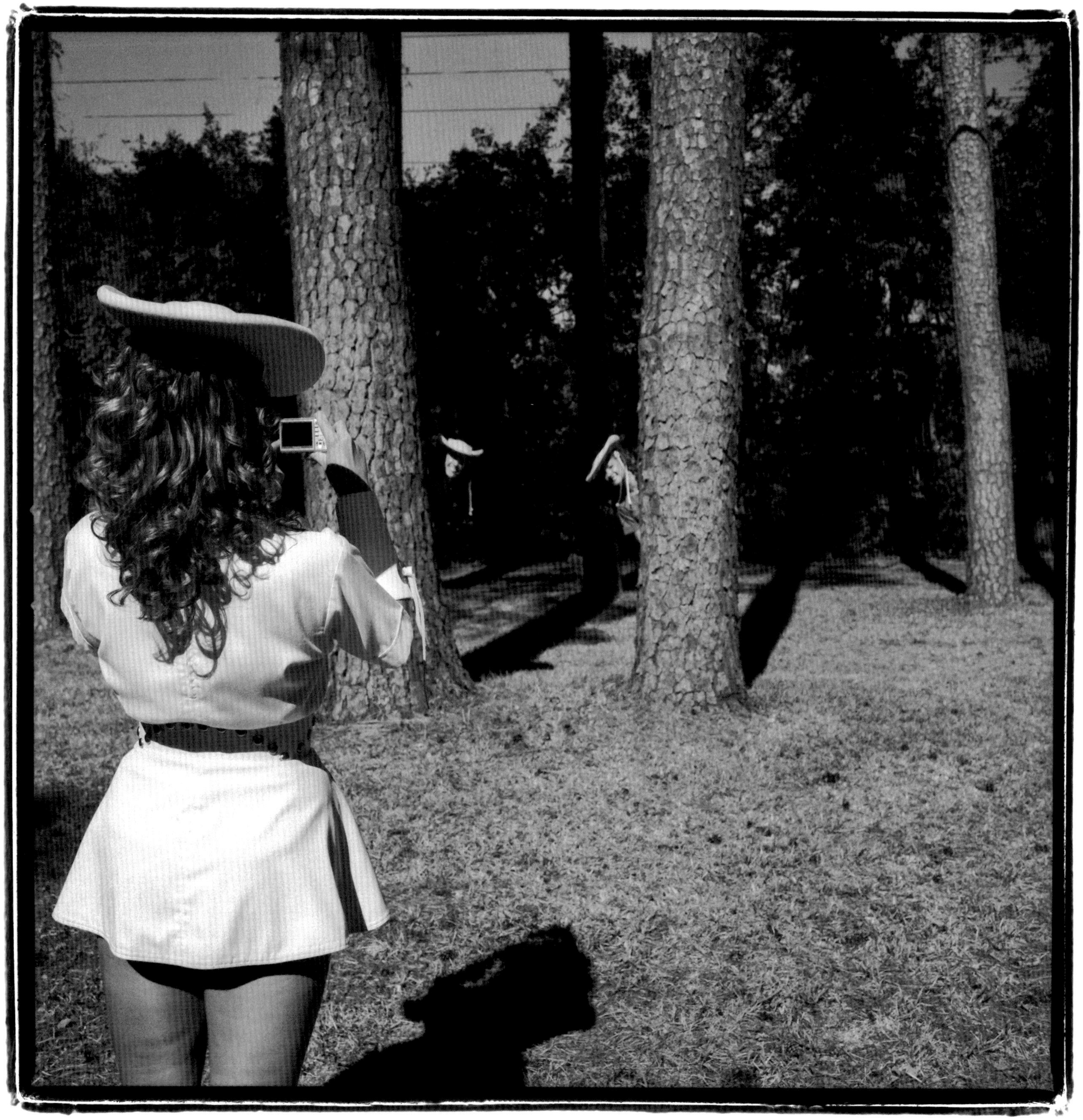

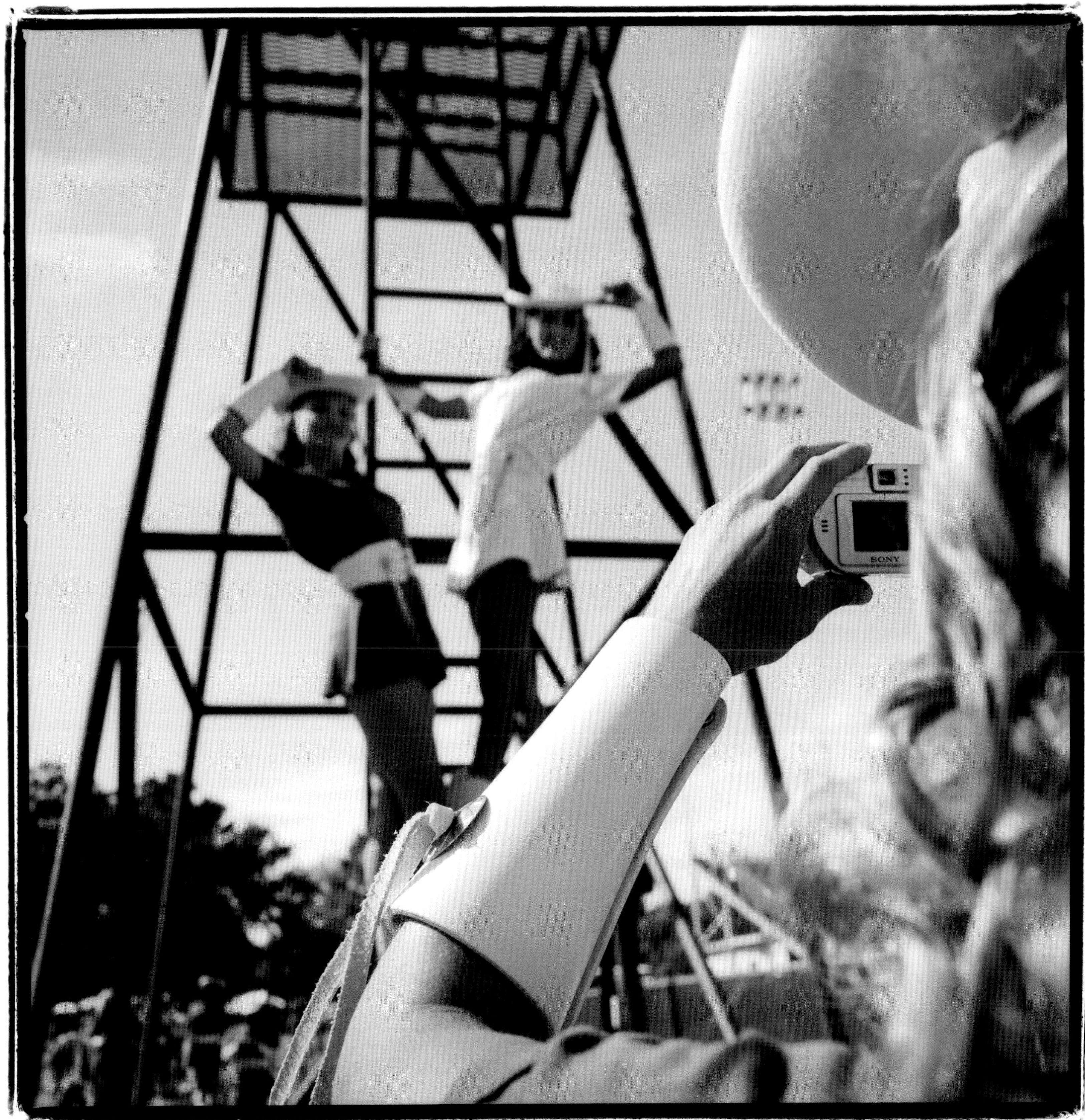
SONY

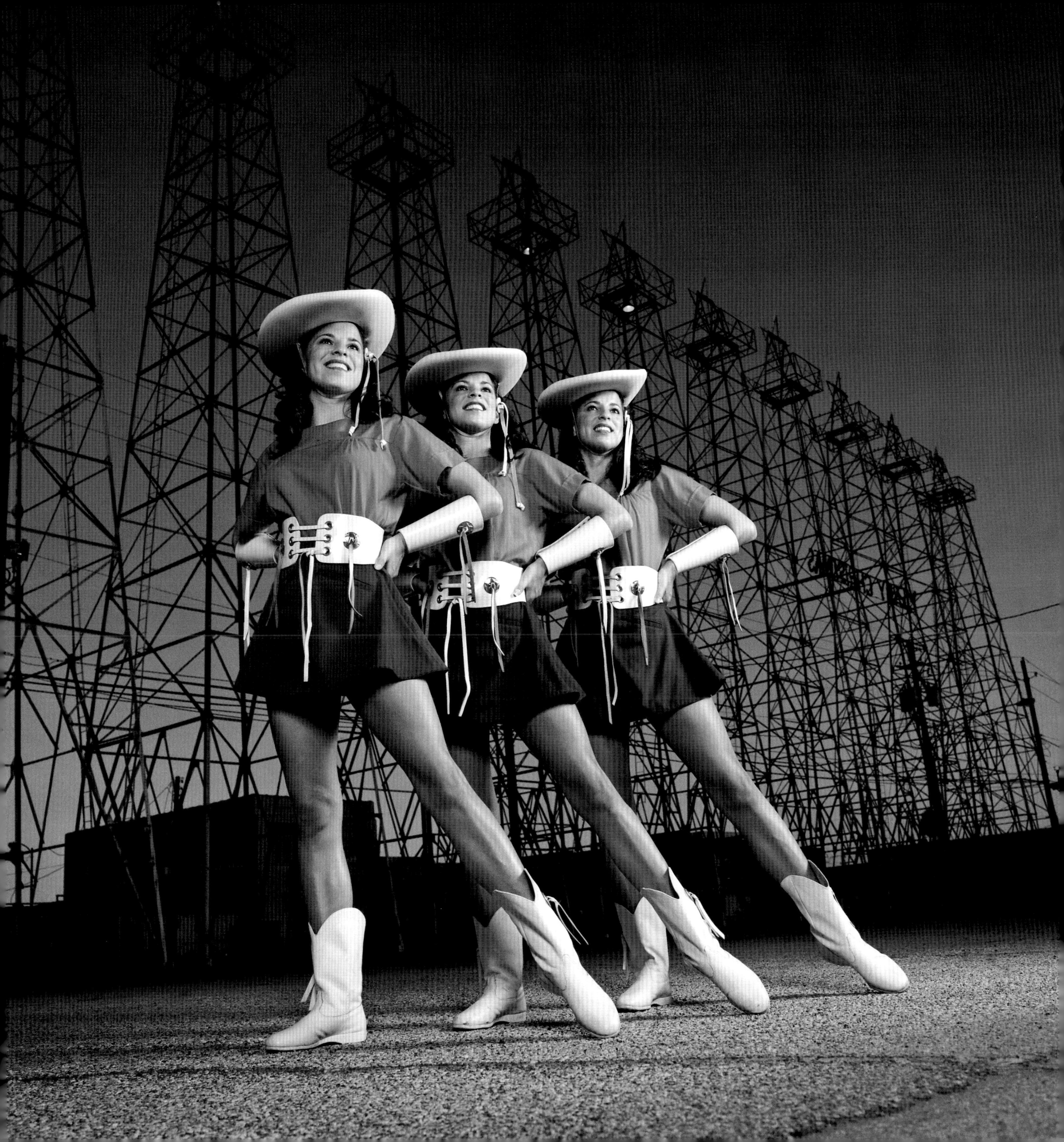

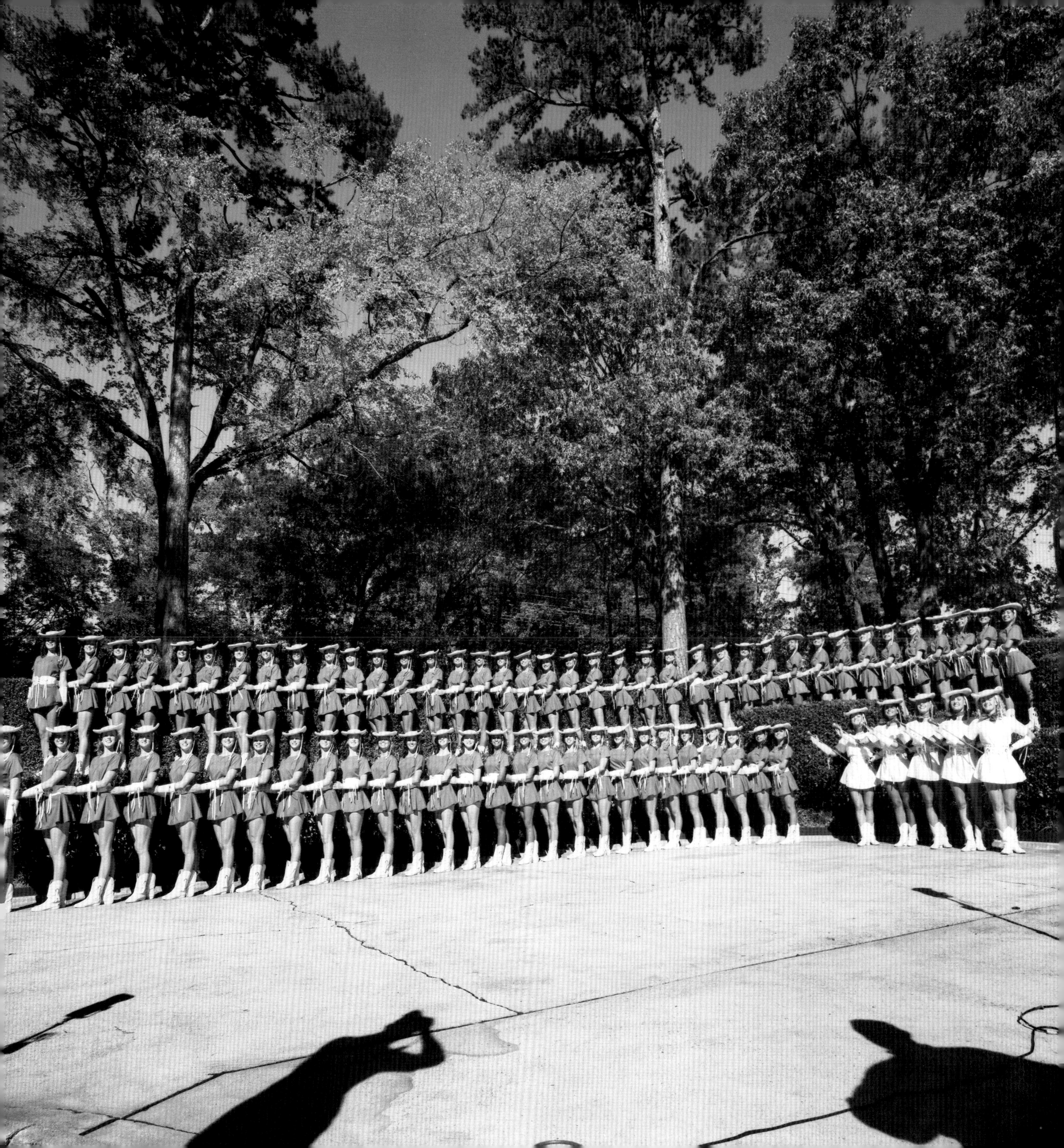

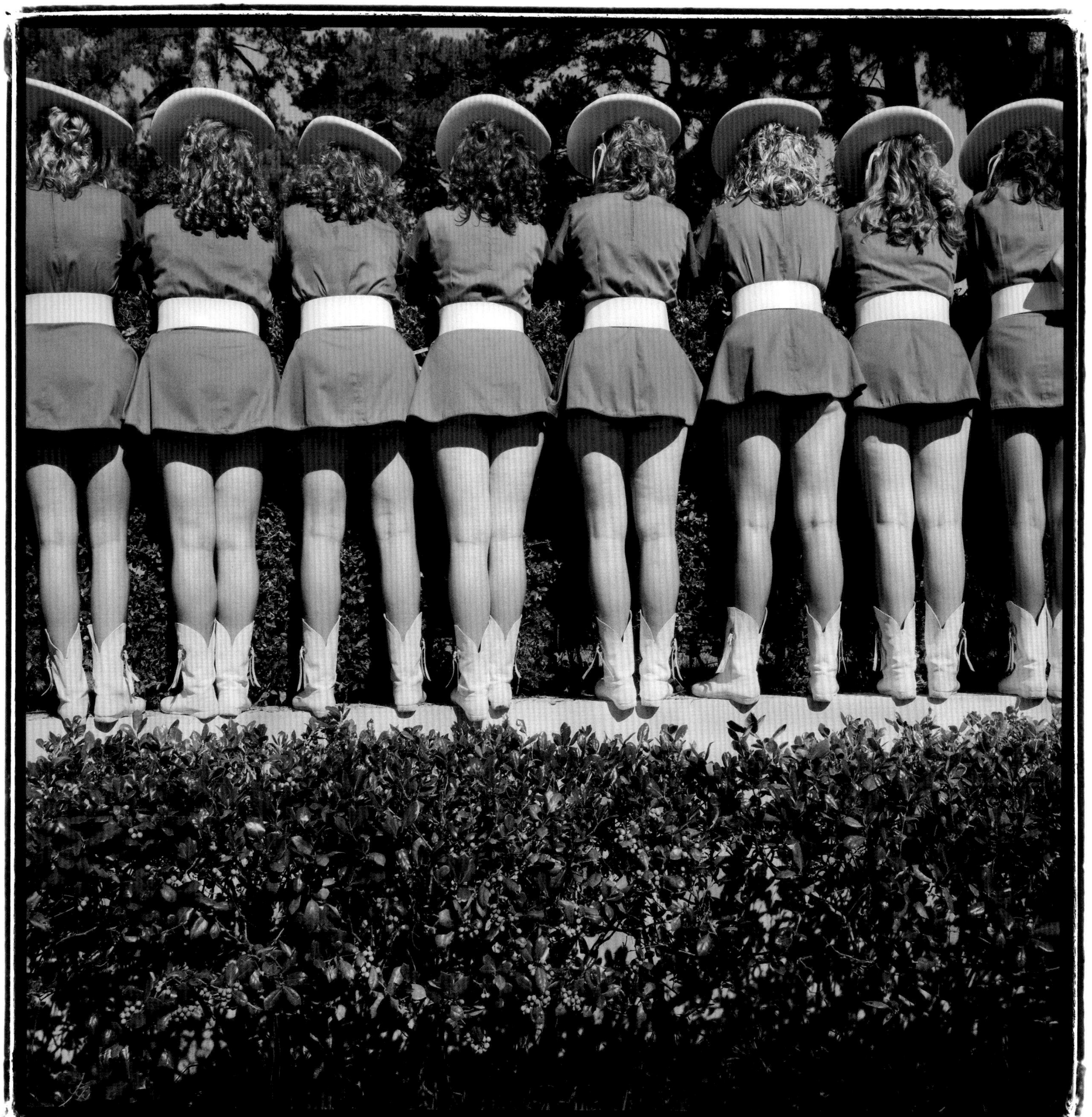

37 **GROUP PICTURE PREP** 2006

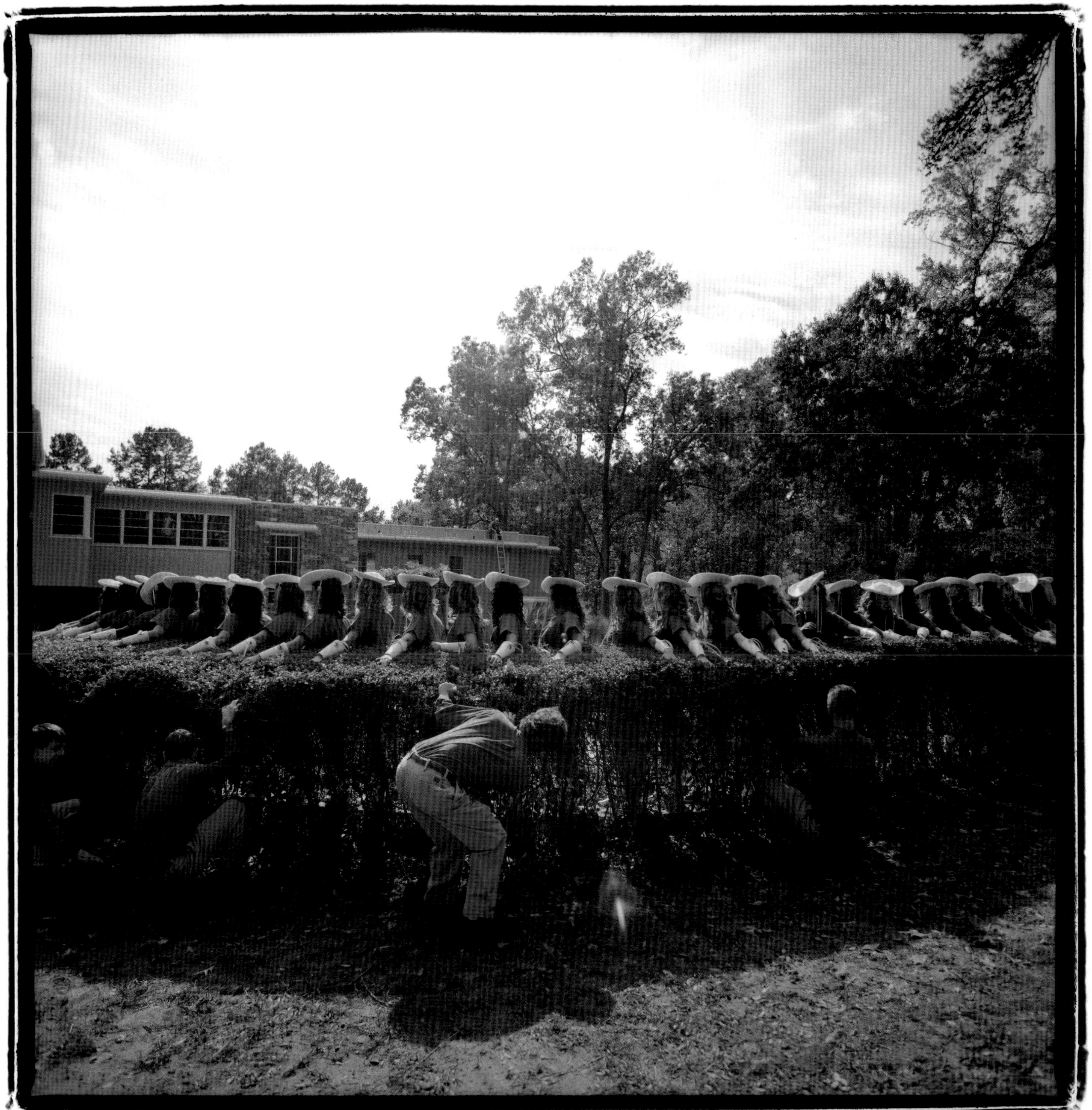

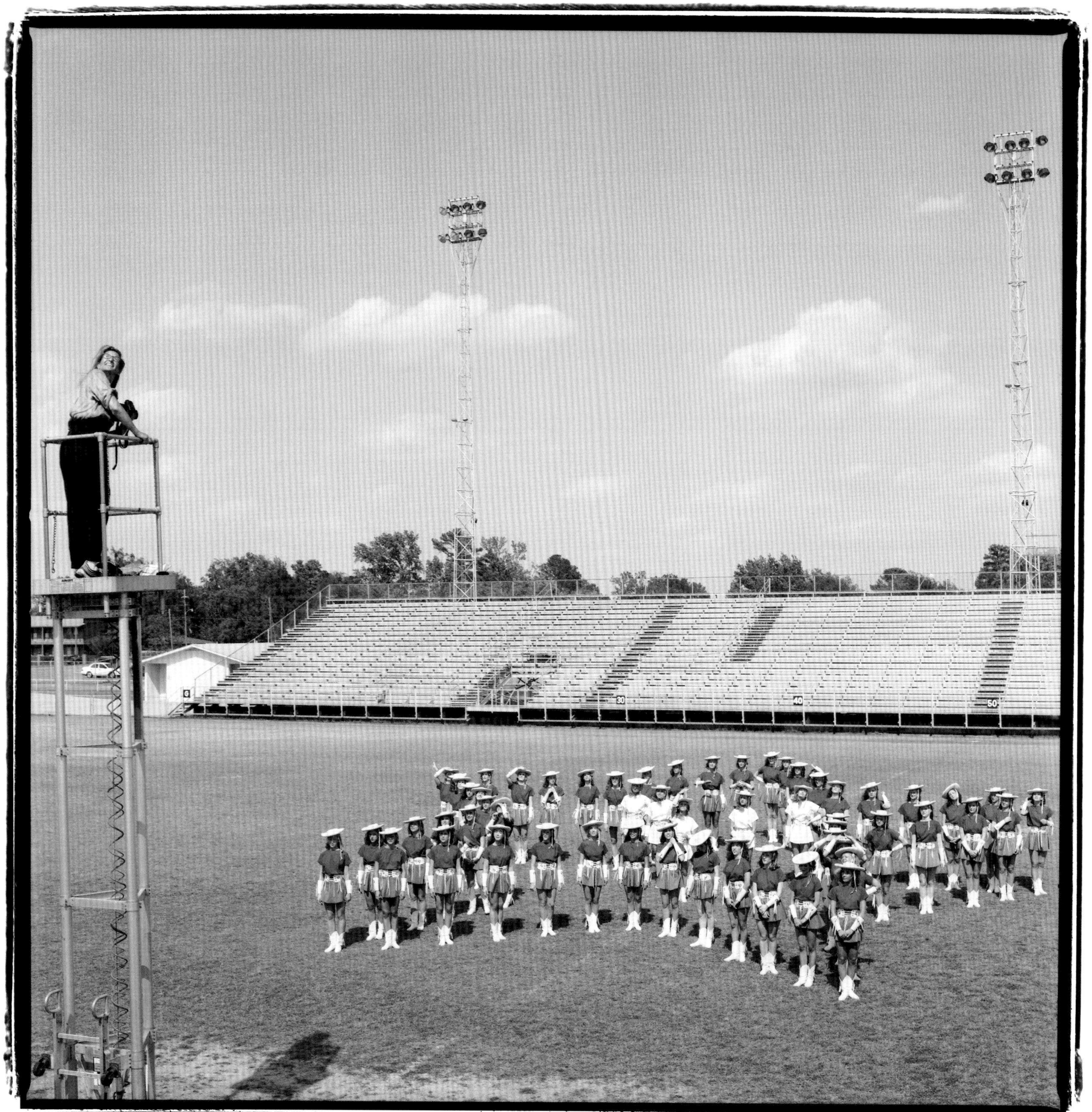

39 **ANNIE LEIBOVITZ** | 1998

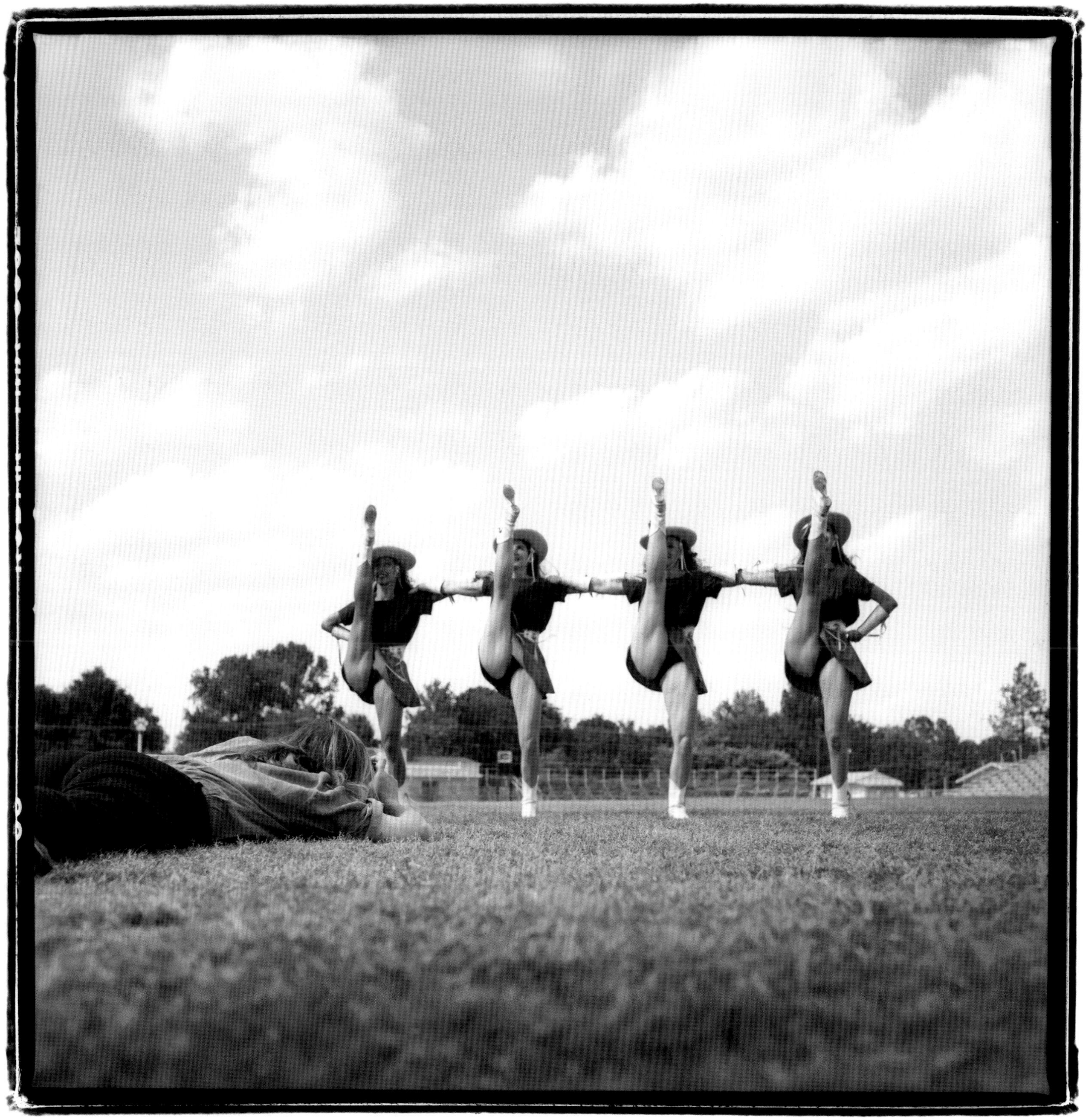

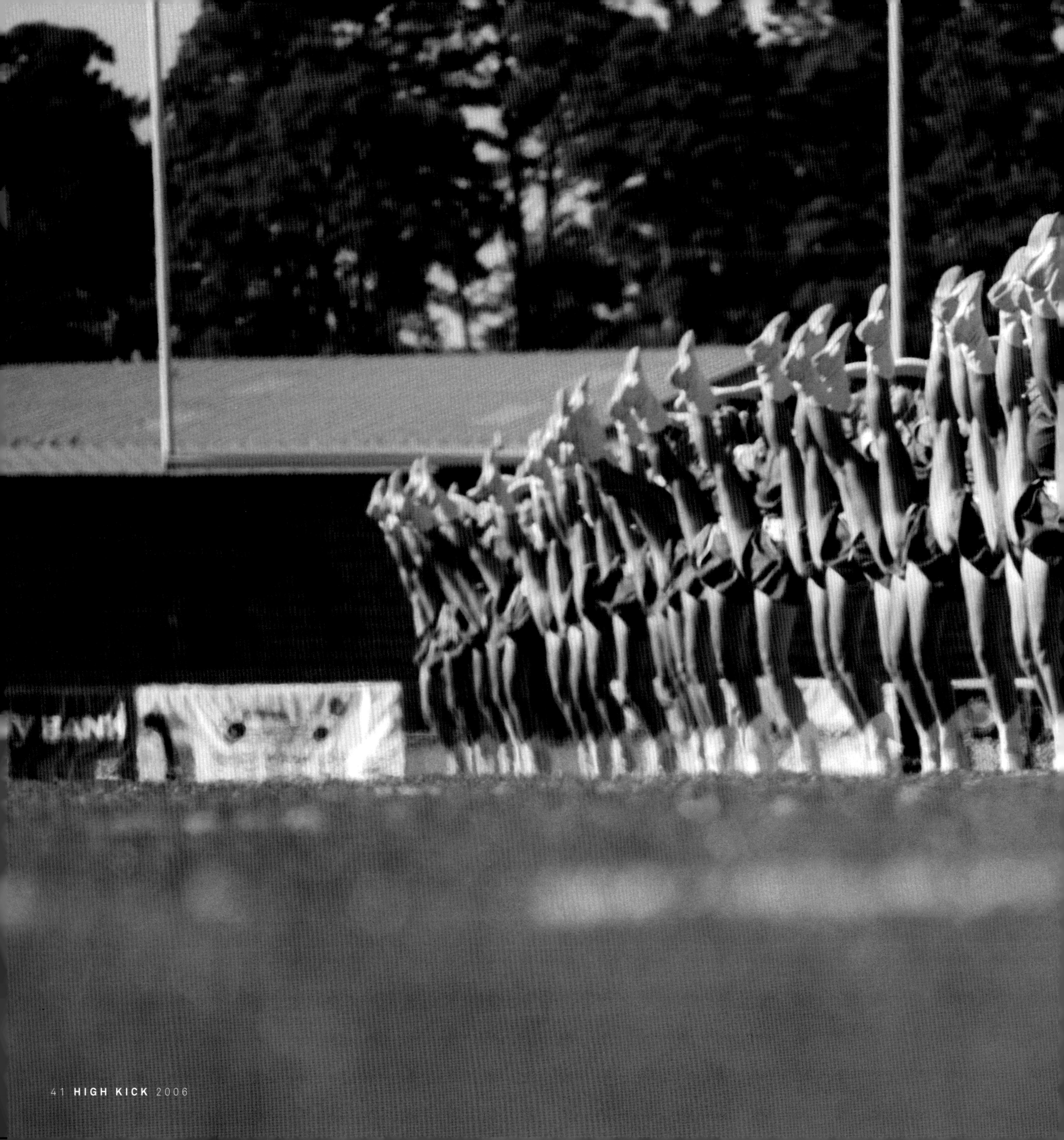

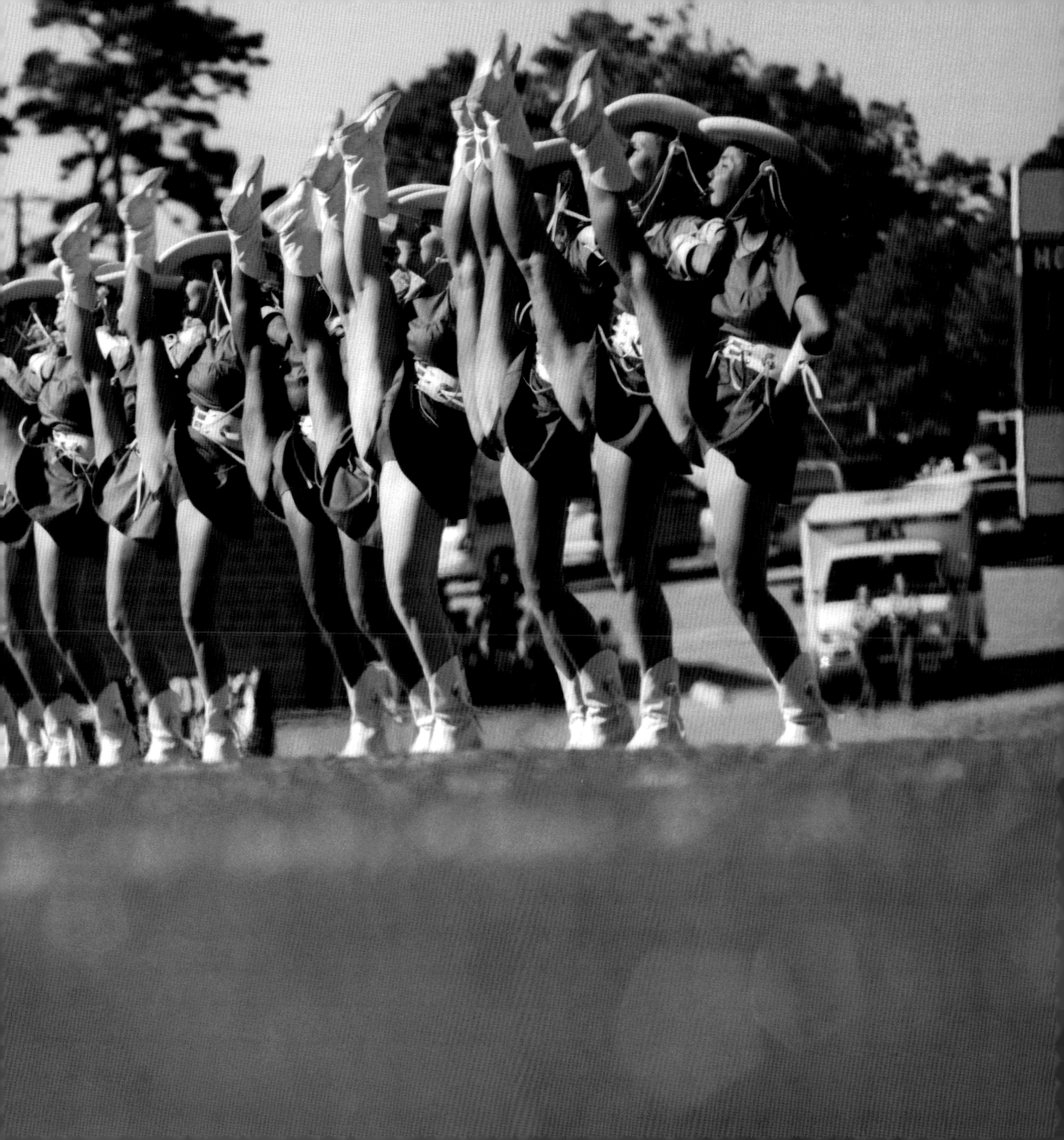

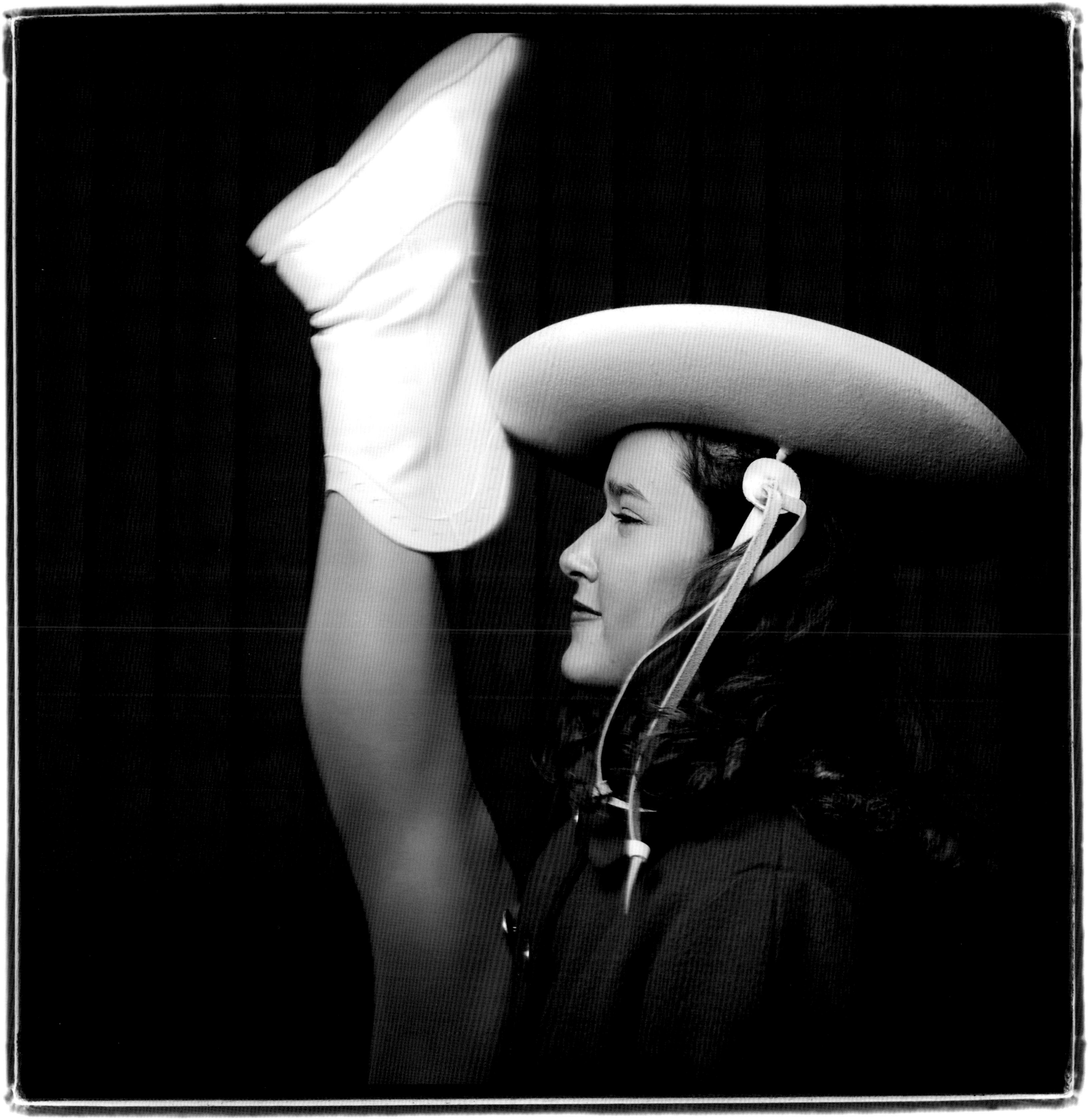

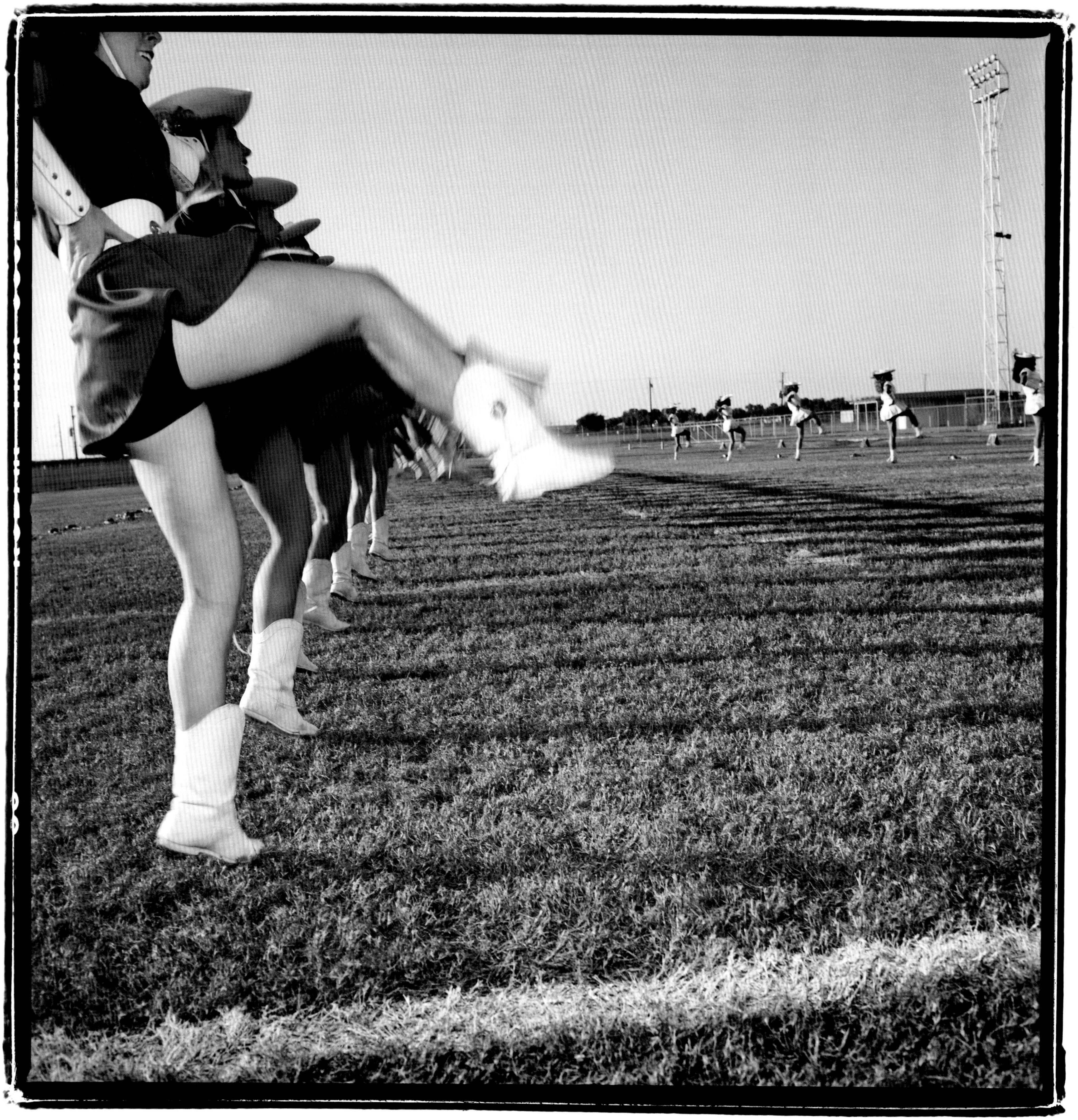

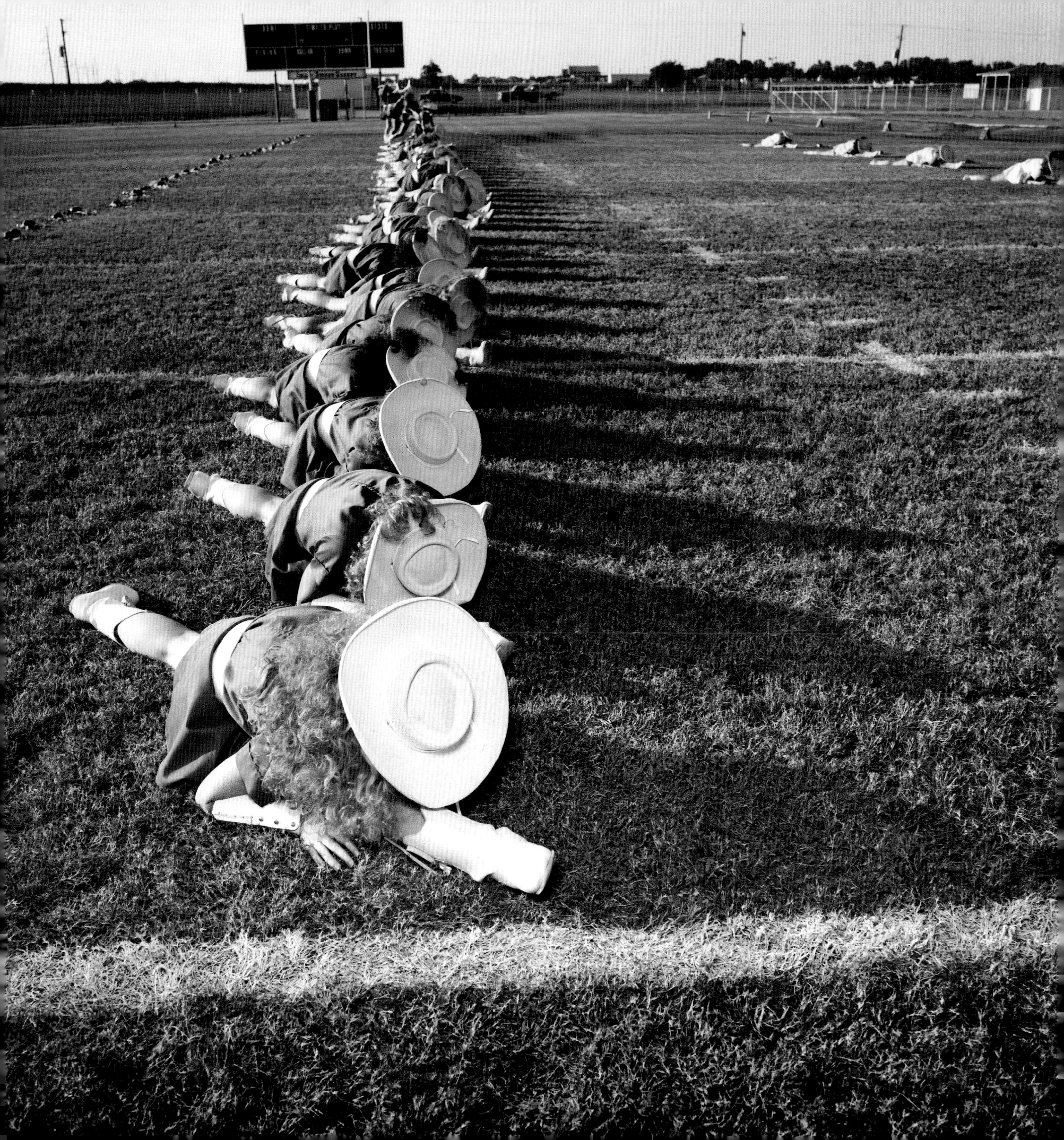

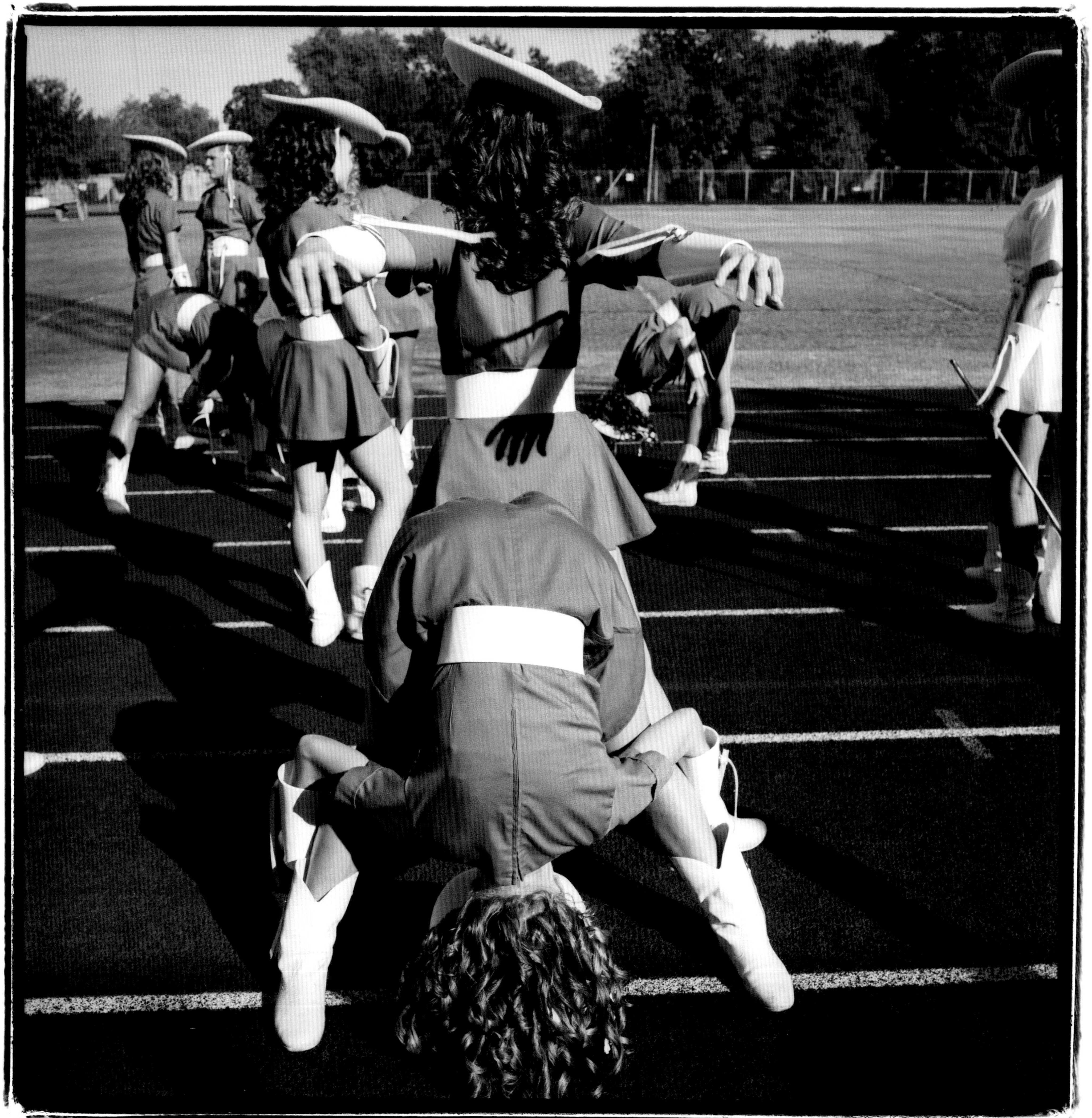

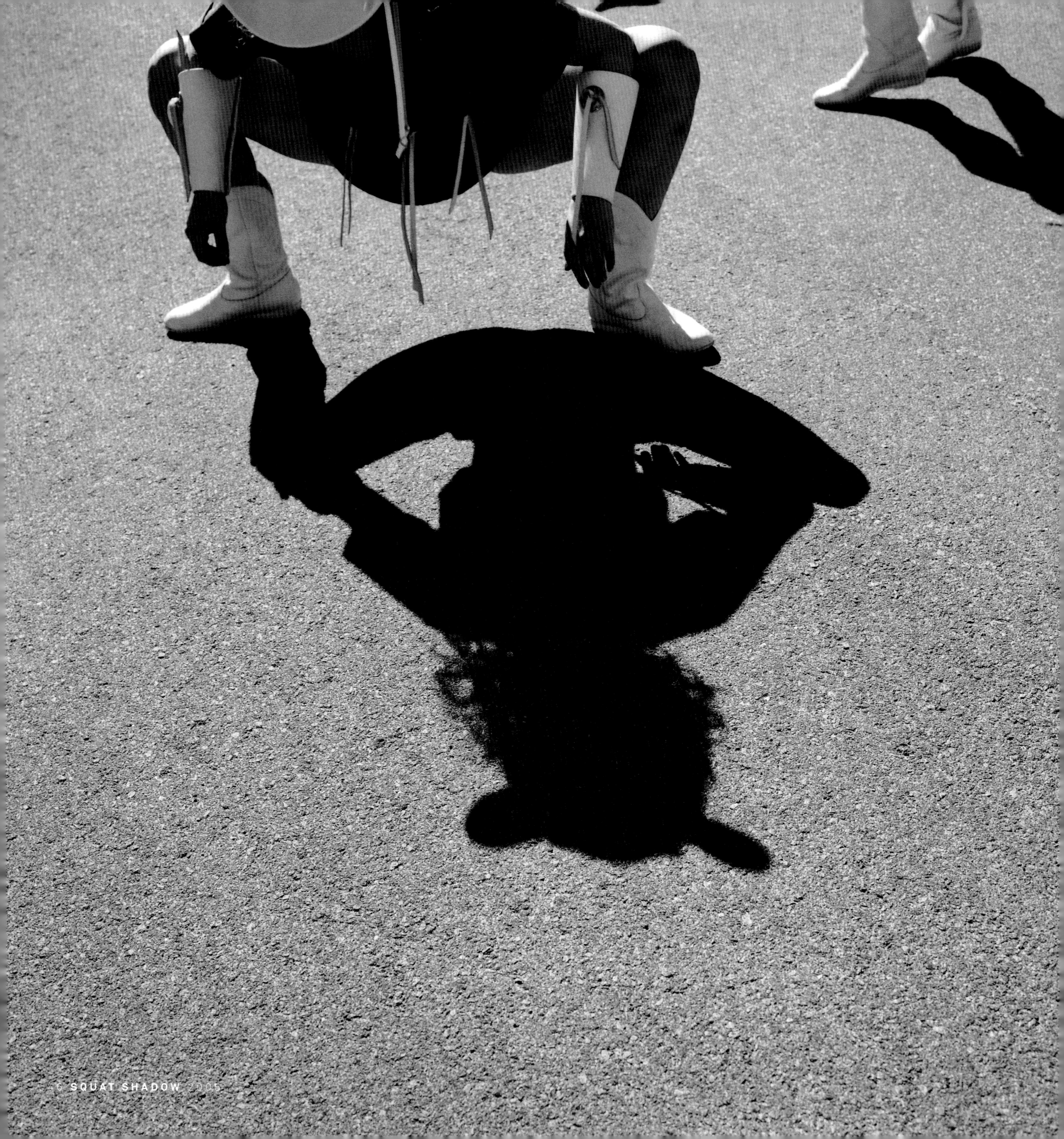

46 **SQUAT SHADOW** 2005

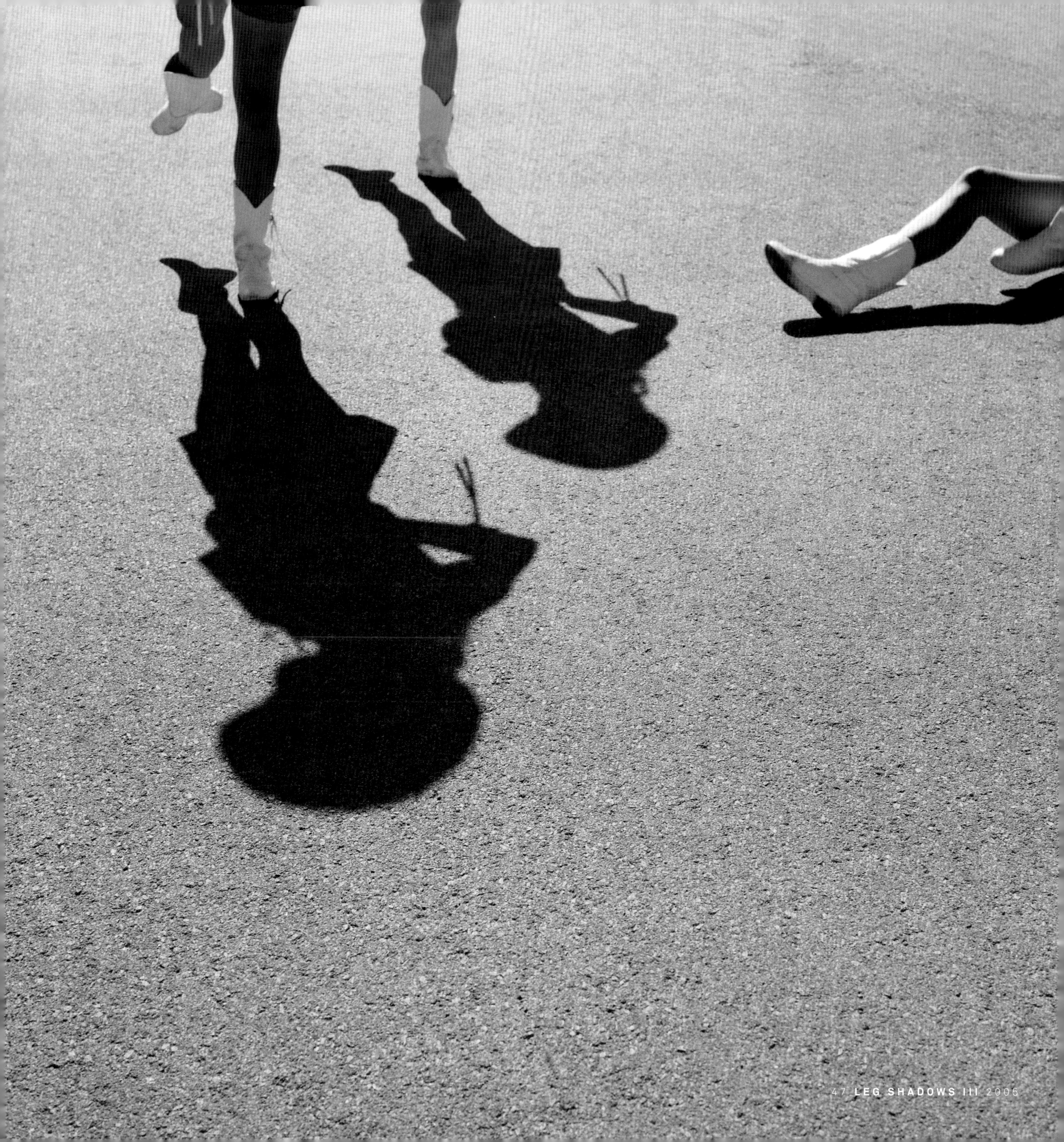

47 **LEG SHADOWS III** 2005

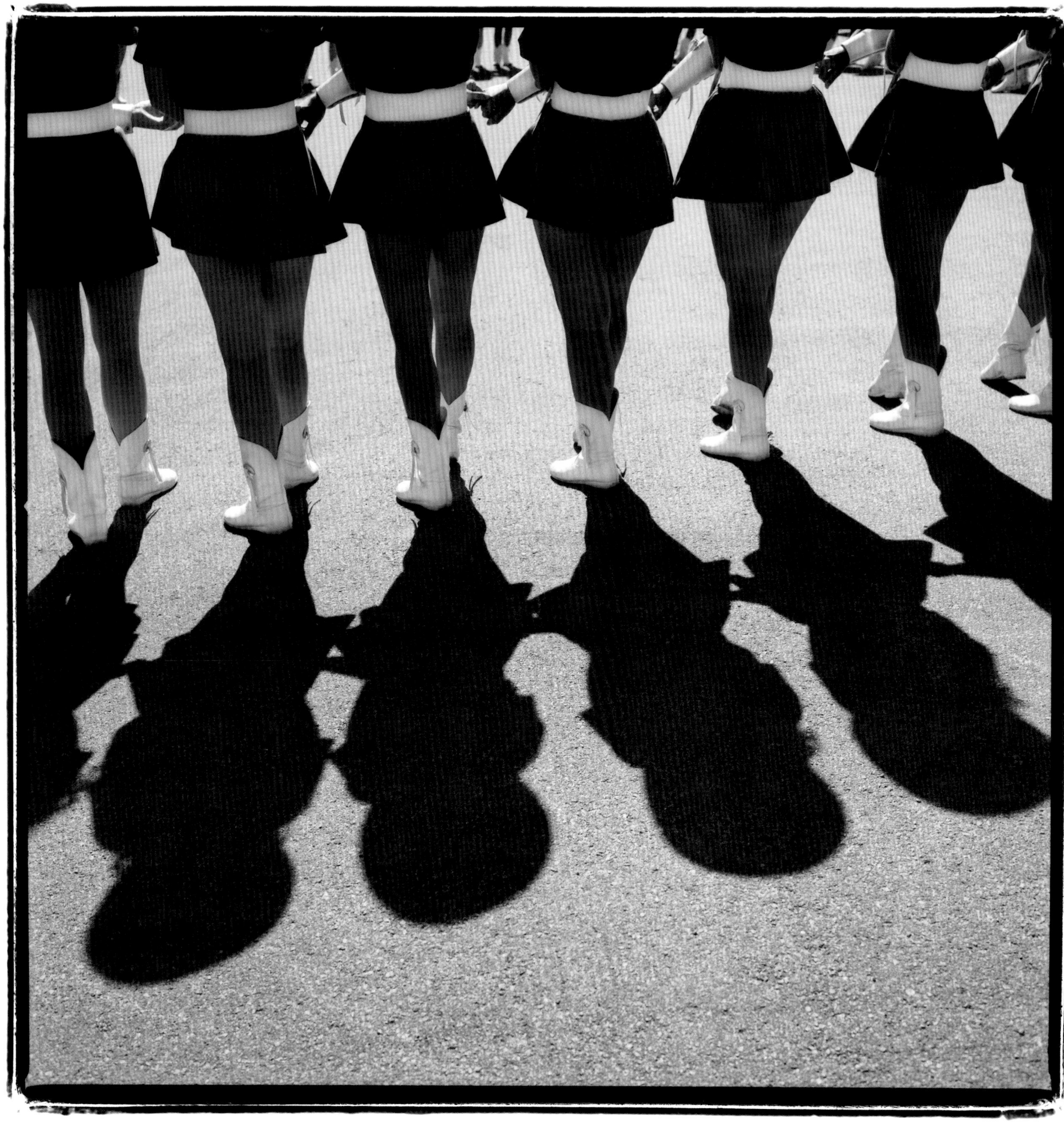

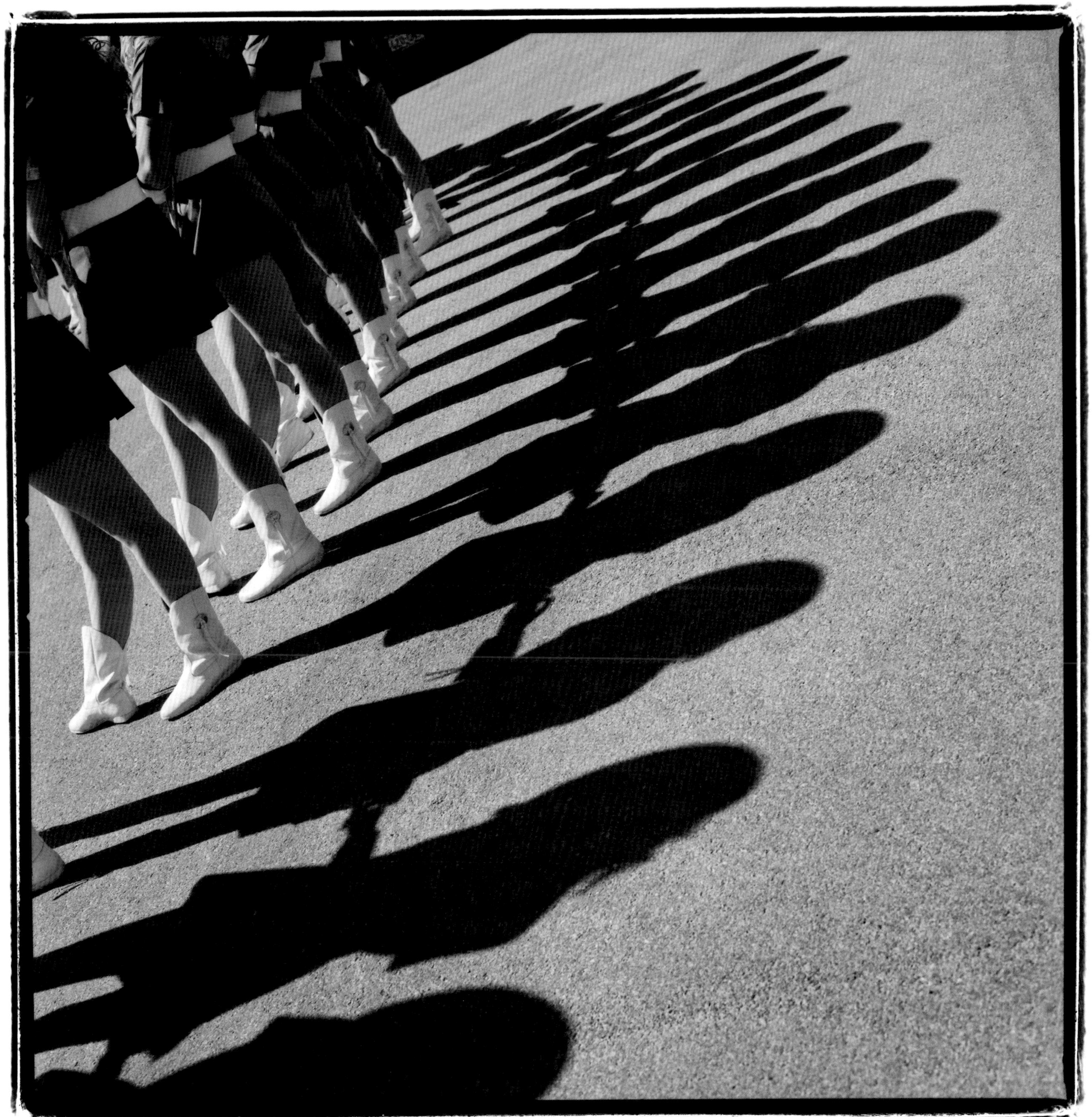

 PRAYER SHADOWS 2005

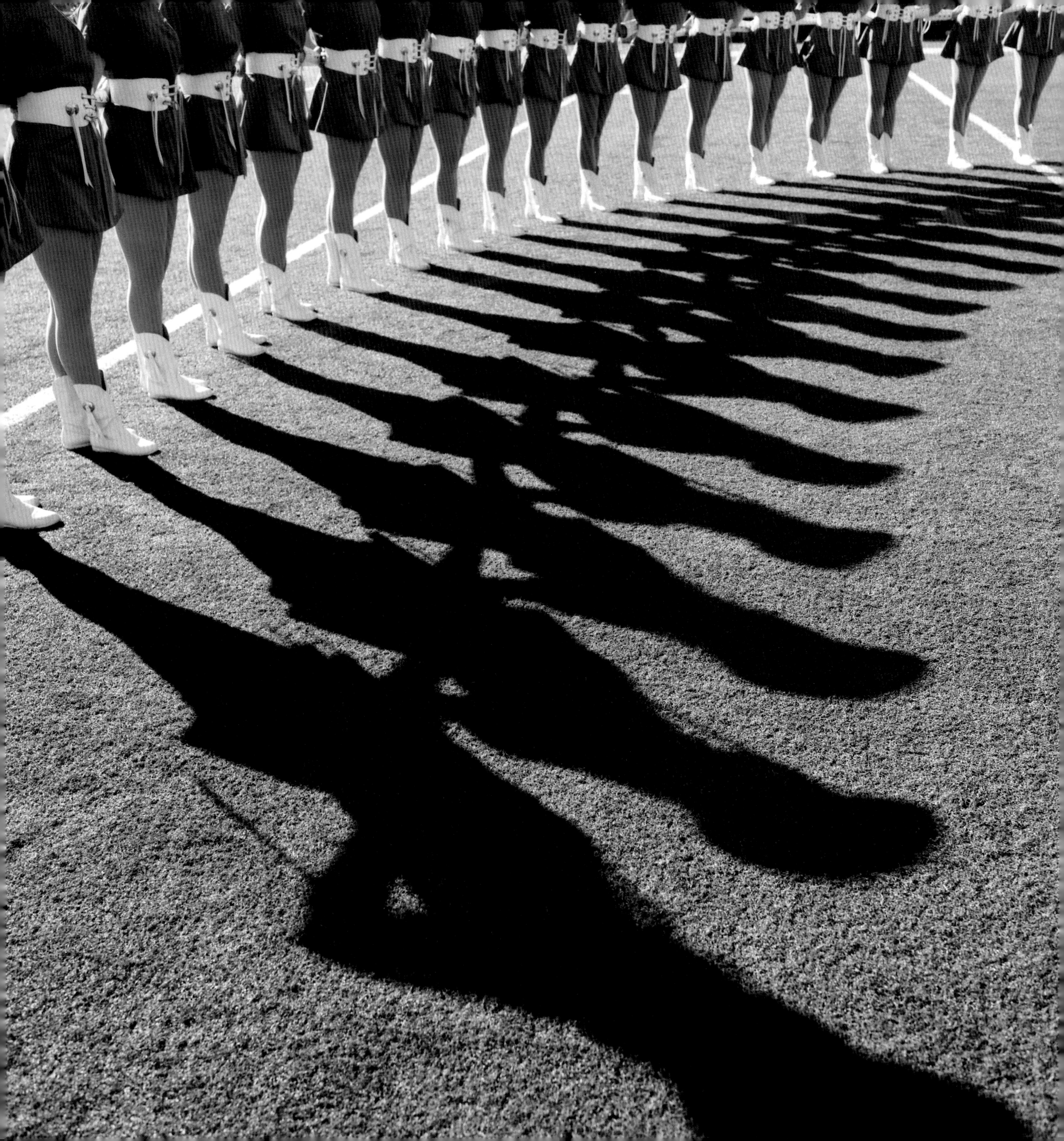

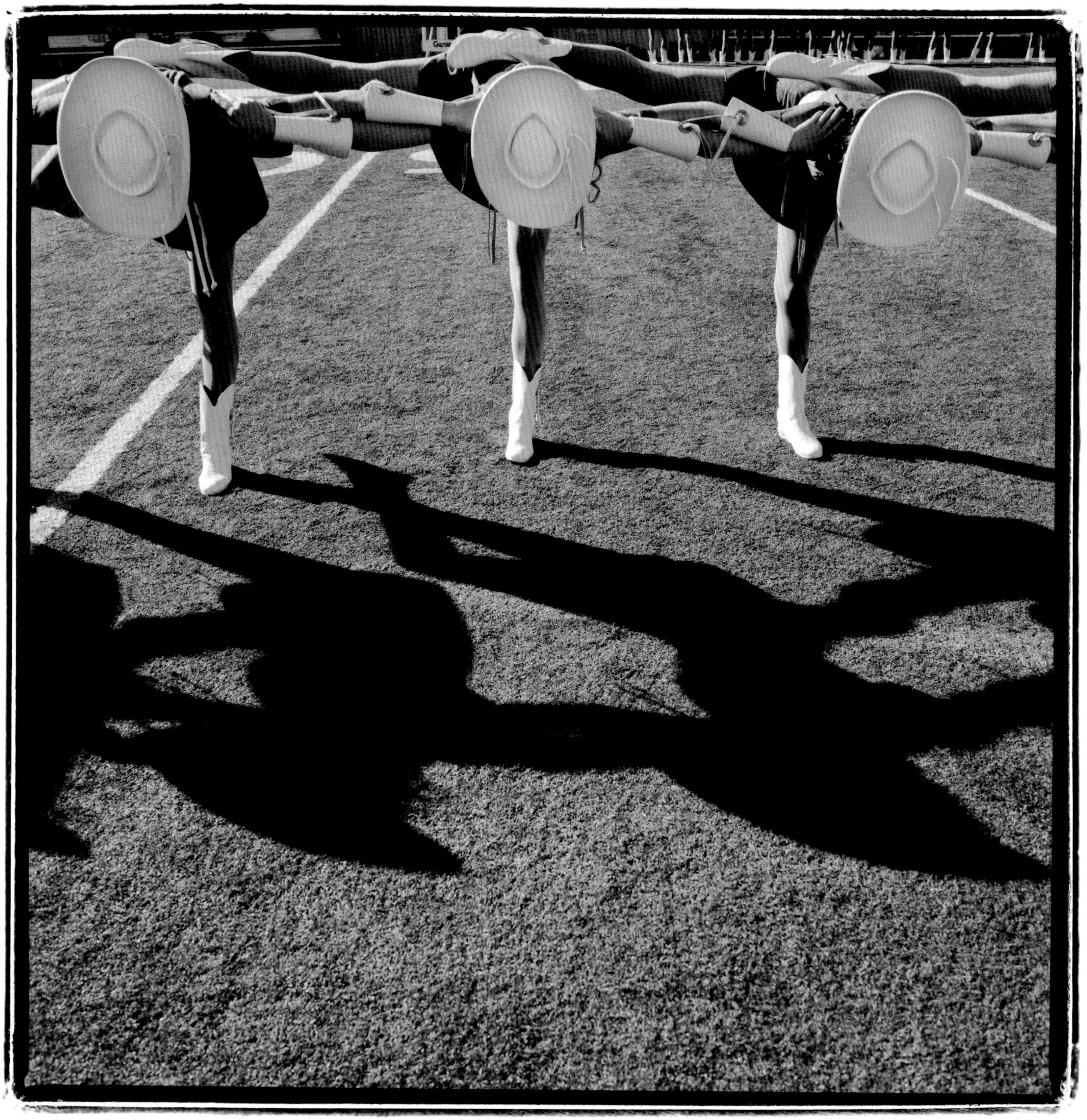

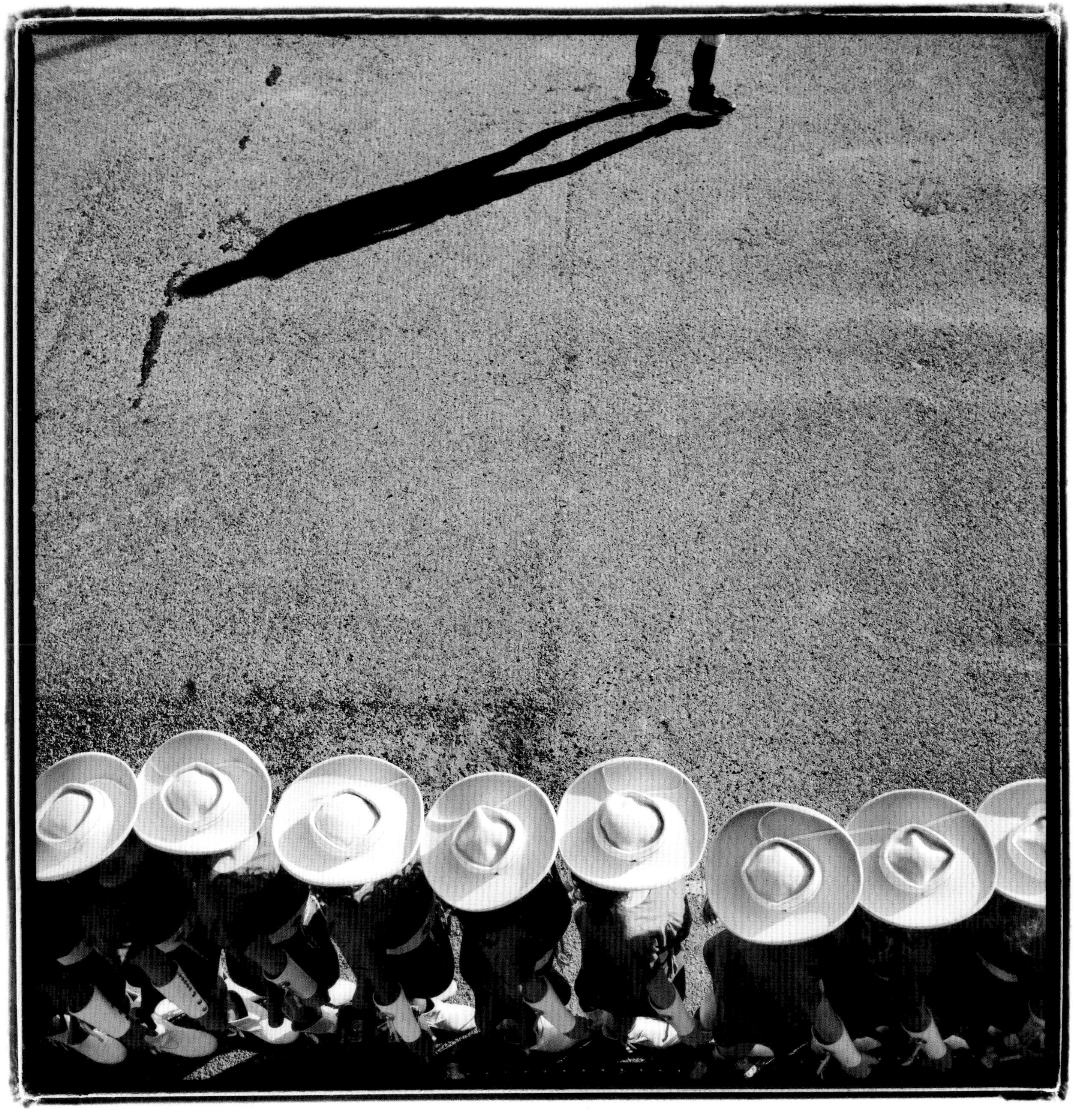

52 **HATS, BALL PLAYER SHADOW** 2006

53 **THREE CHAIRS RANGERETTE REVELS** 2003

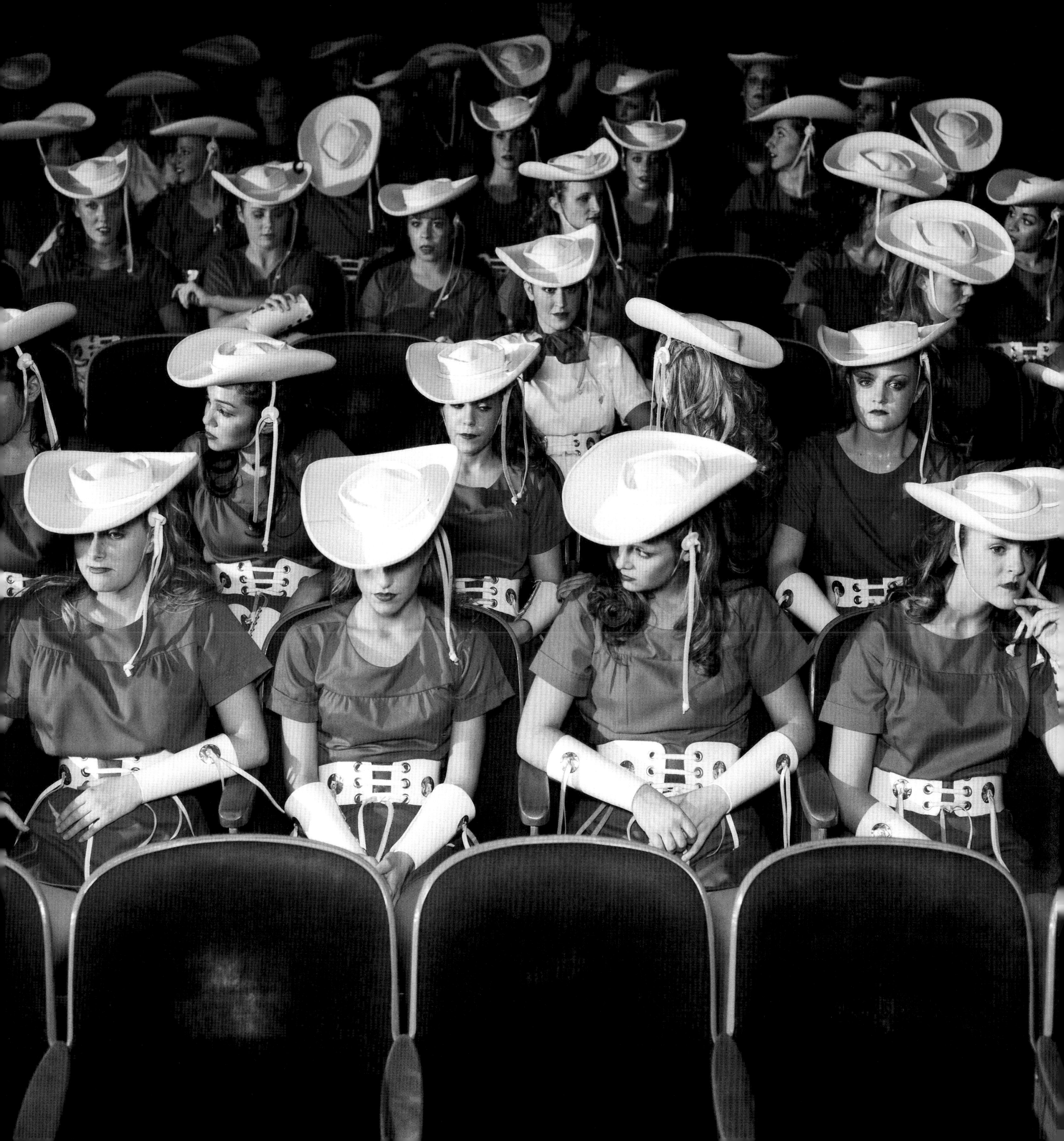

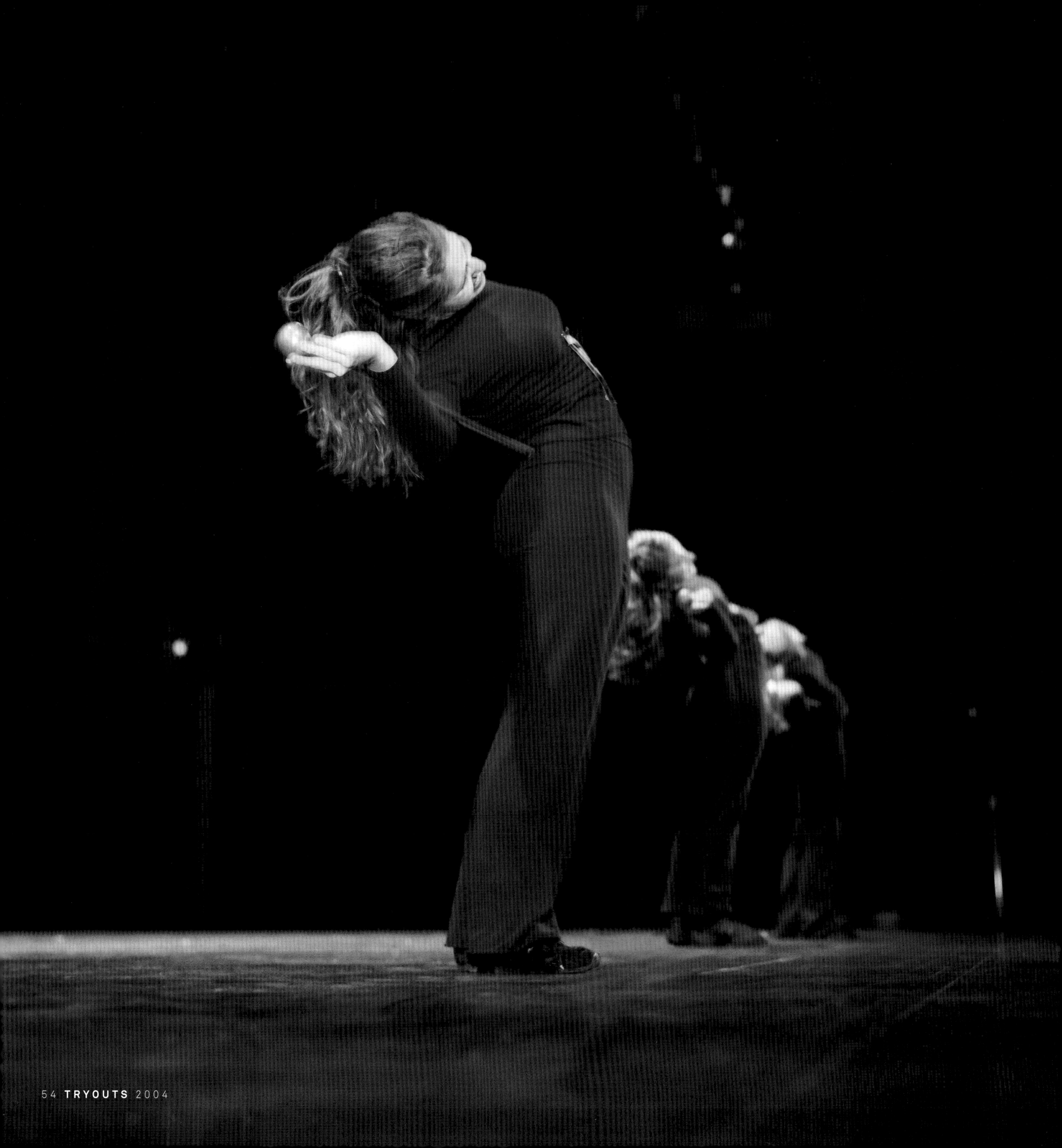

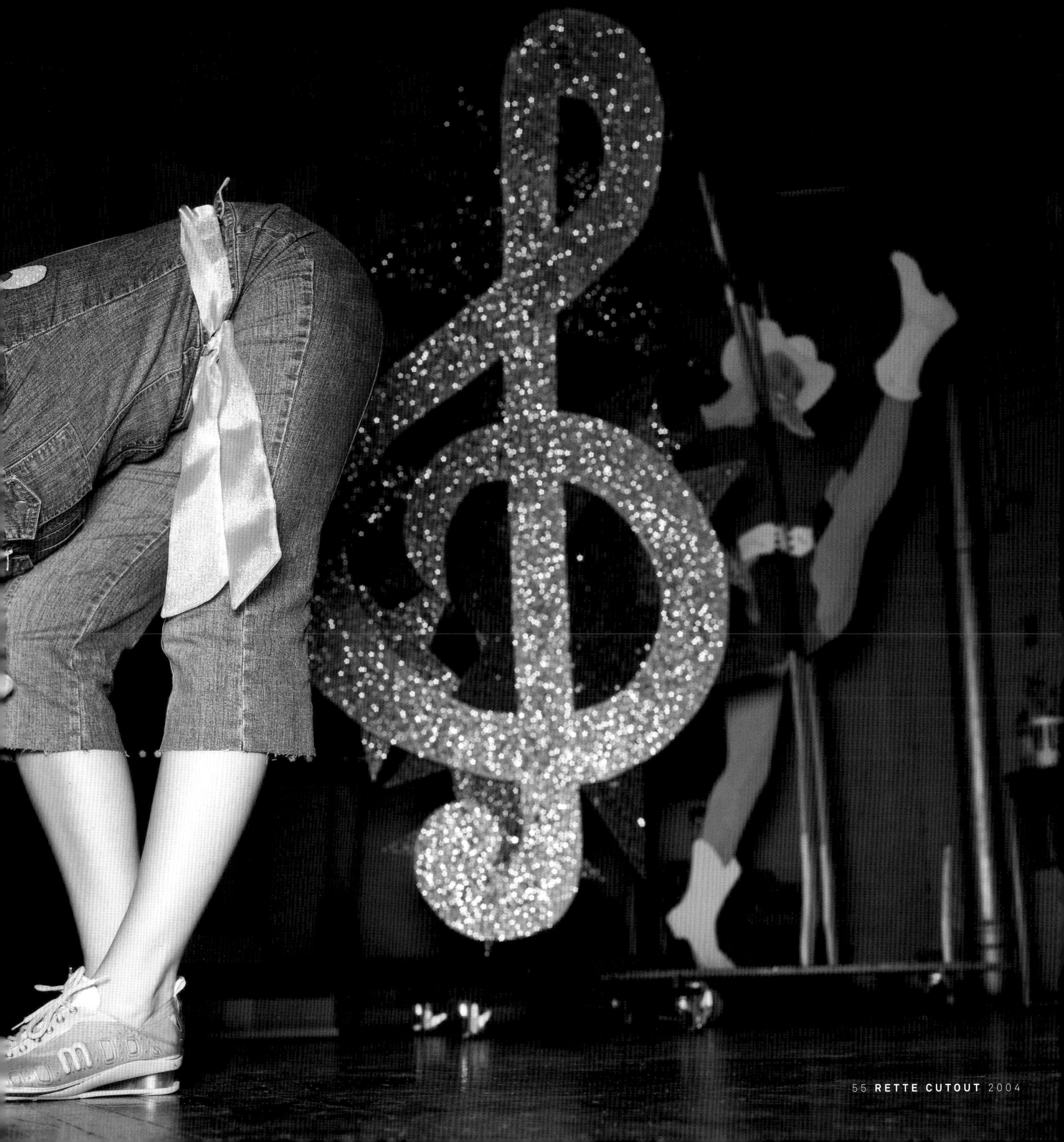

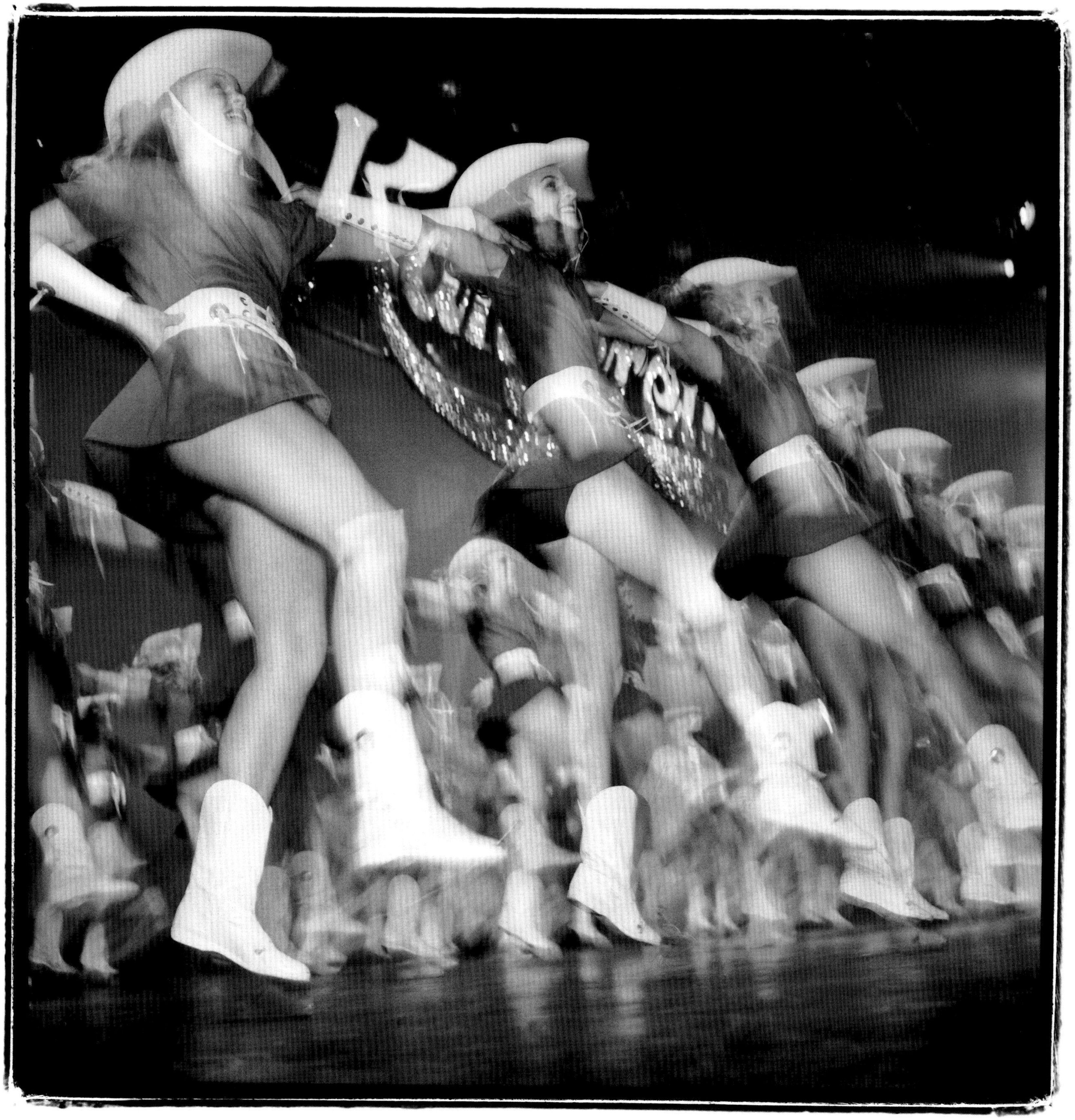

 RANGERETTE REVELS KICK 2004

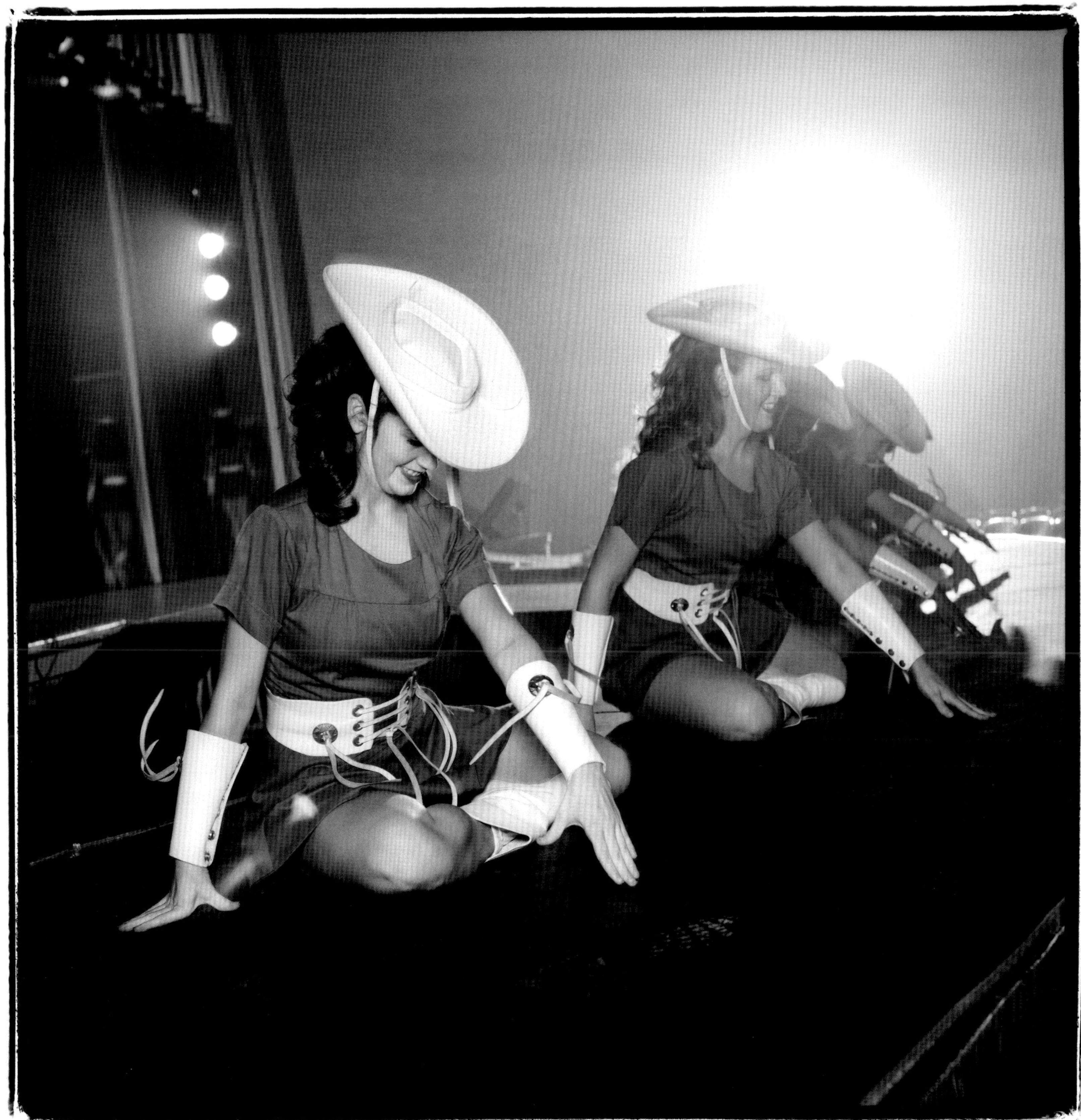

57 **RANGERETTE REVELS STAGE** 2004

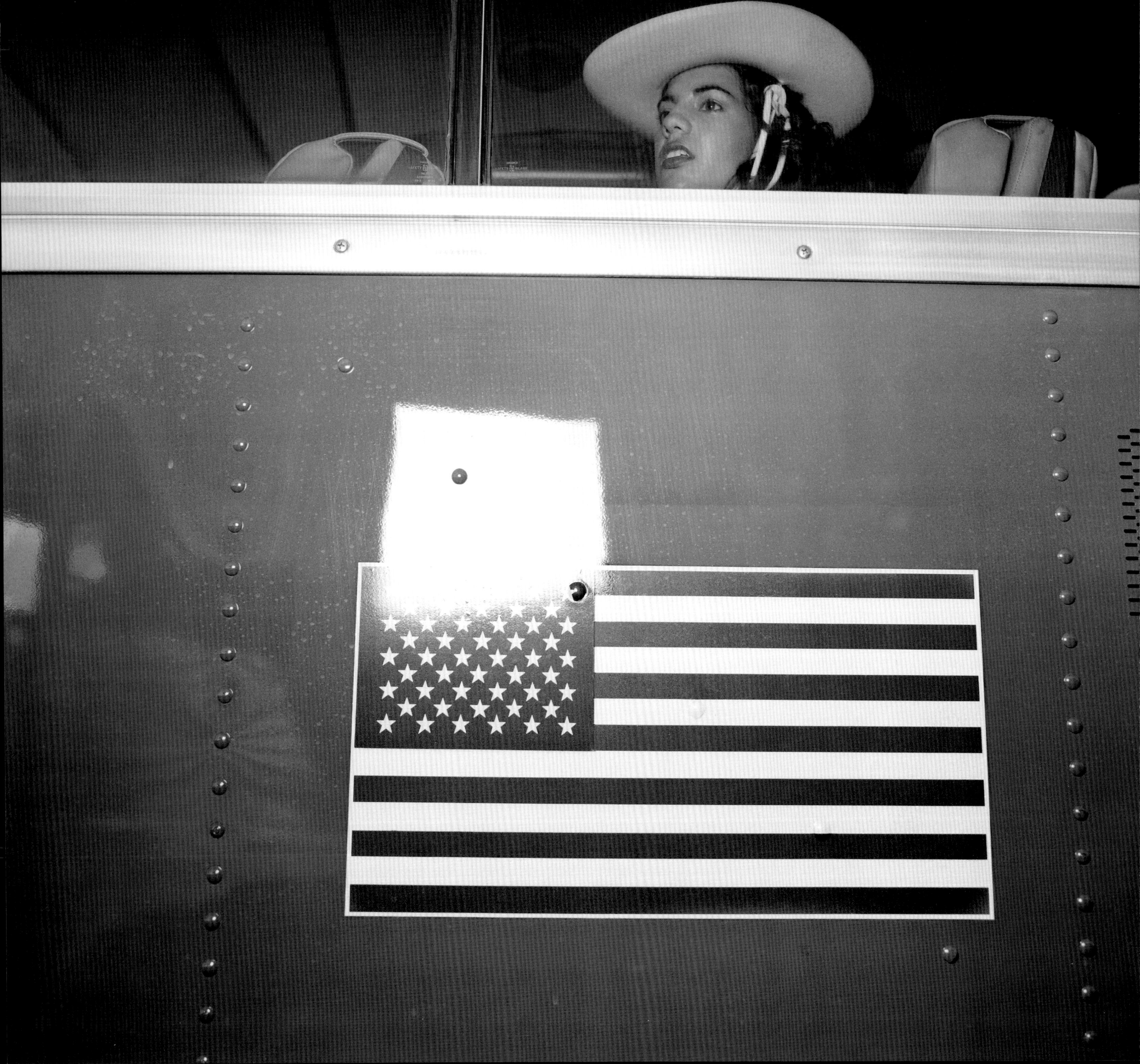

58 BUS FLAG 1989

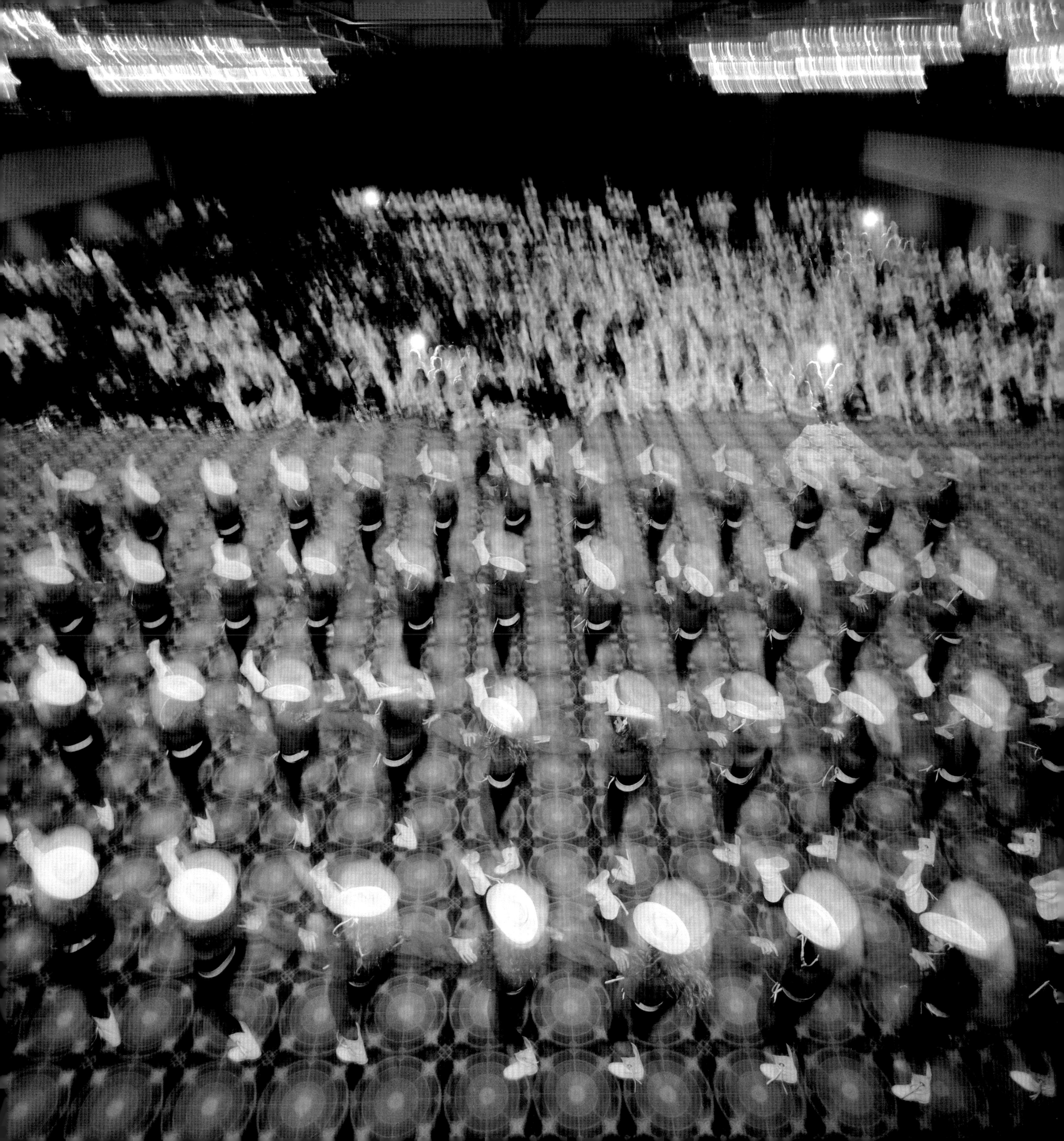

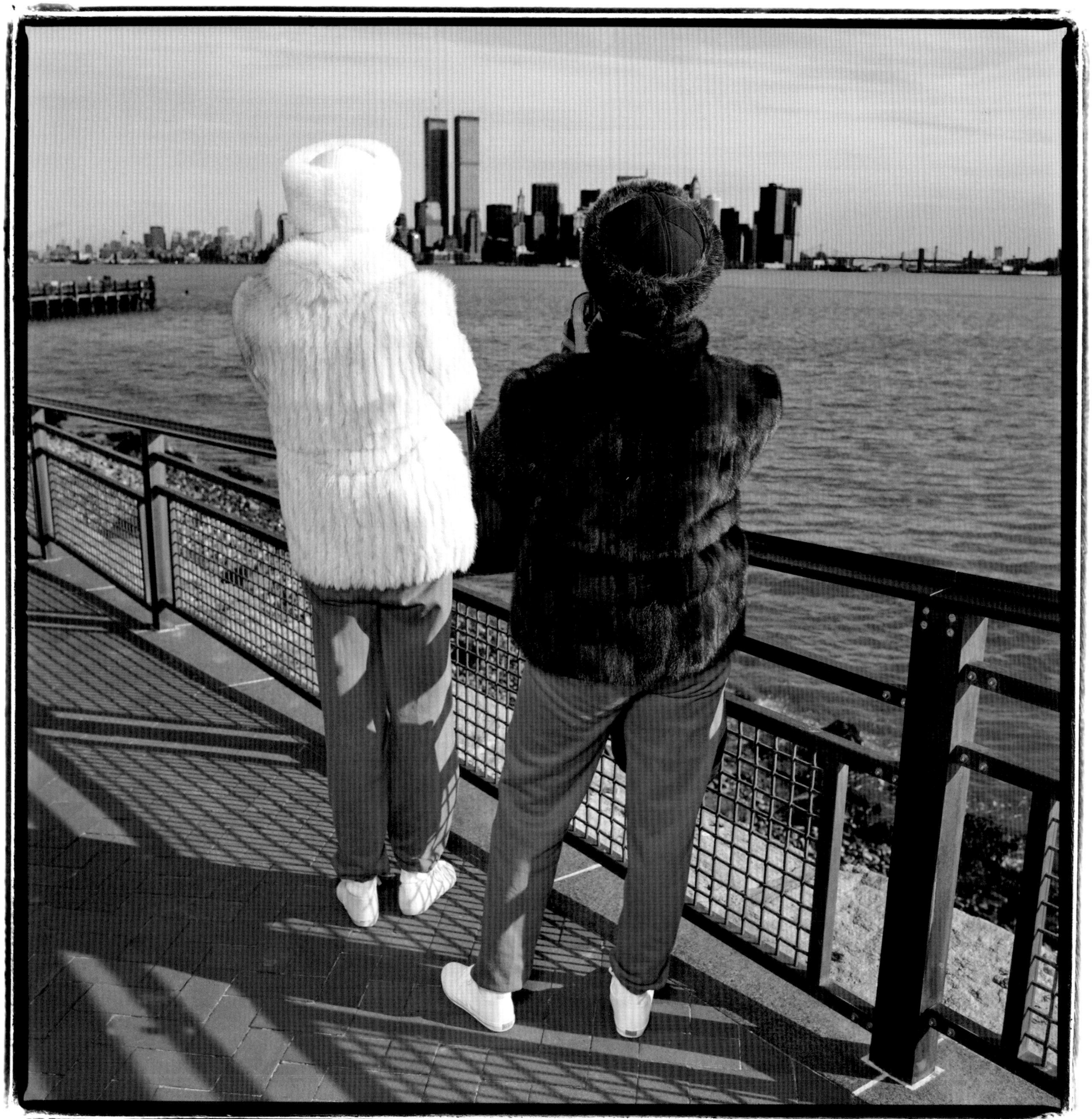

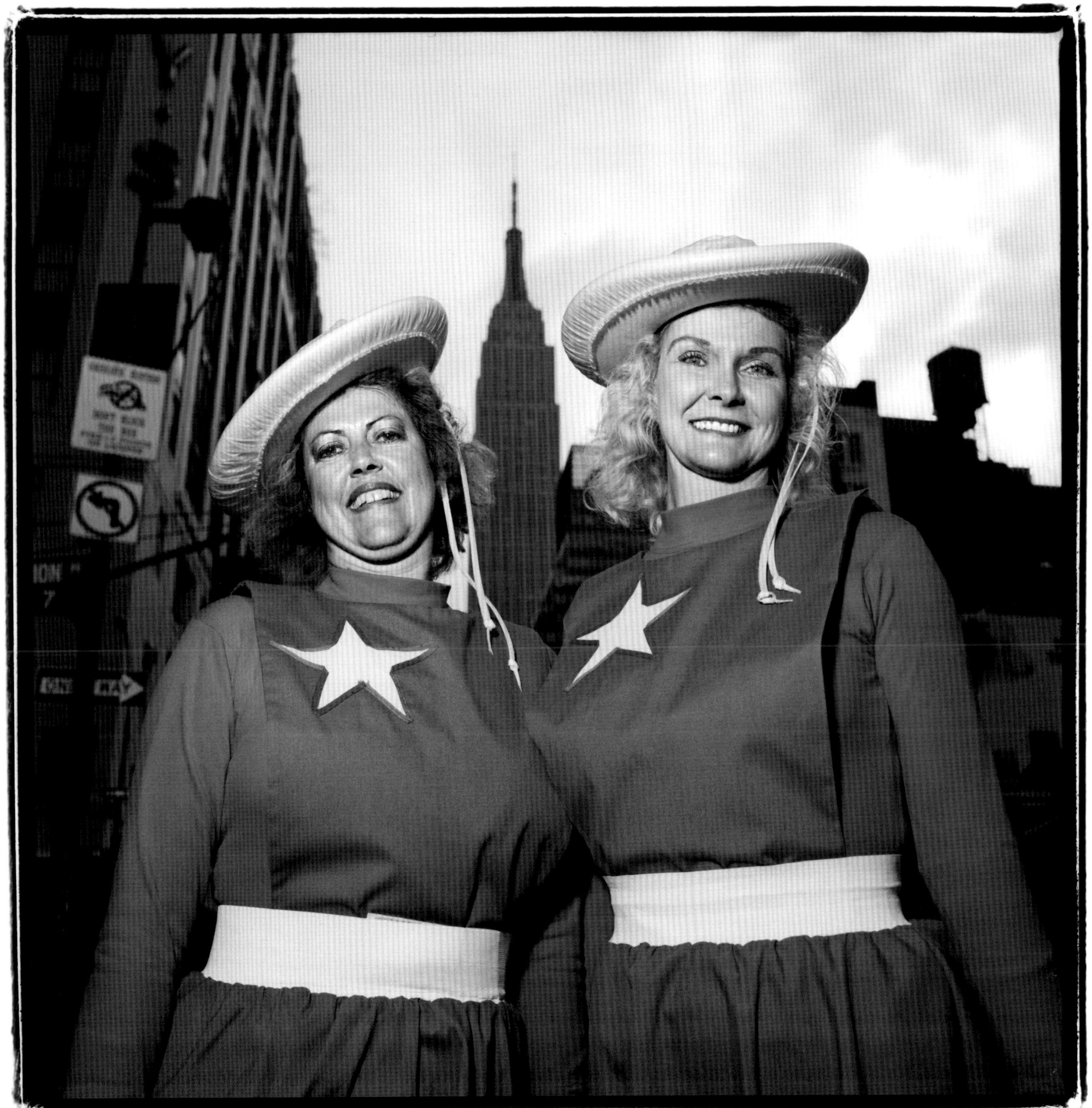

61 **EMPIRE STATE BUILDING** 1989

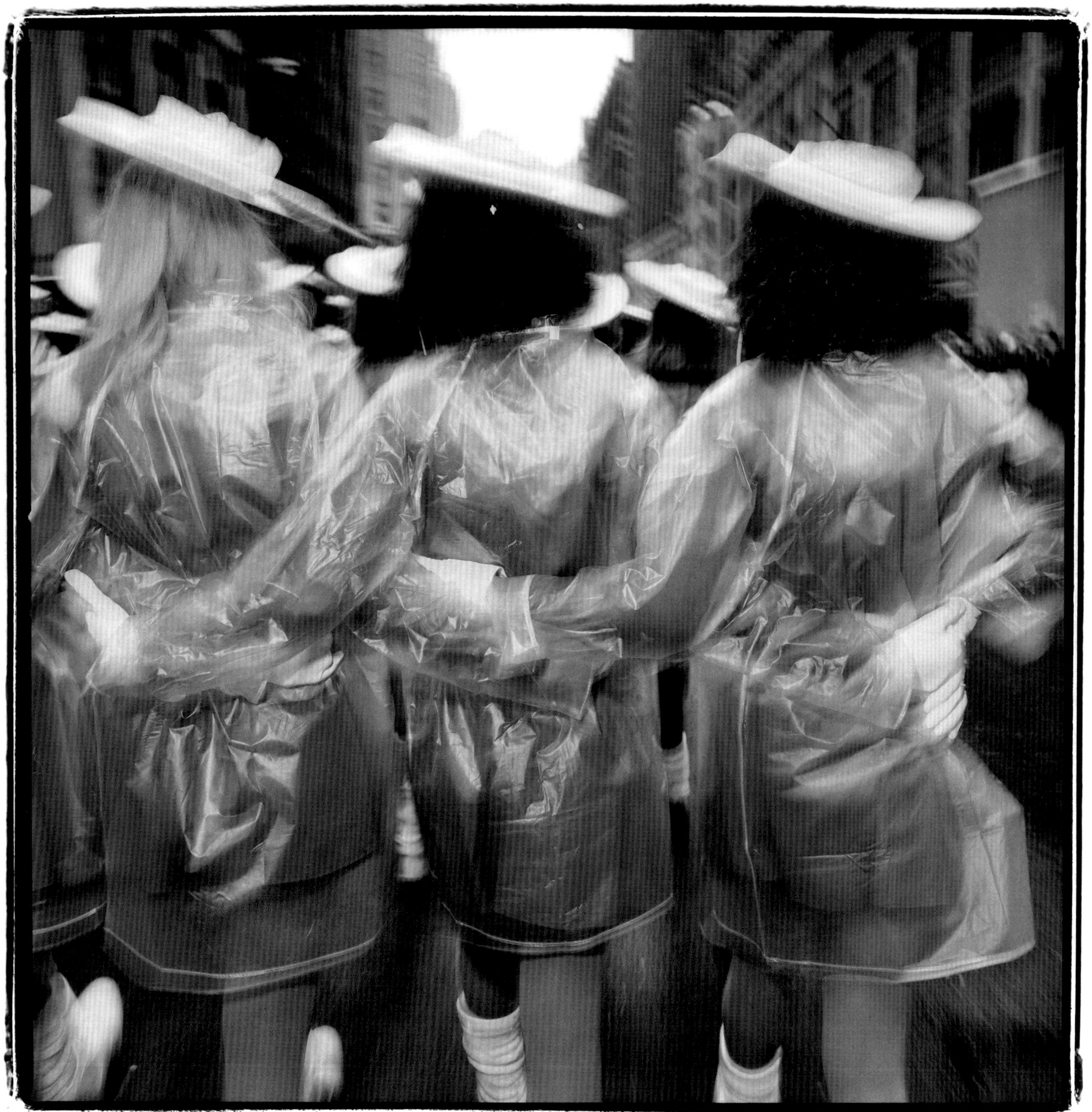

 RETTE FOREVER MACY'S 1989

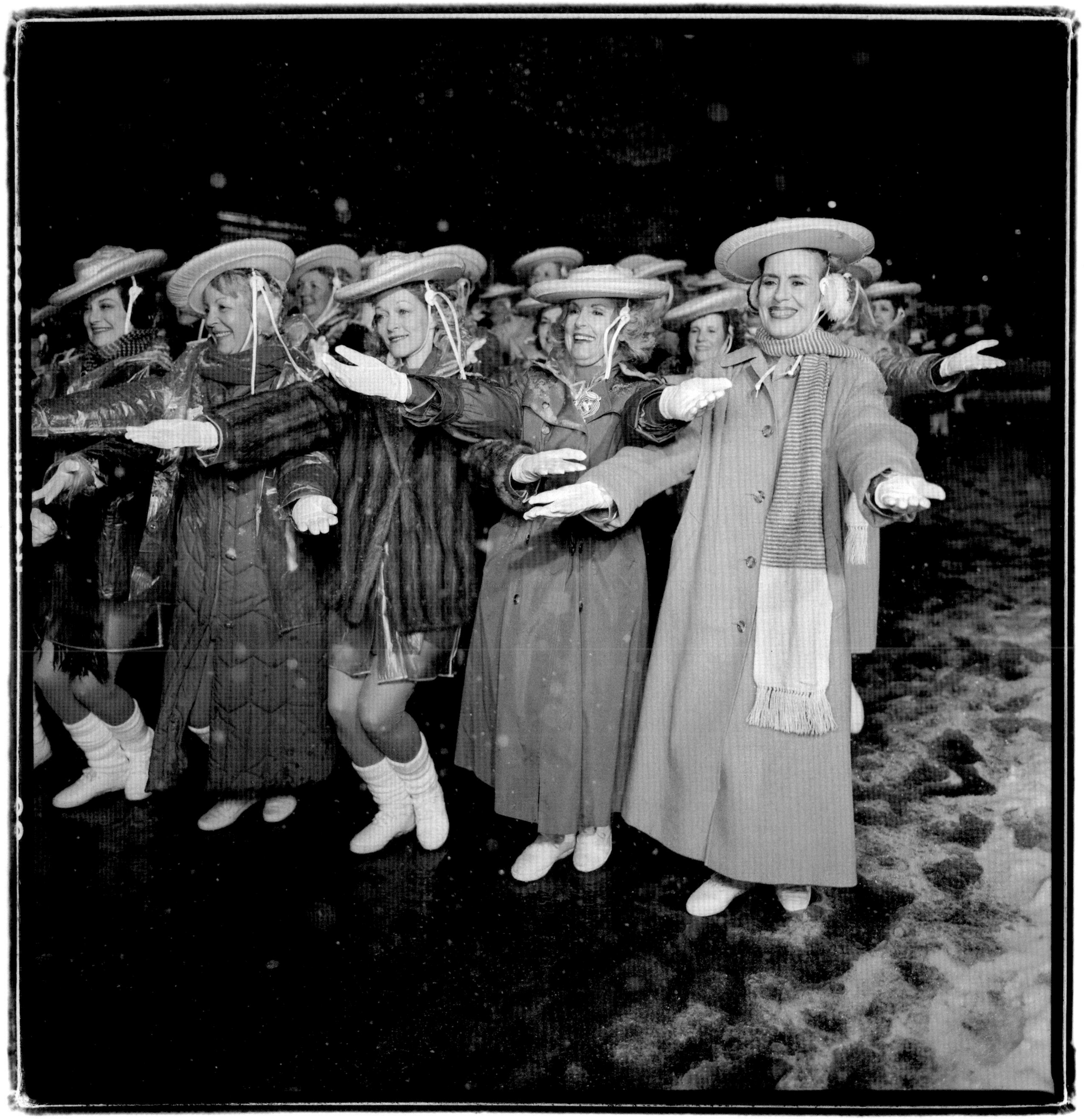

63 **FOREVER SNOW** 1989

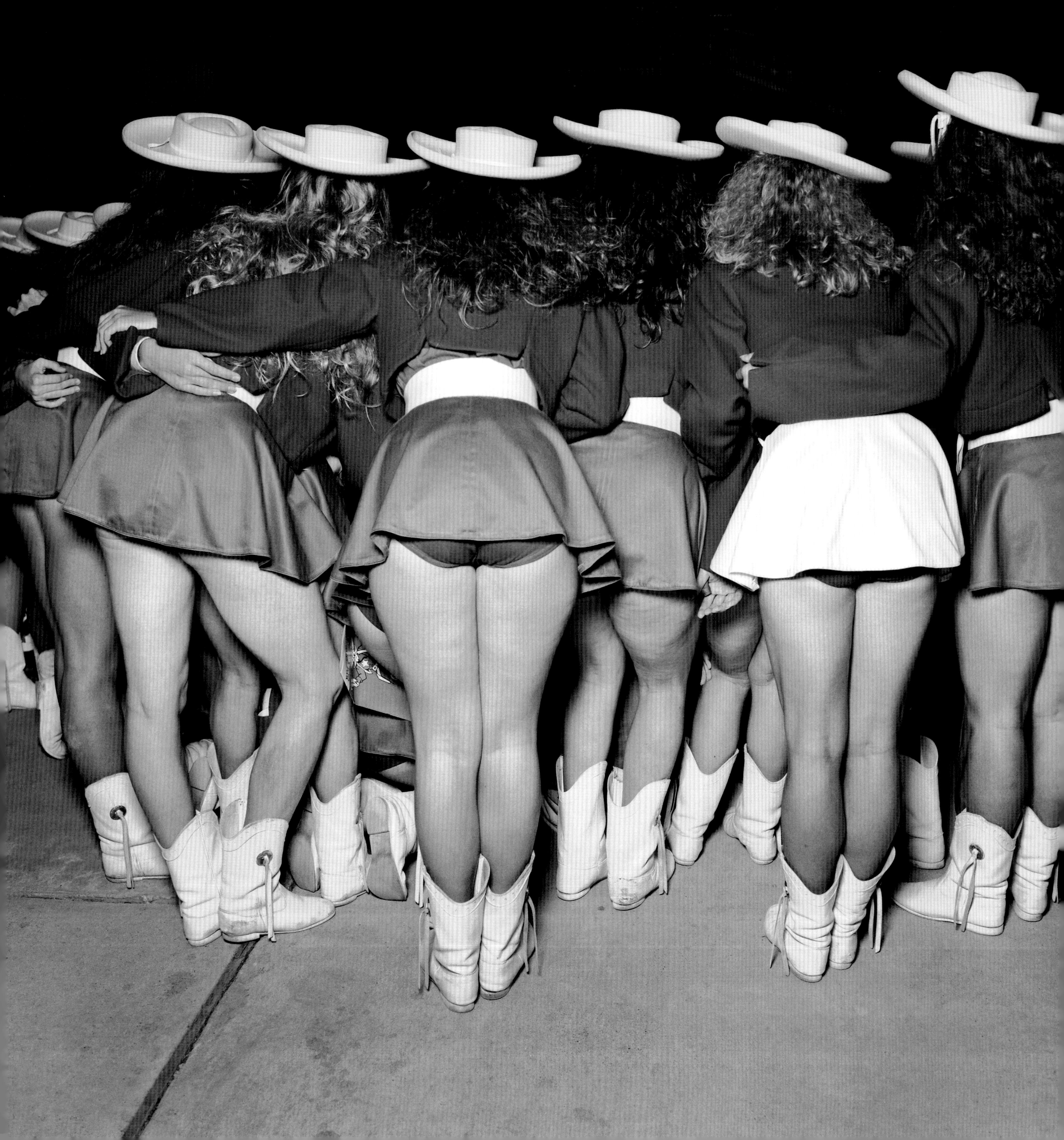

64 **GROUP PICTURE** 1989

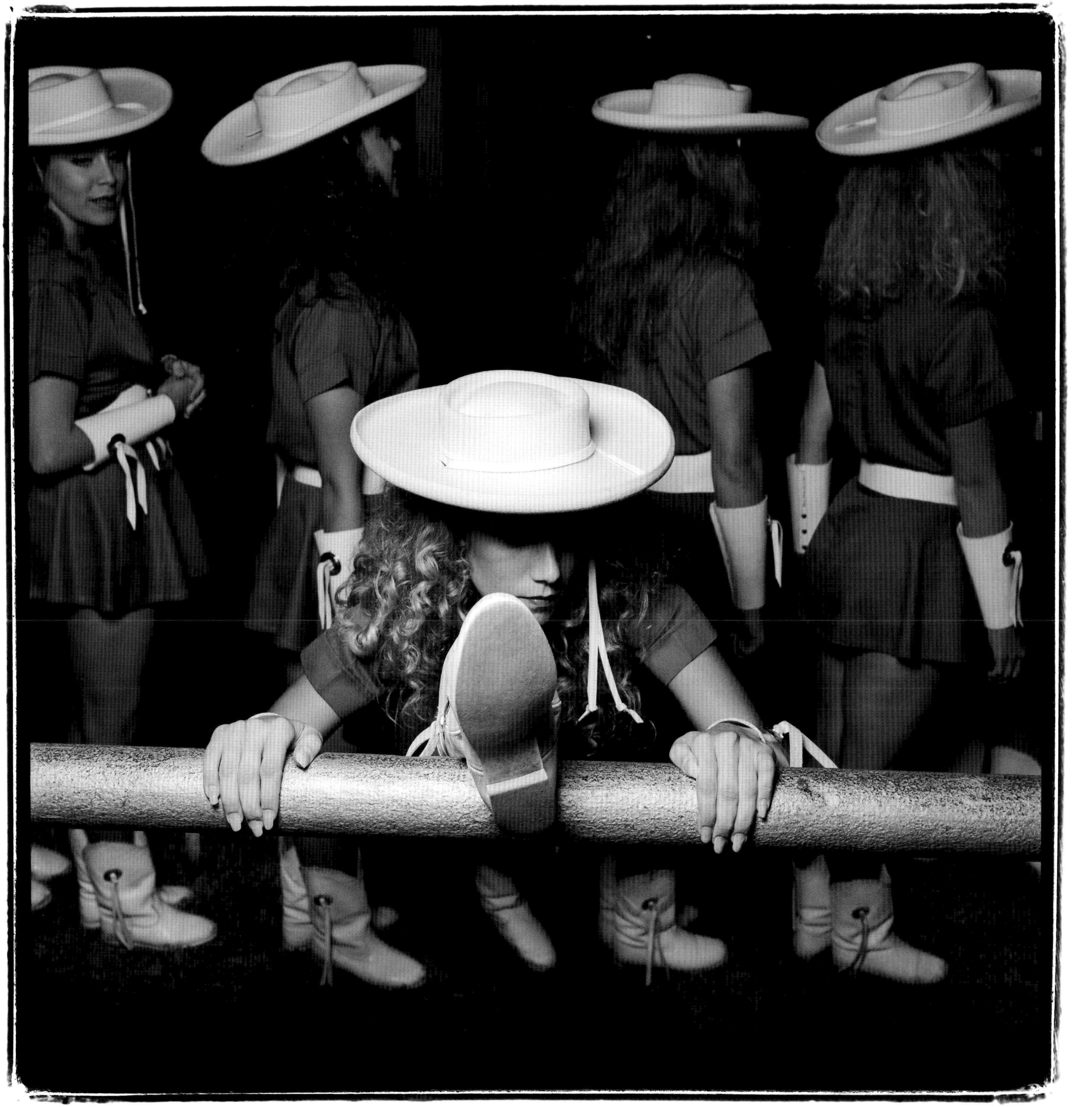

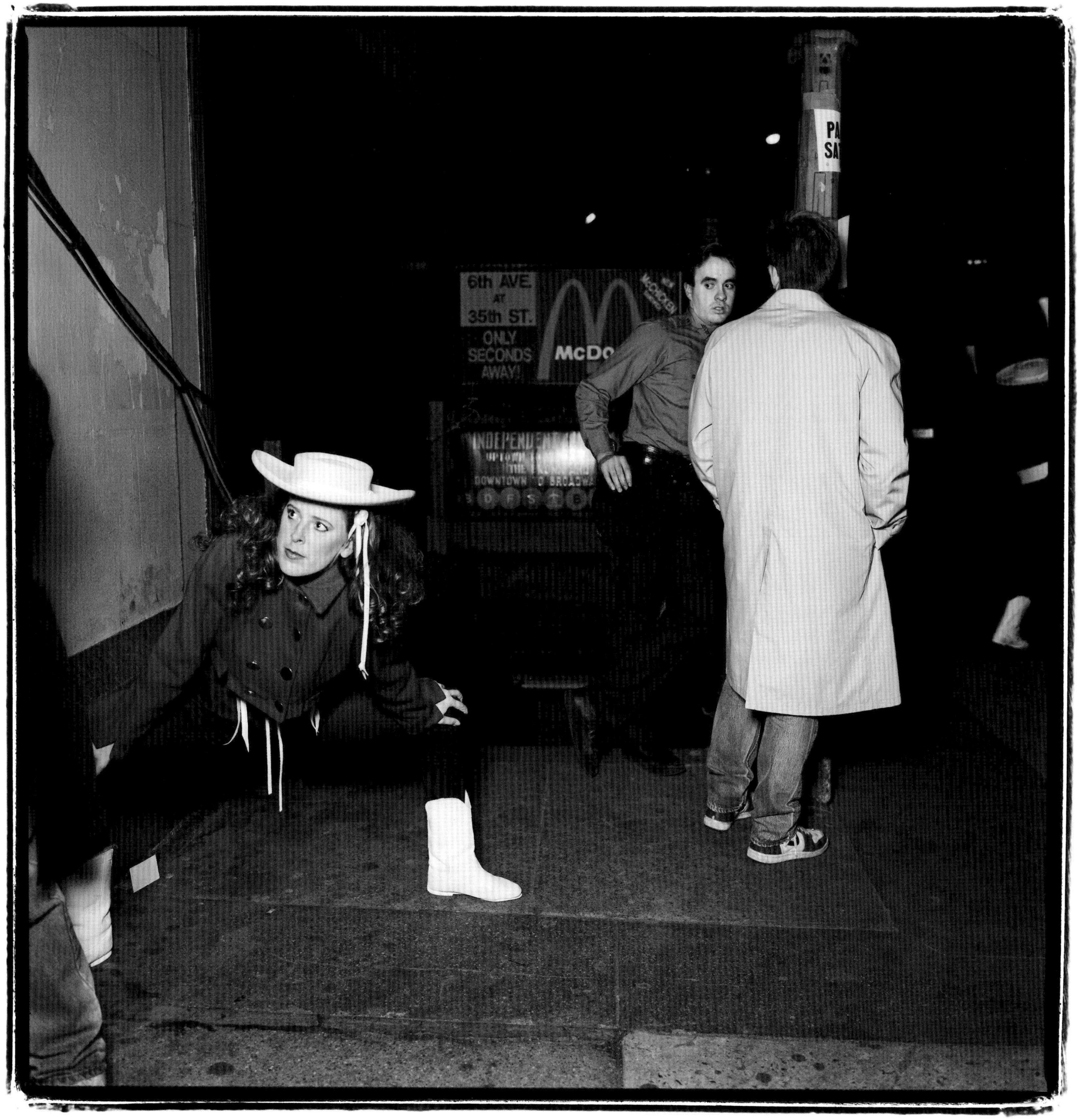
6th AVE.
AT
35th ST.
ONLY
SECONDS
AWAY!

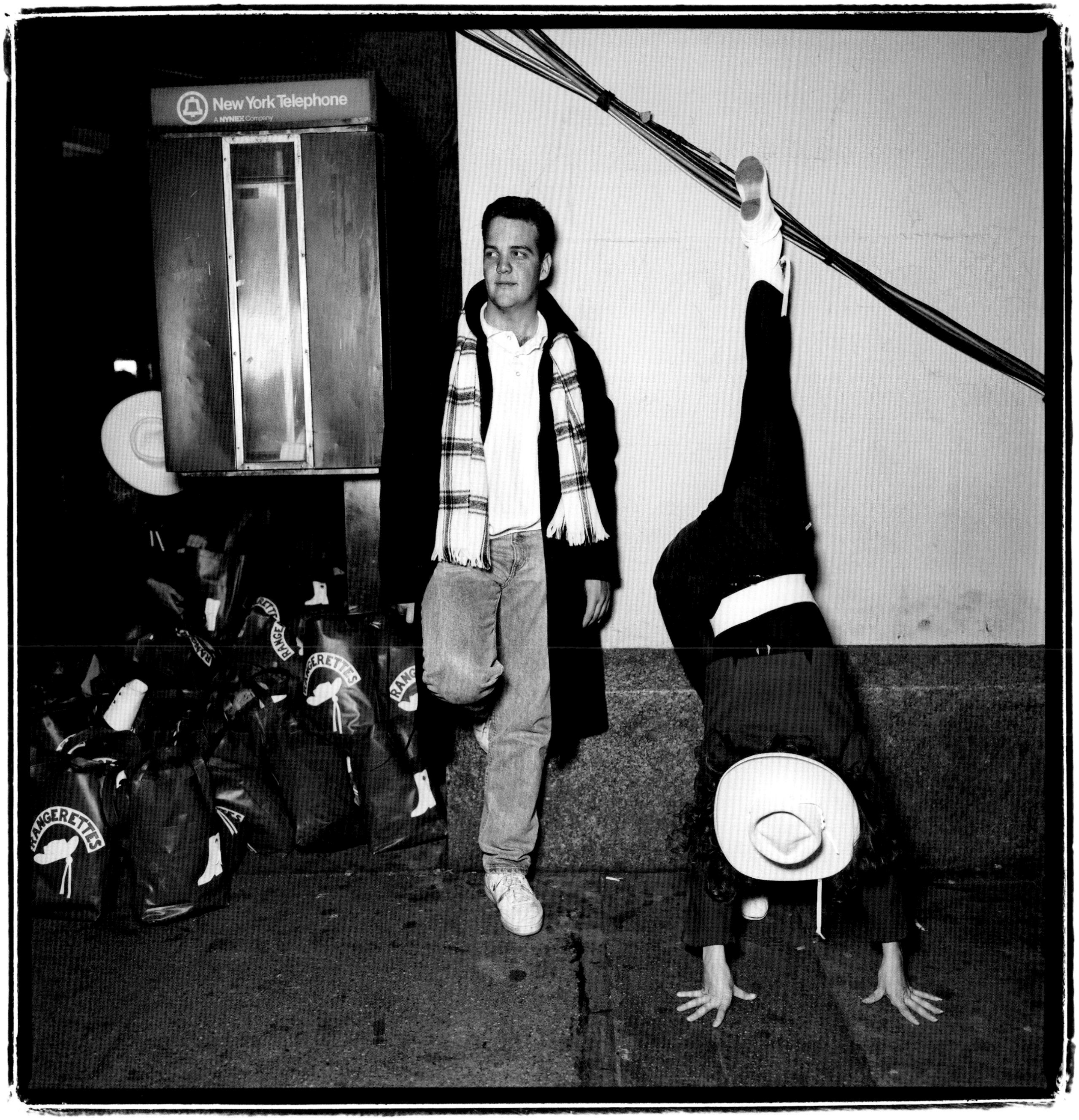
New York Telephone
A NYNEX Company
RANGERETTES

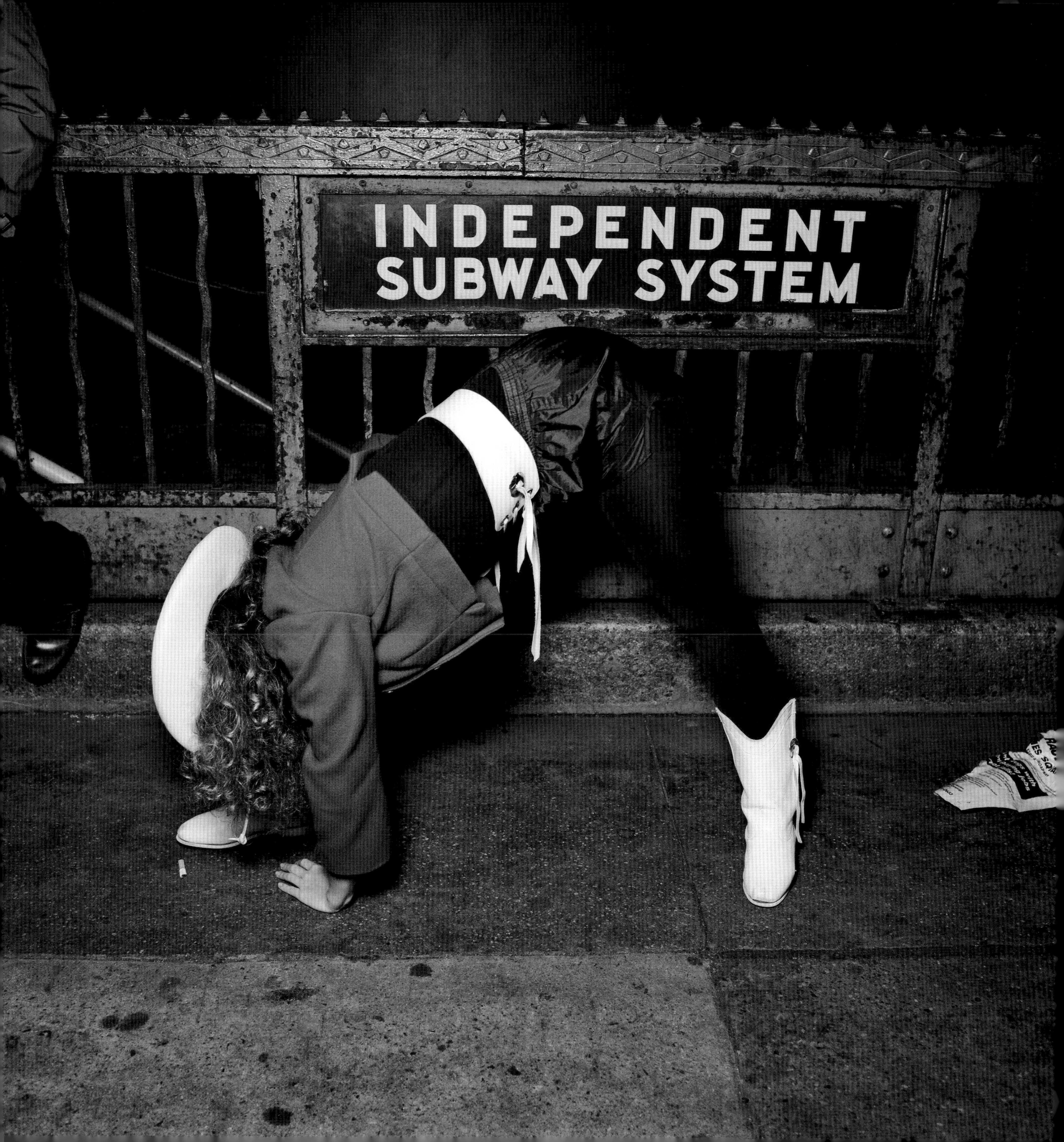
INDEPENDENT
SUBWAY SYSTEM

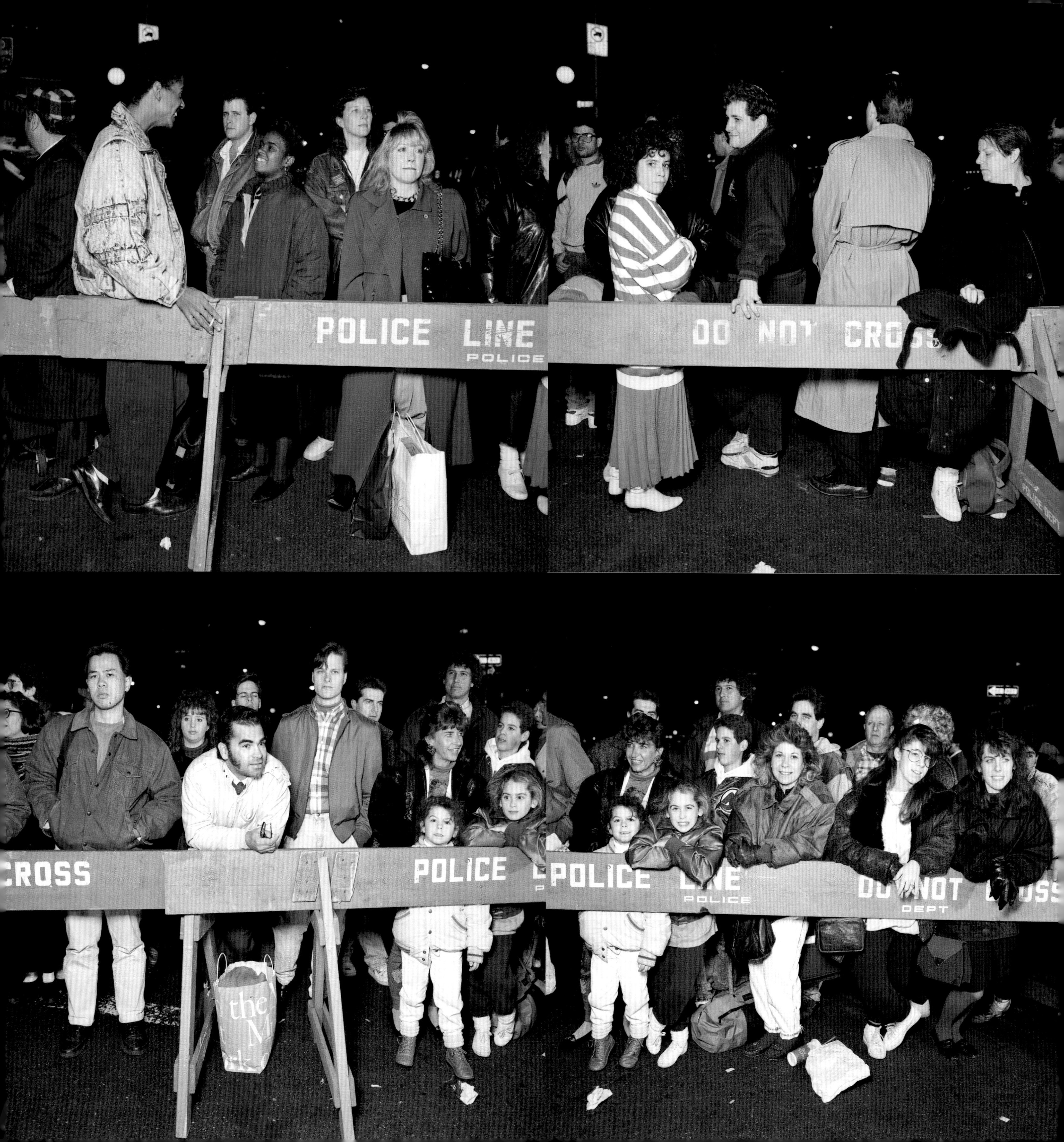
POLICE LINE
POLICE
DO NOT CROSS
CROSS
POLICE
POLICE LINE
POLICE
DO NOT CROSS
DEPT

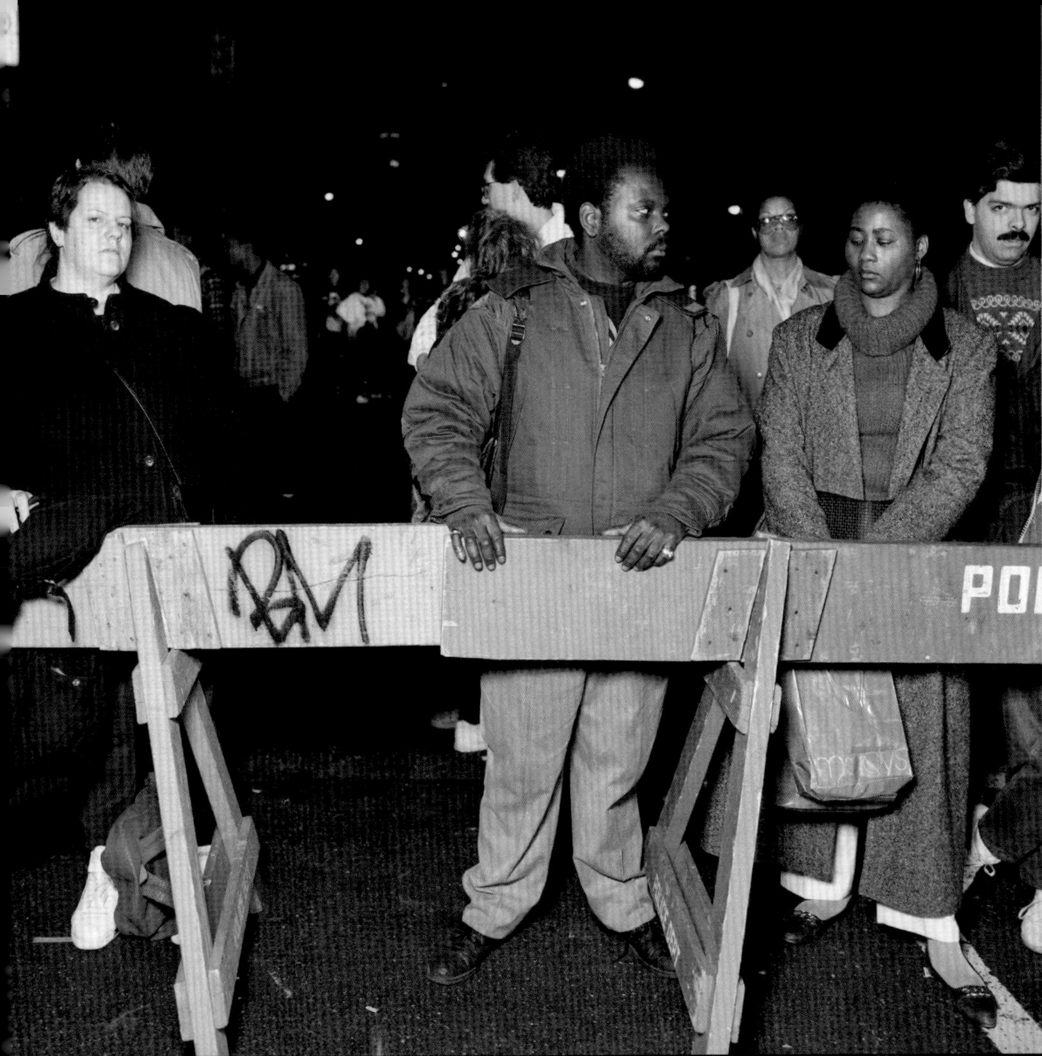

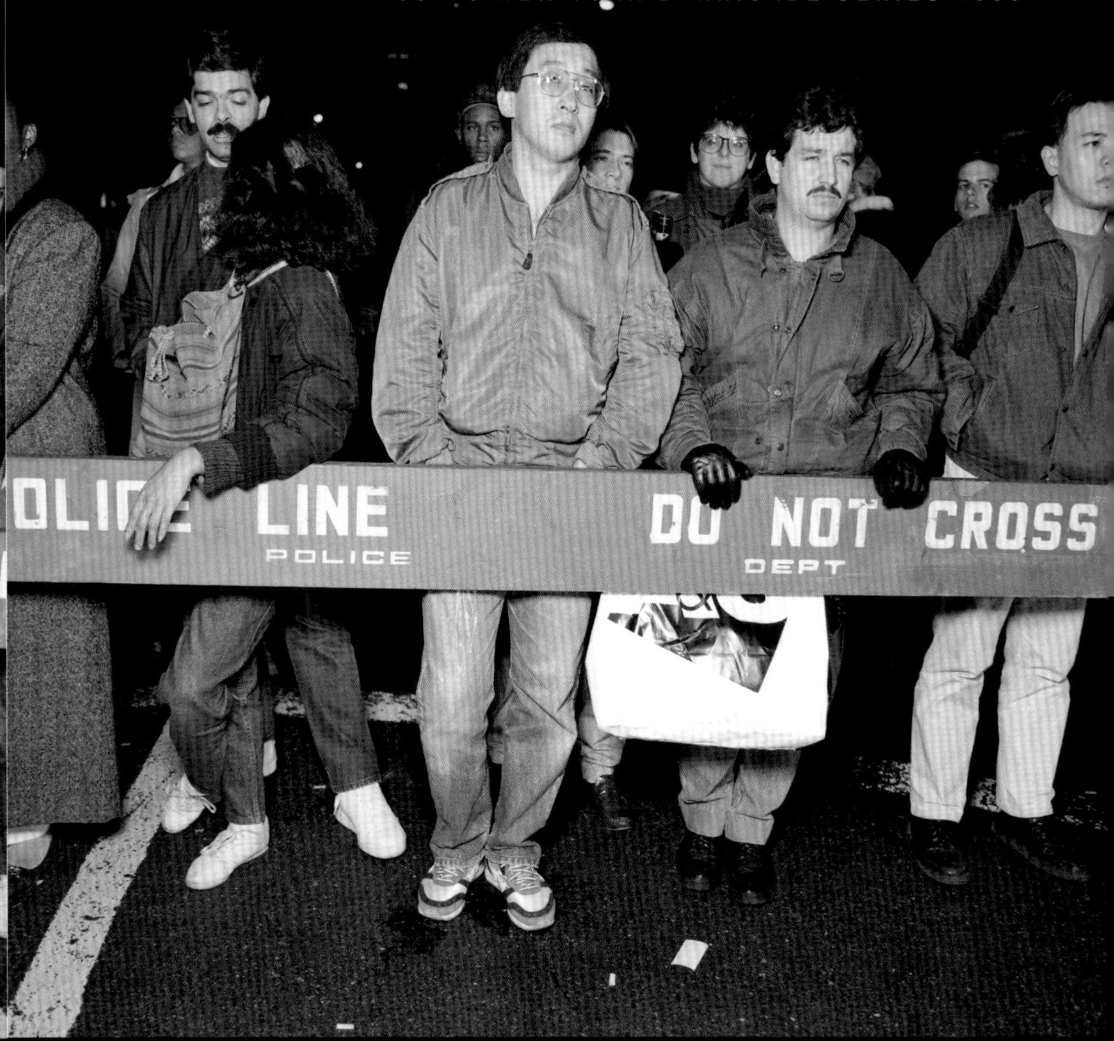
POLICE
DO NOT CROSS
DEPT

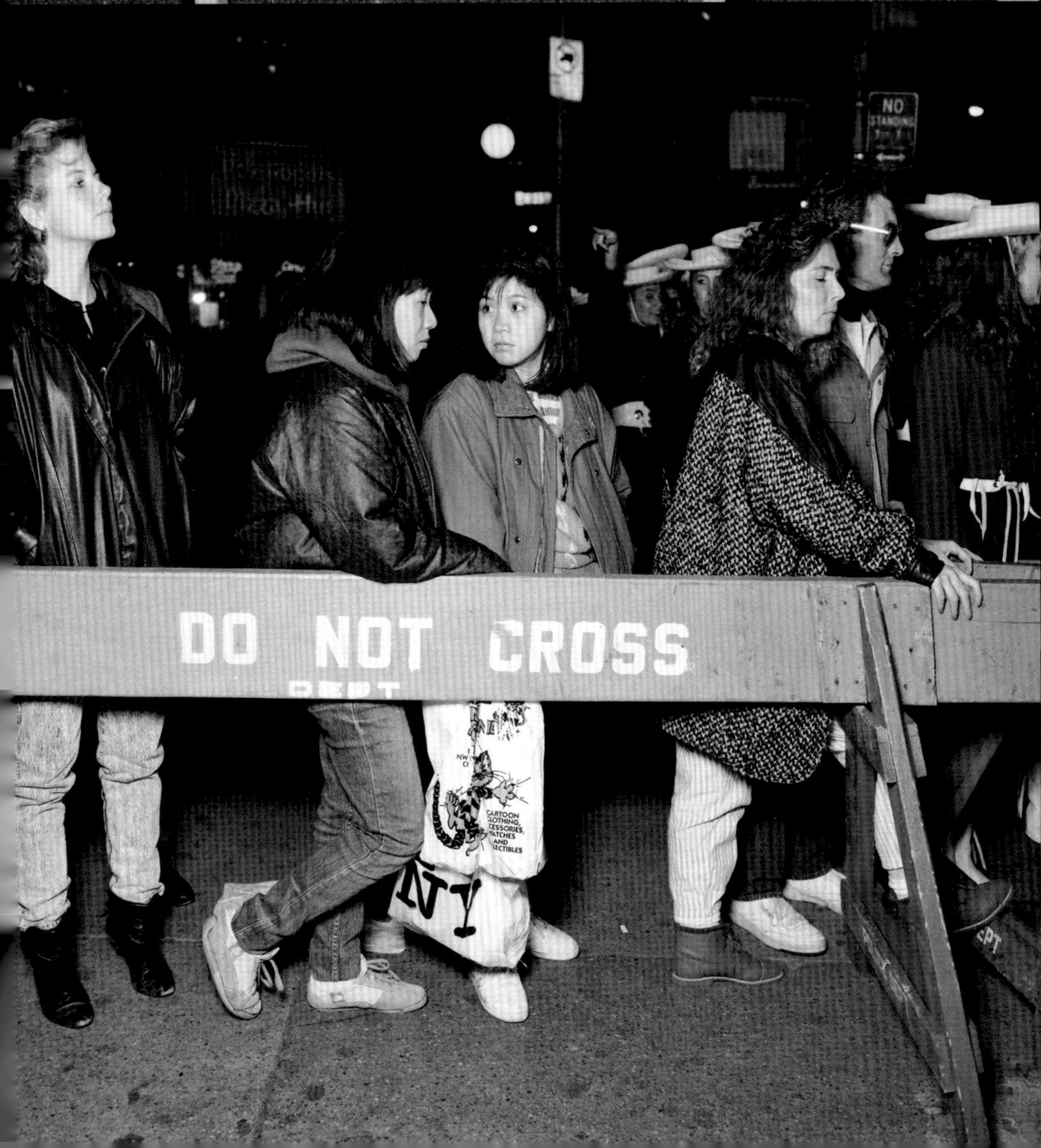
NO STANDING
DO NOT CROSS

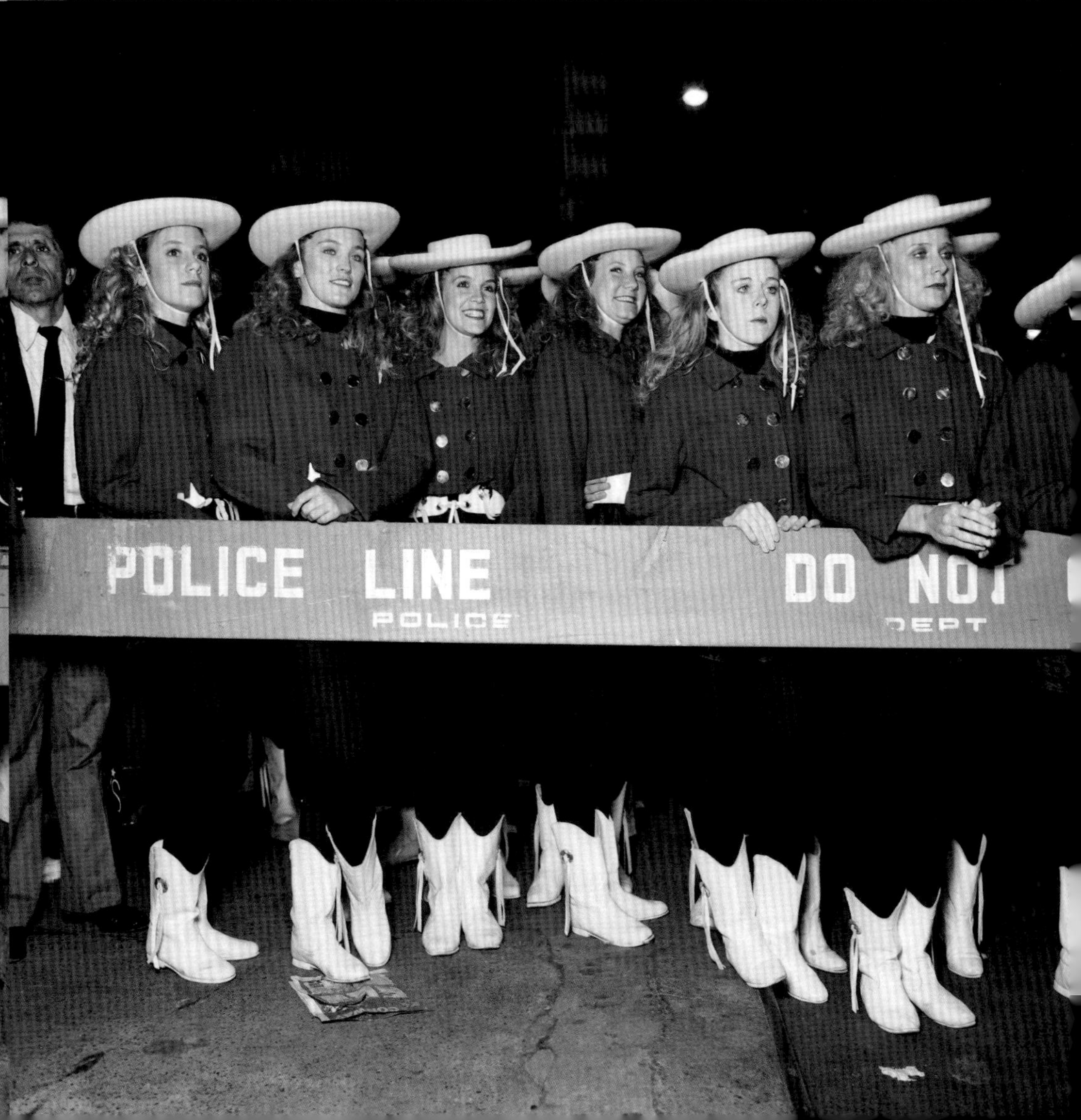
POLICE LINE

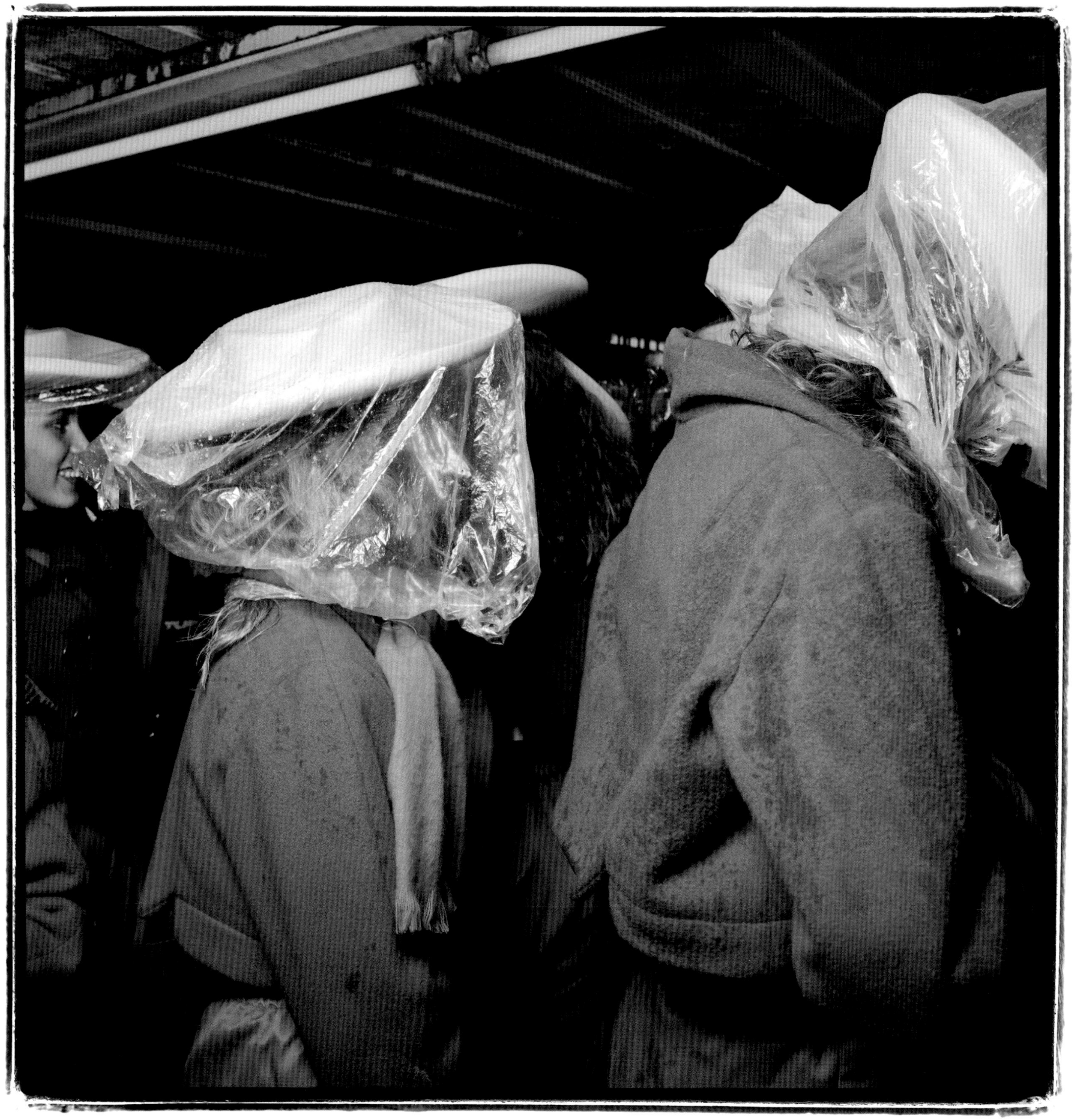

77 **NEW YORK RAIN** 1989

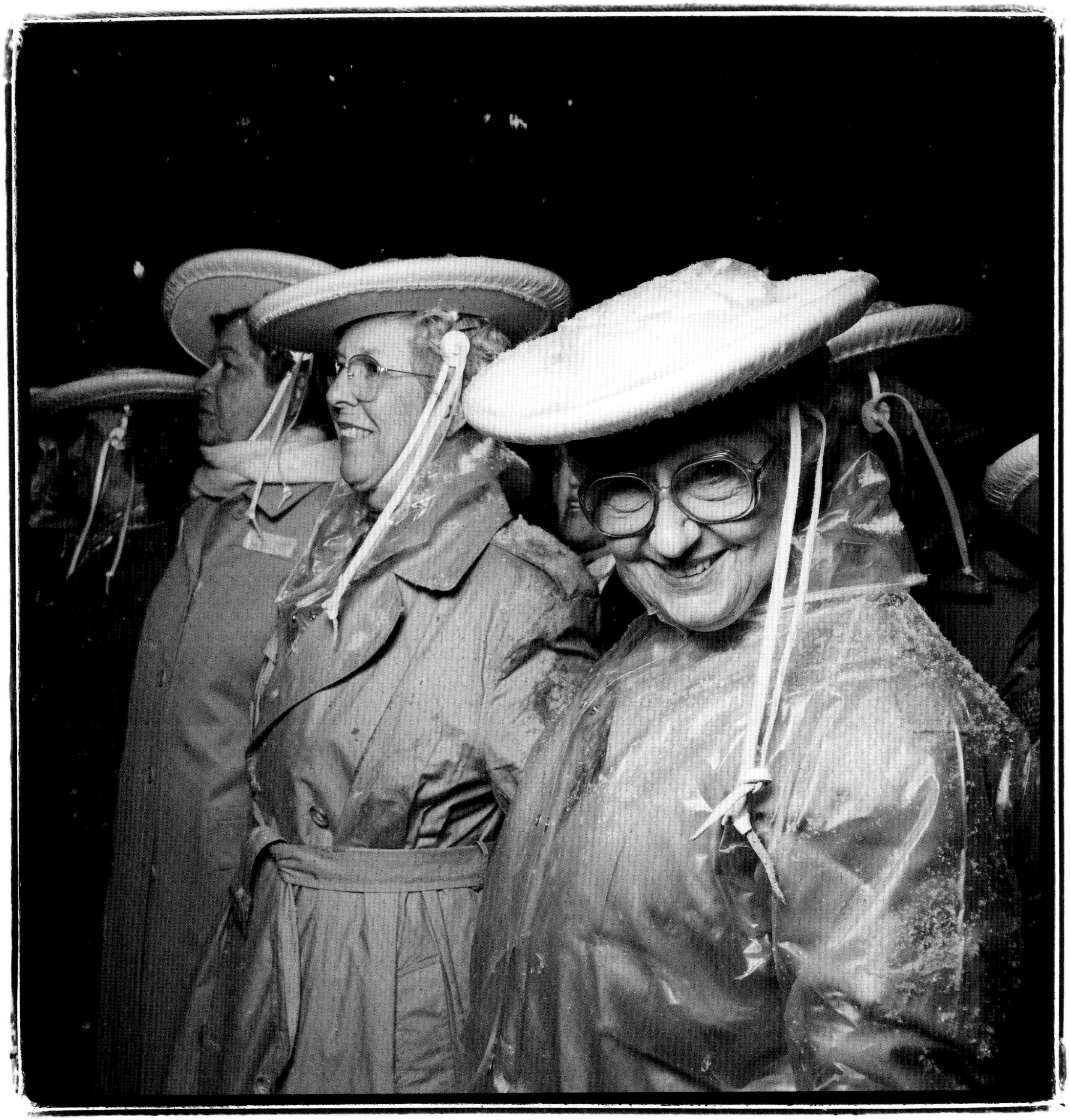

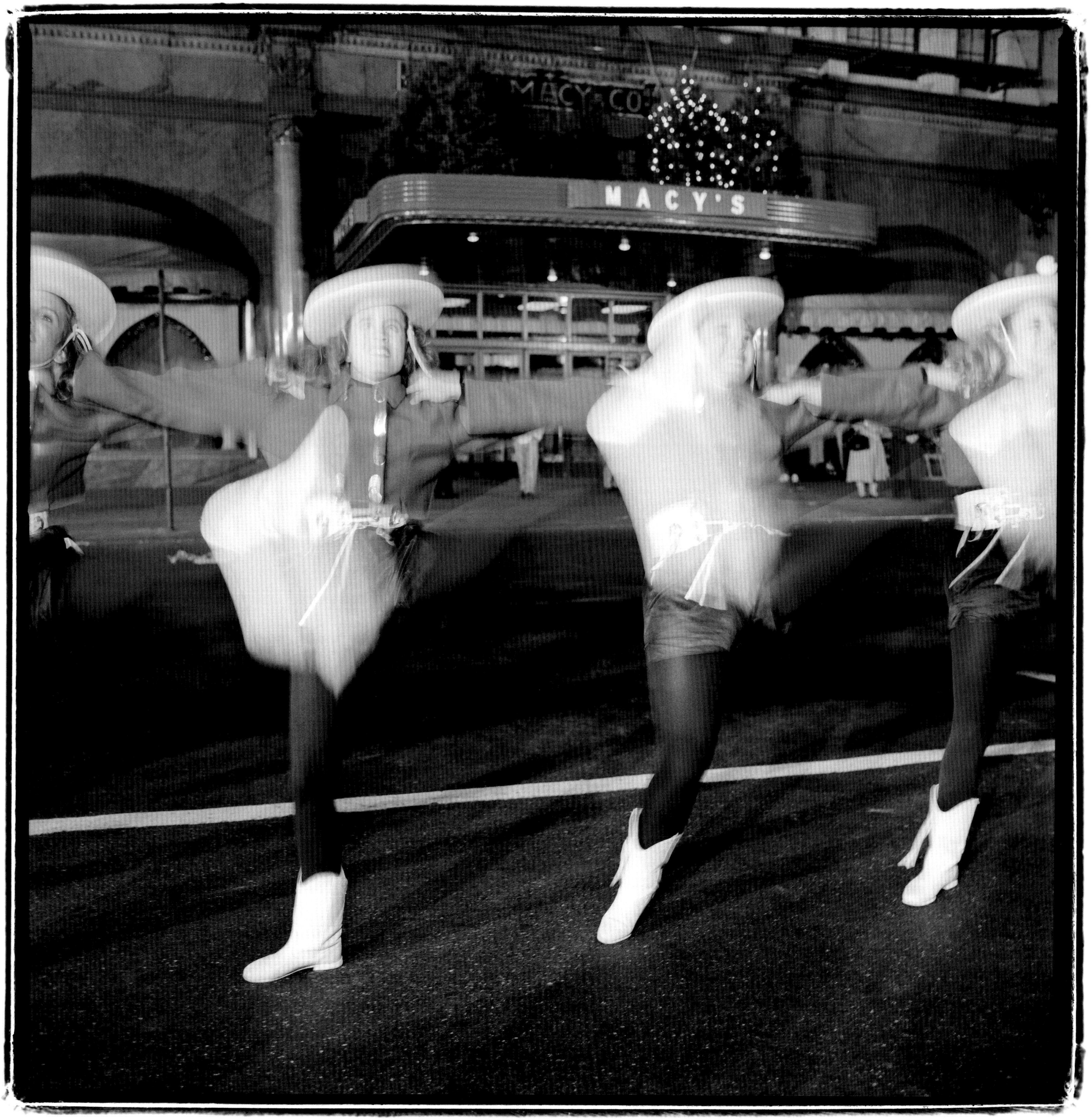
MACY'S

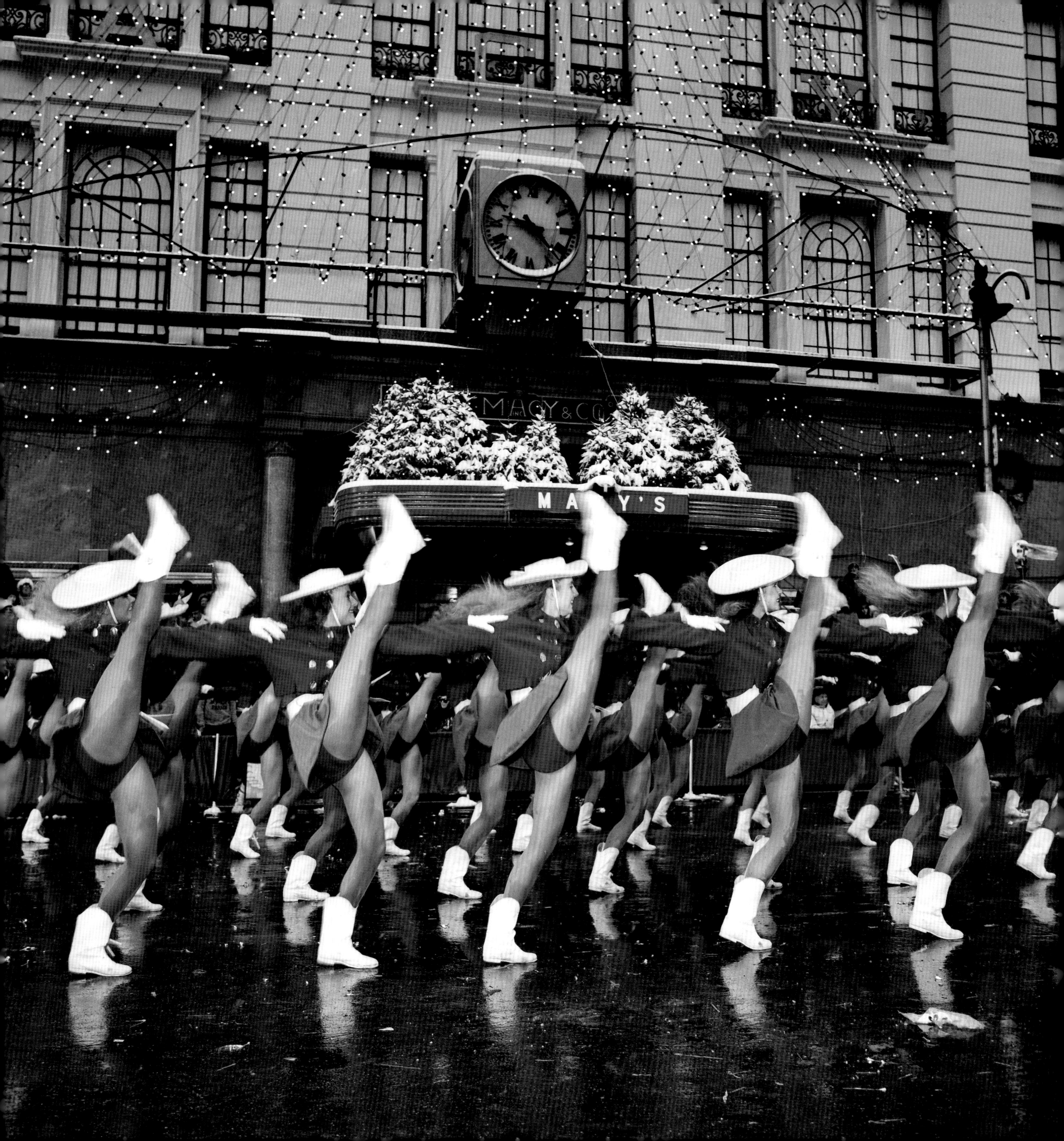
MACY & CO

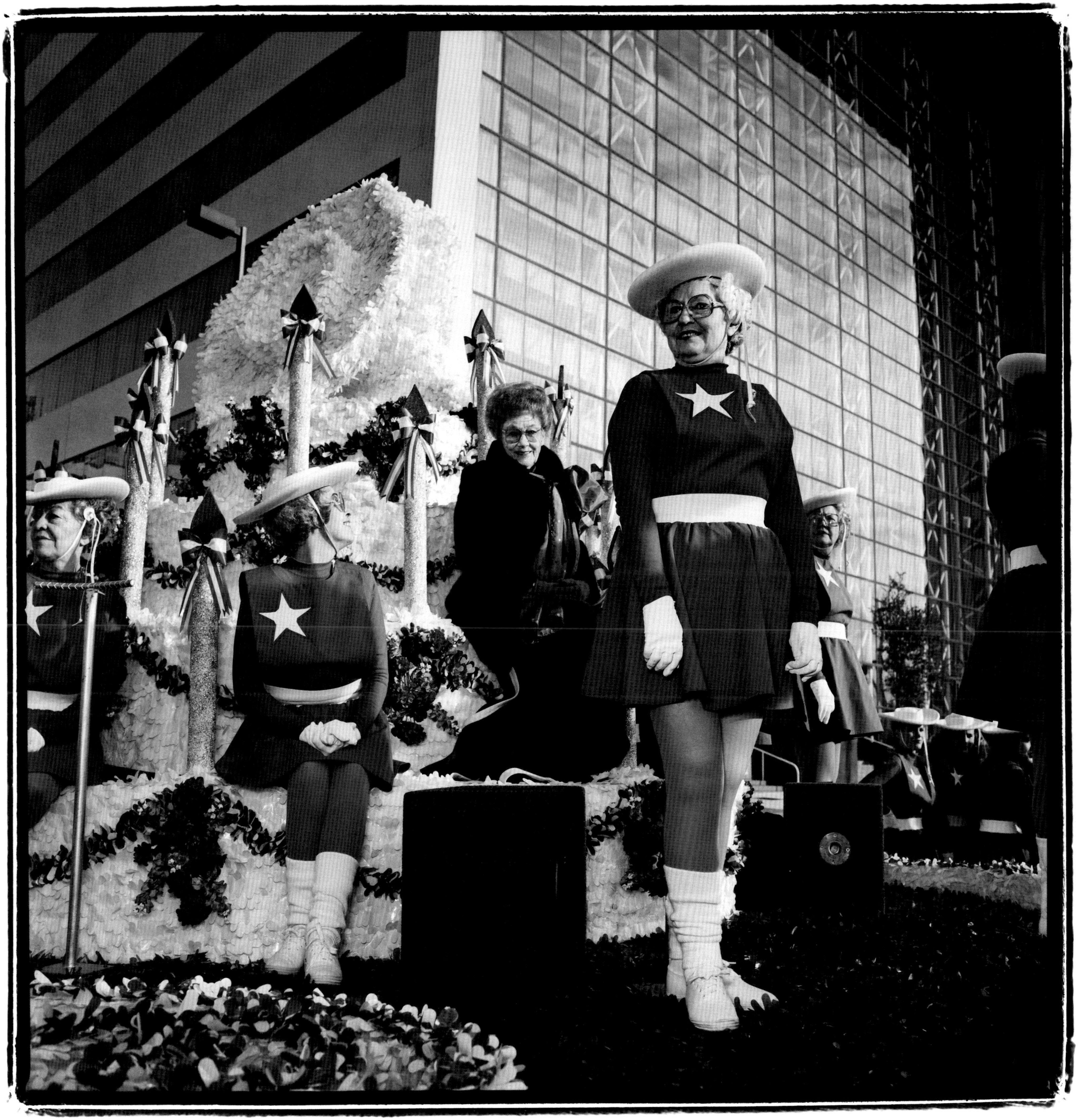

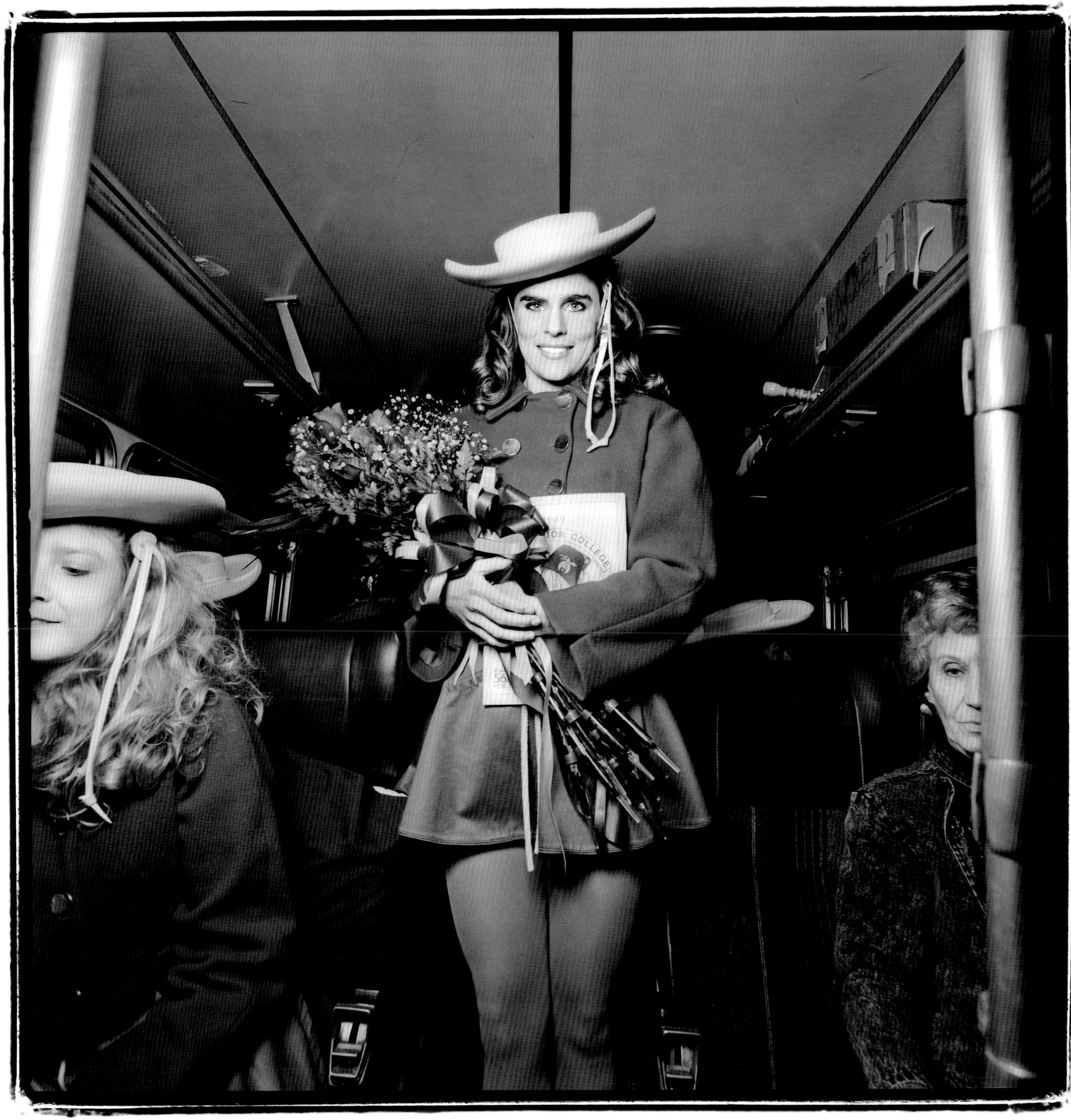
1989
COLLEGE

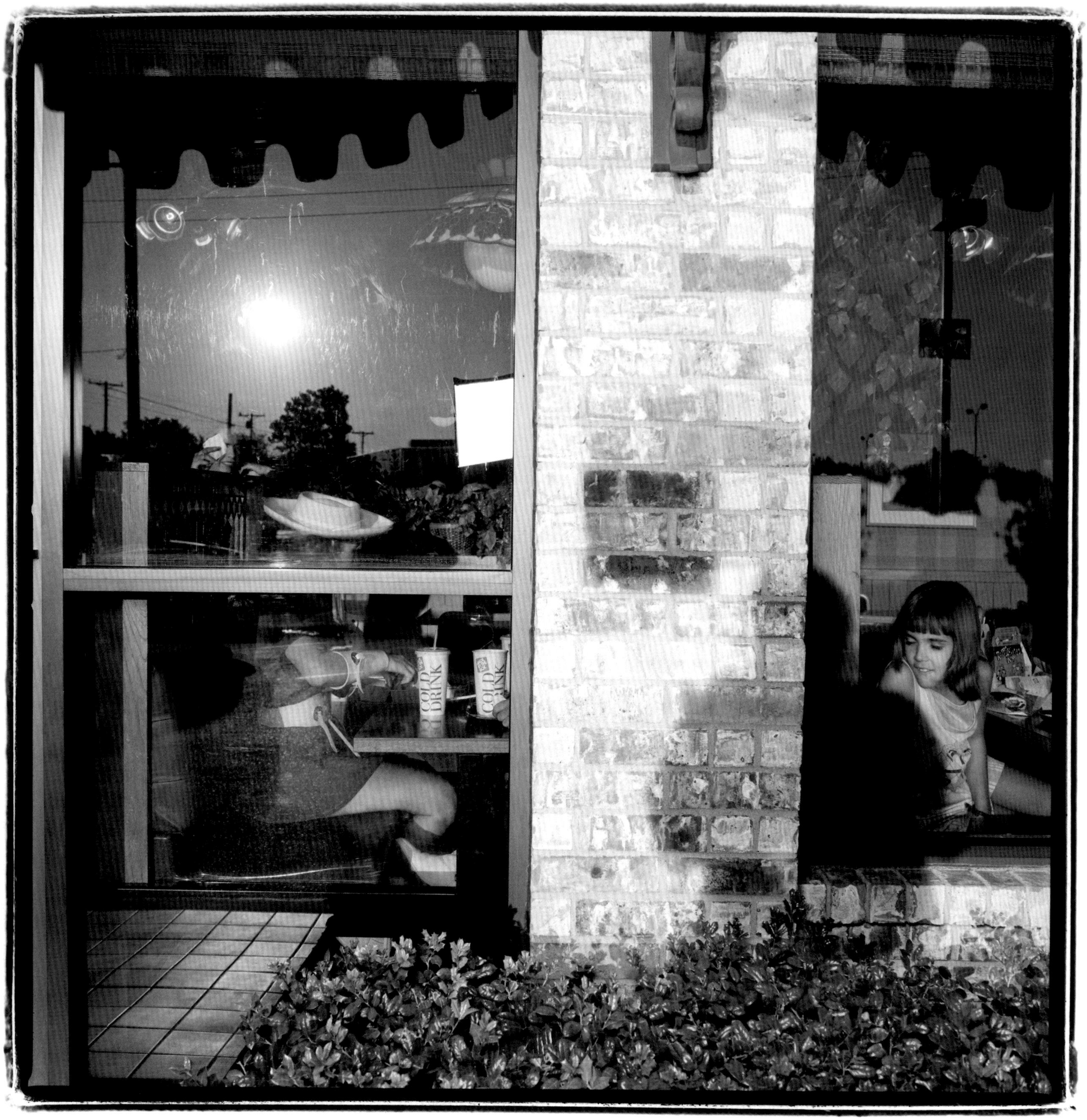

83 **COLD DRINK** 1989

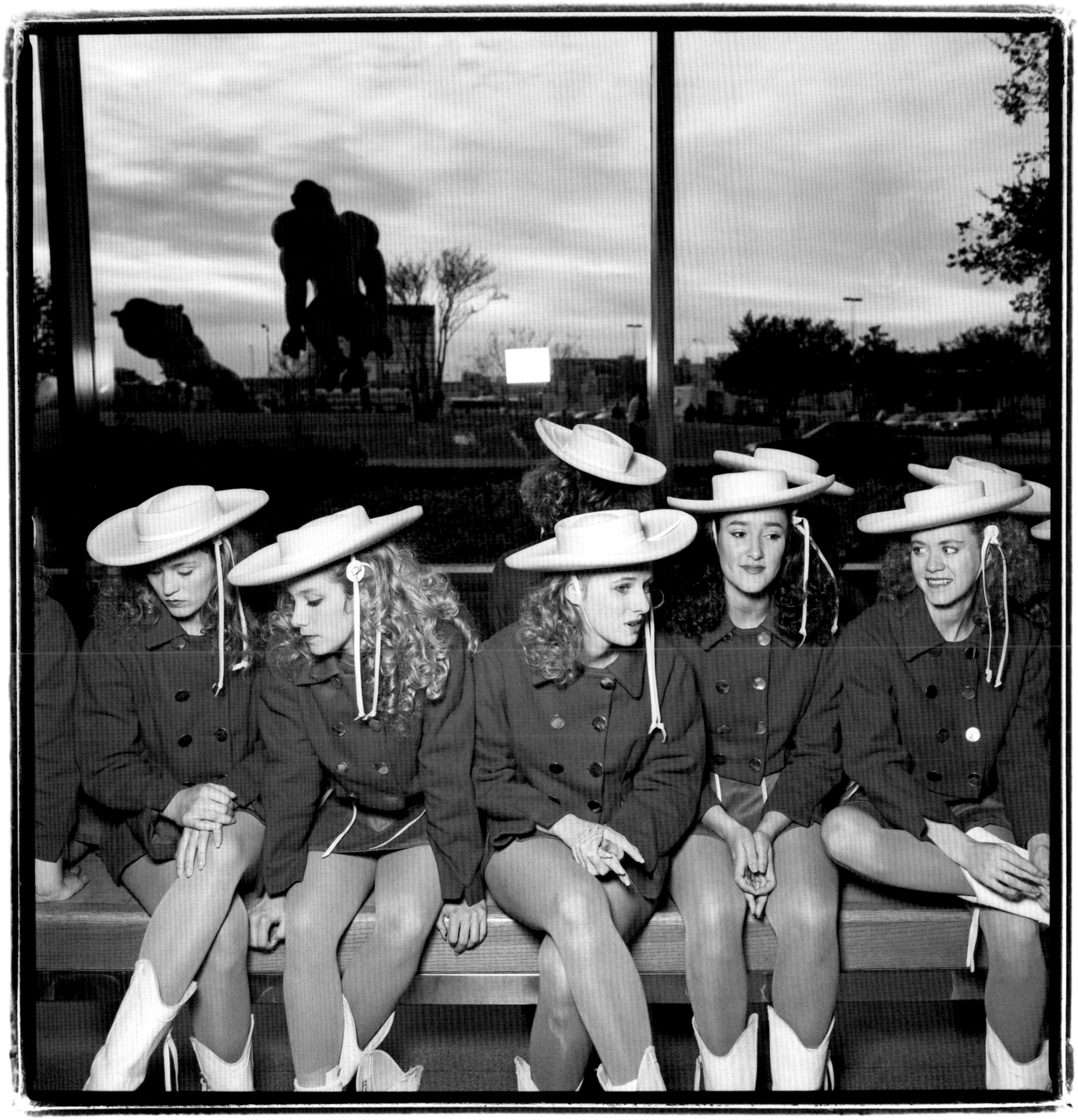

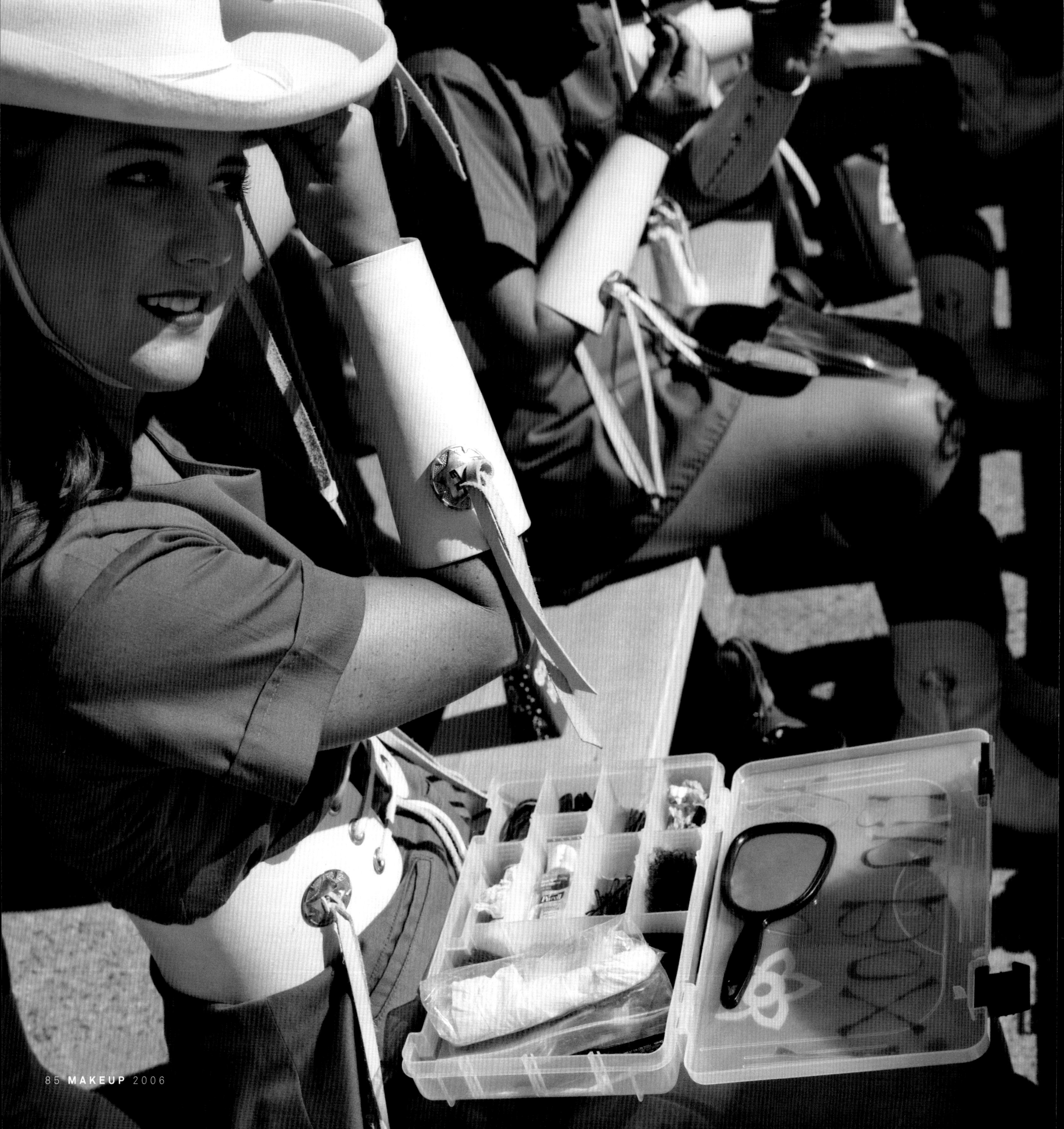

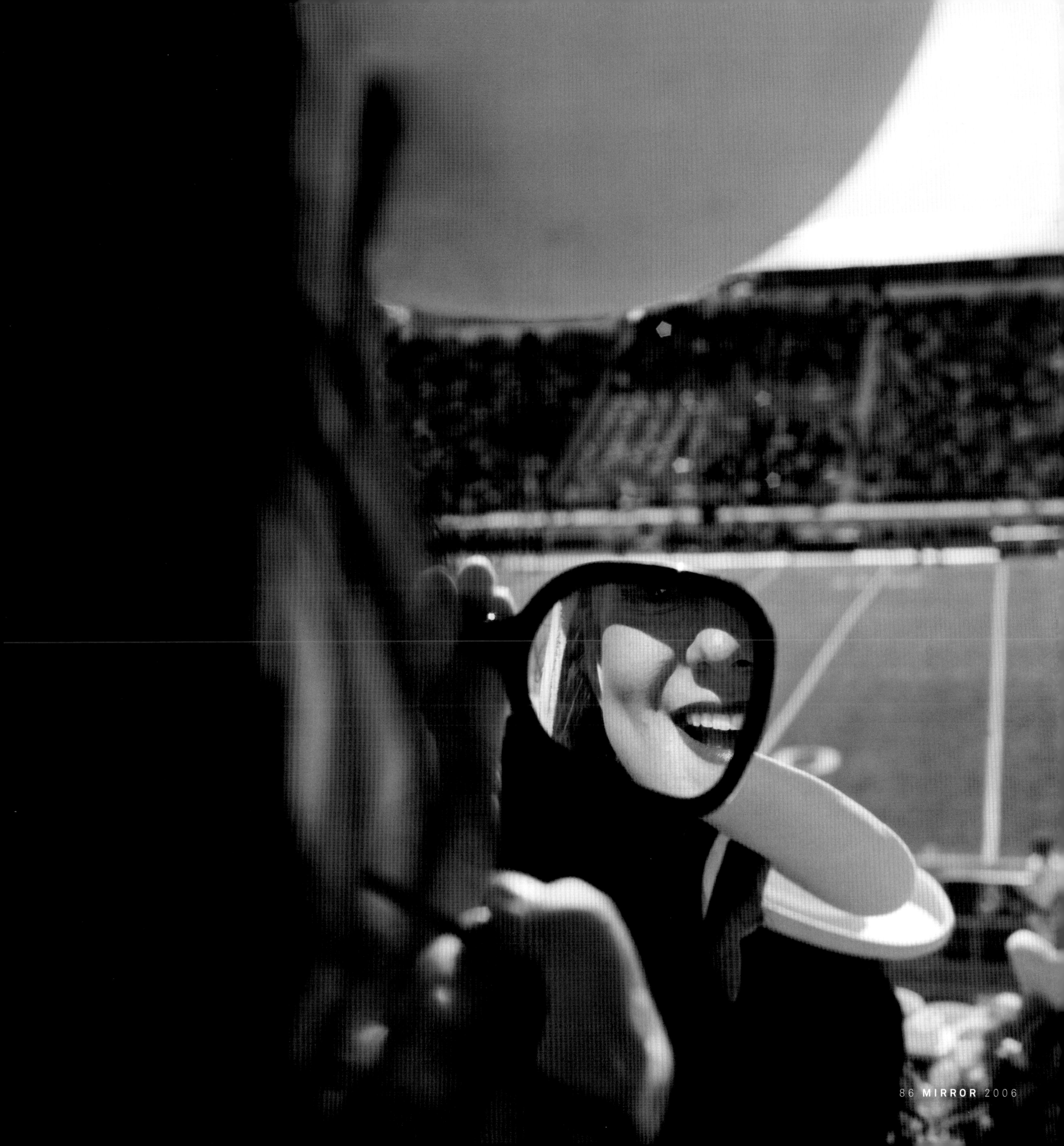

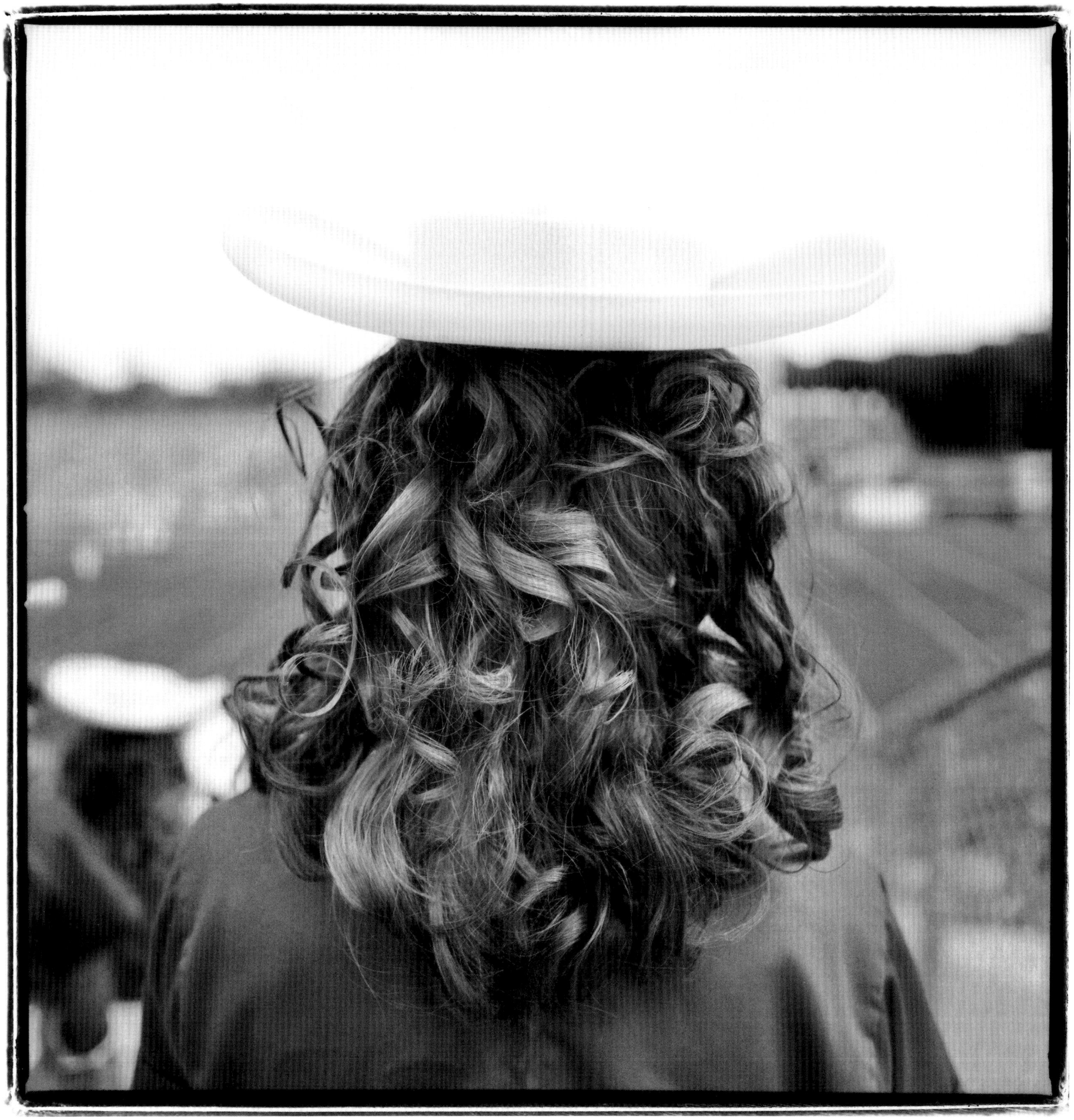

87 **BRUNETTE** 2006

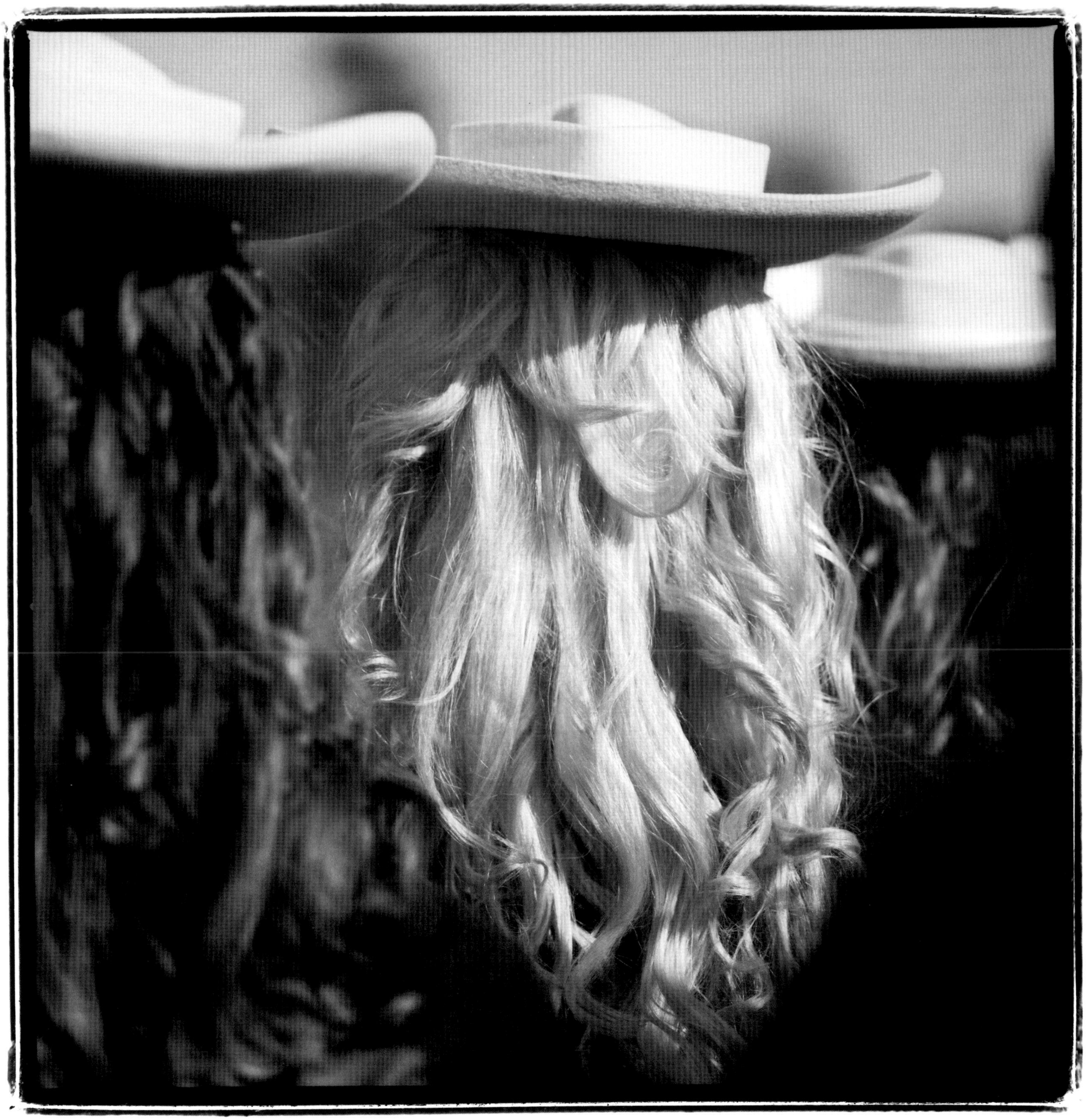

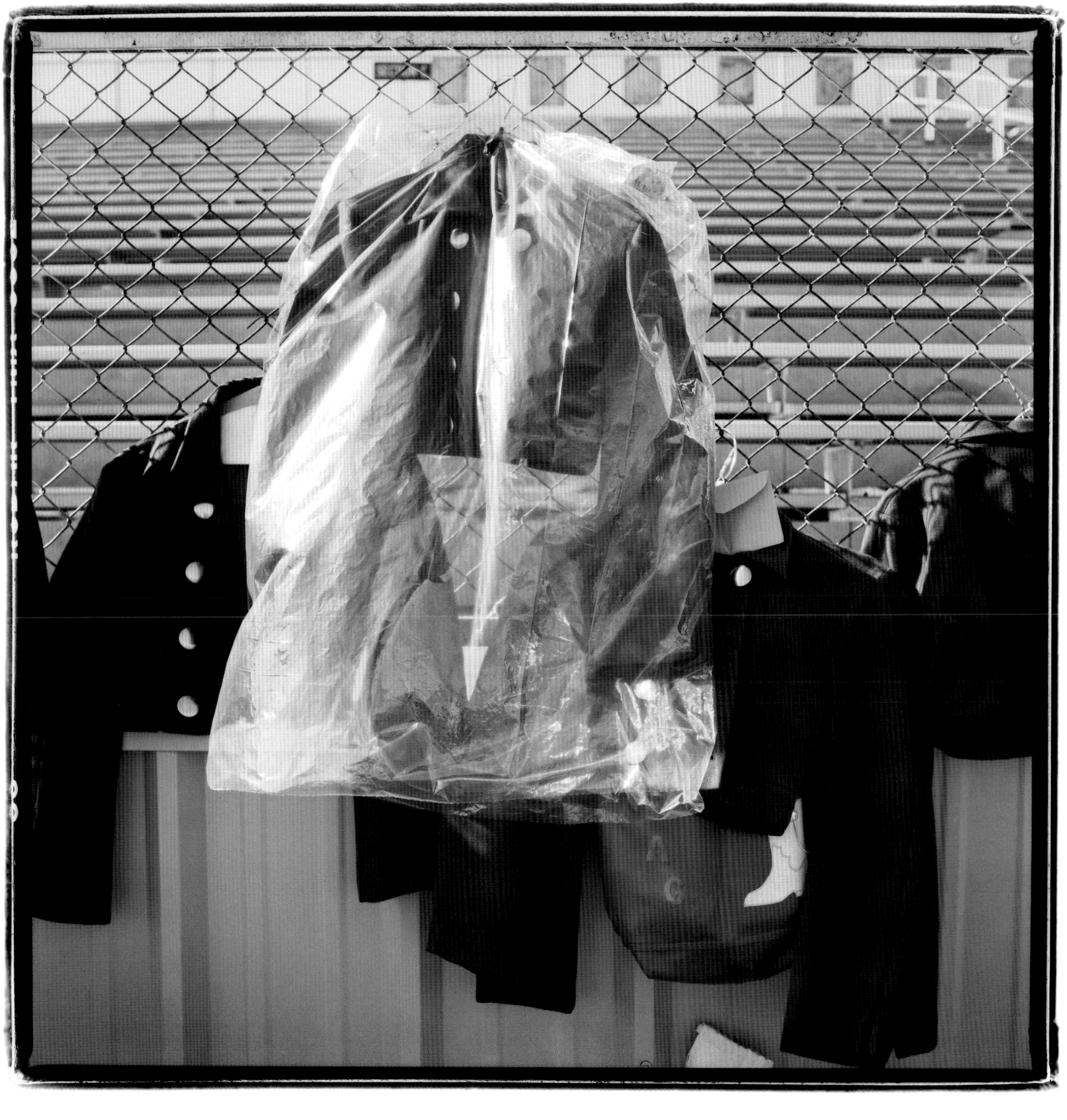

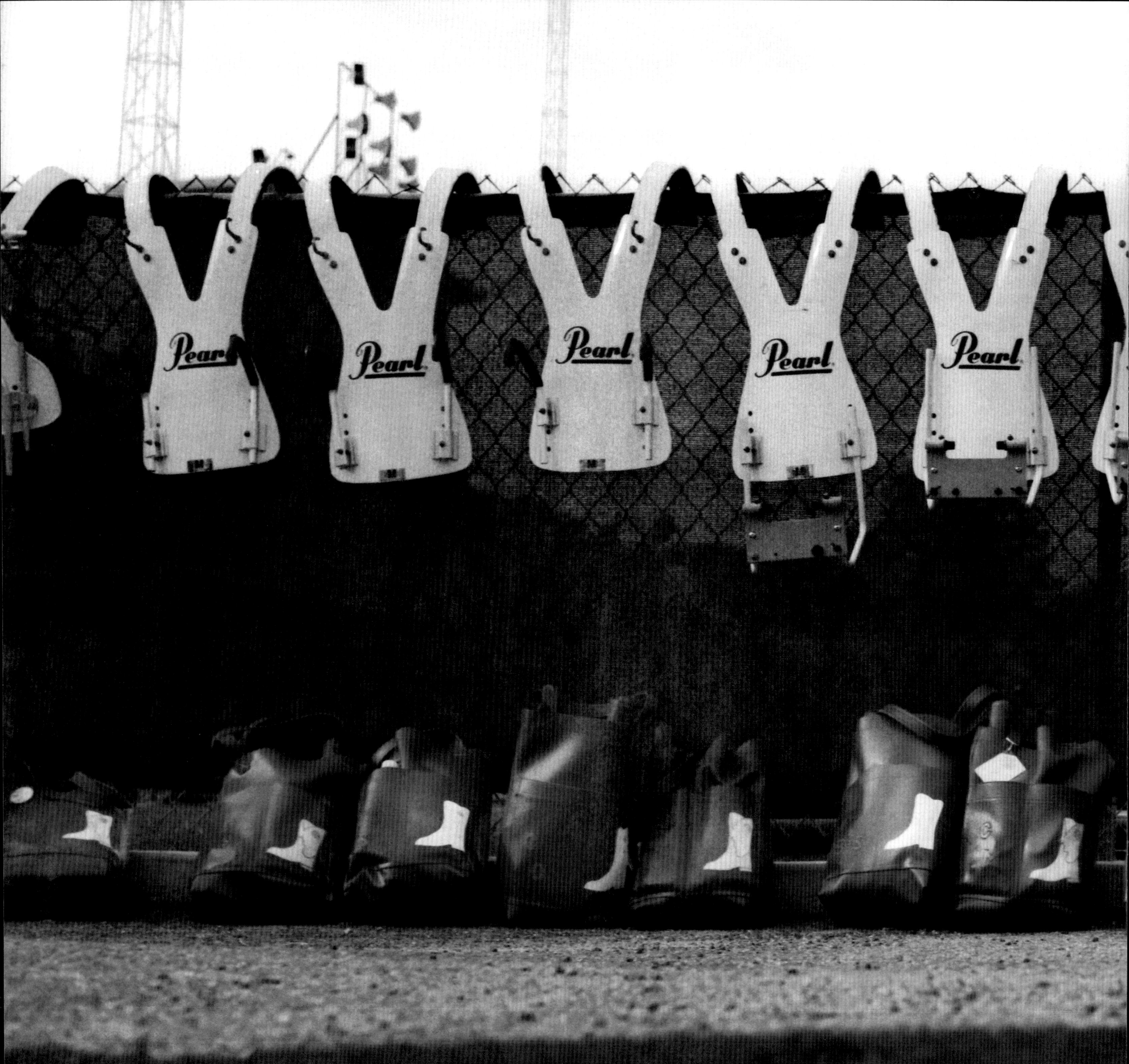
Pearl
Pearl
Pearl
Pearl

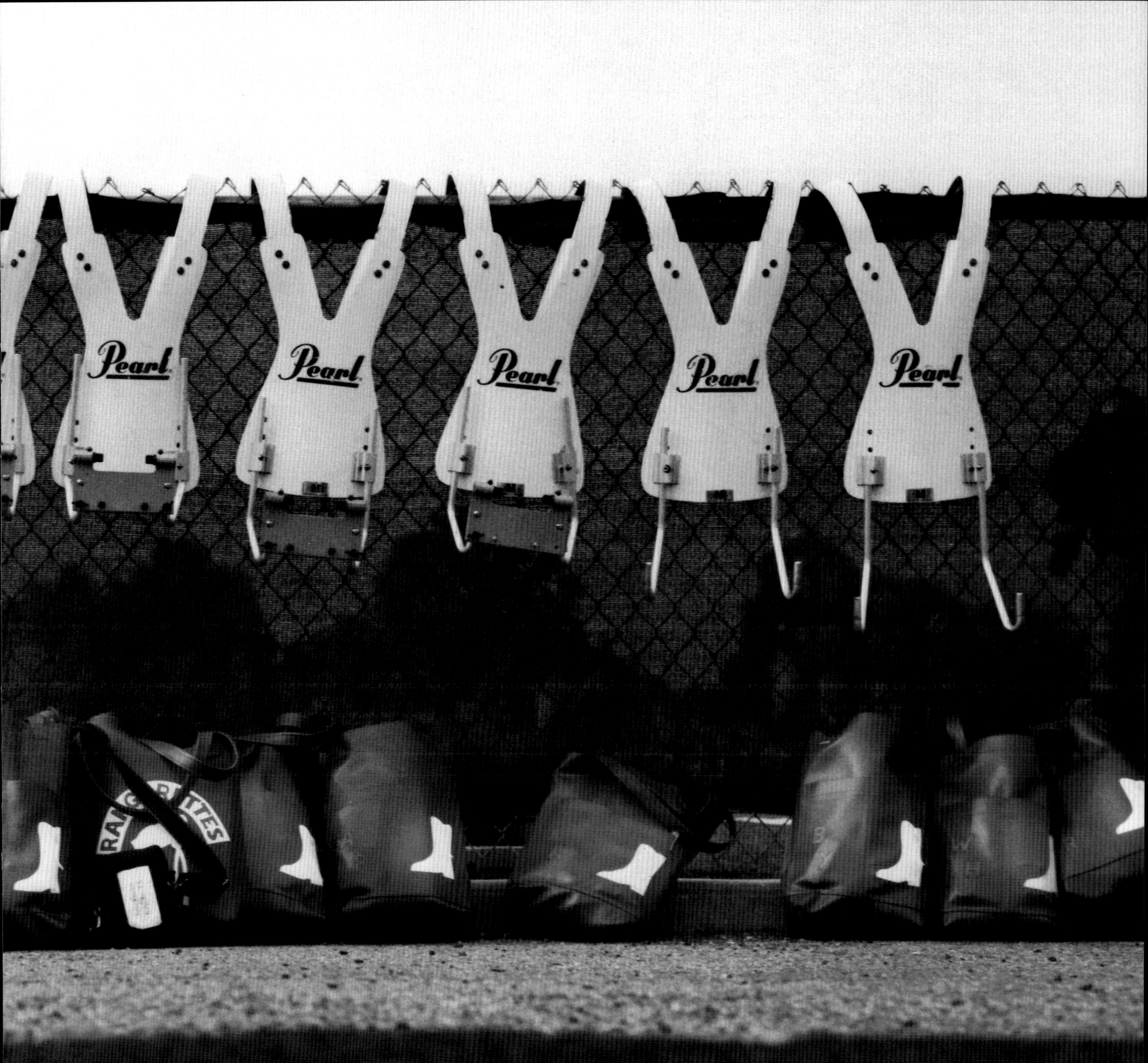
Pearl
Pearl
Pearl
Pearl
Pearl

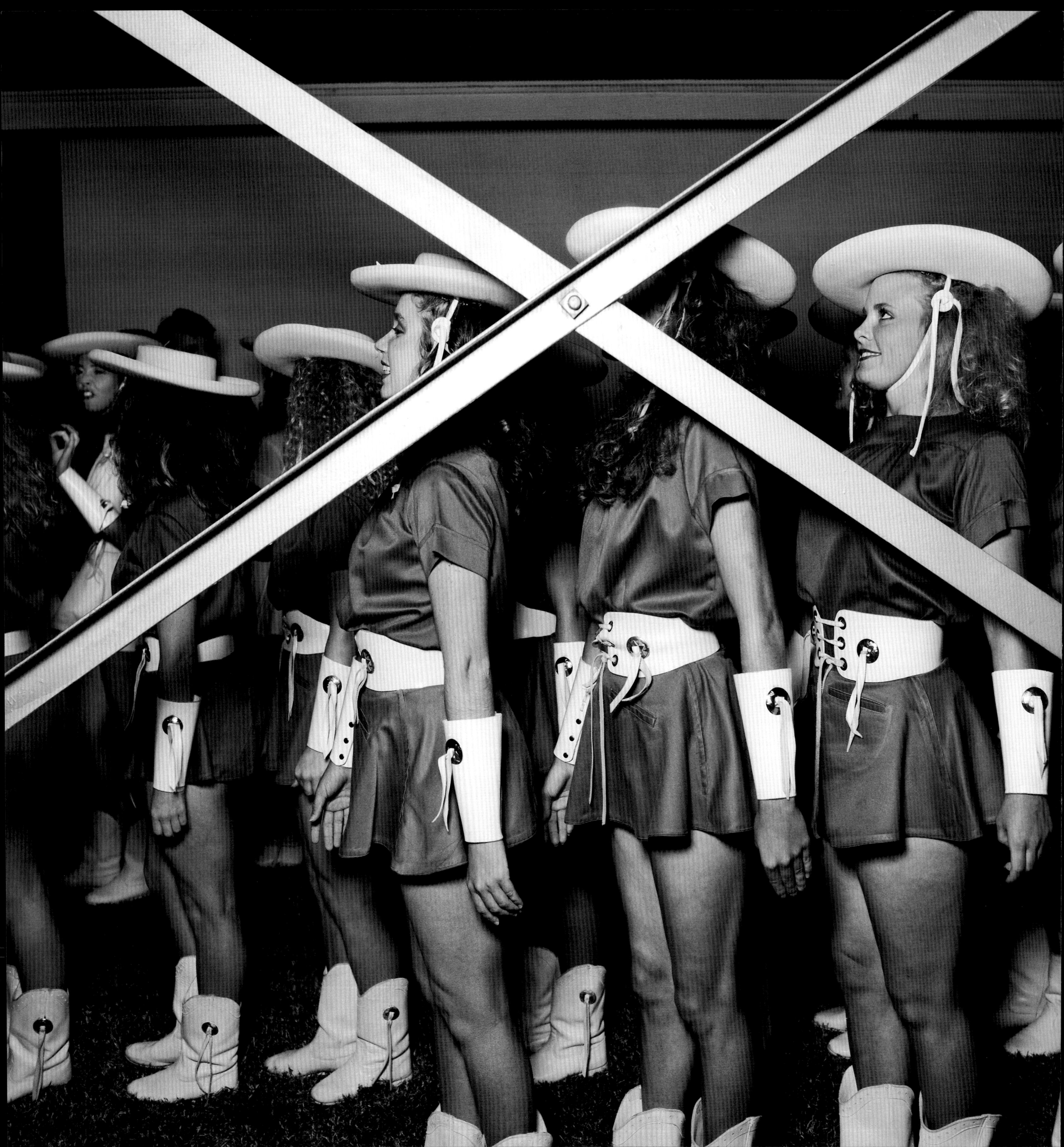

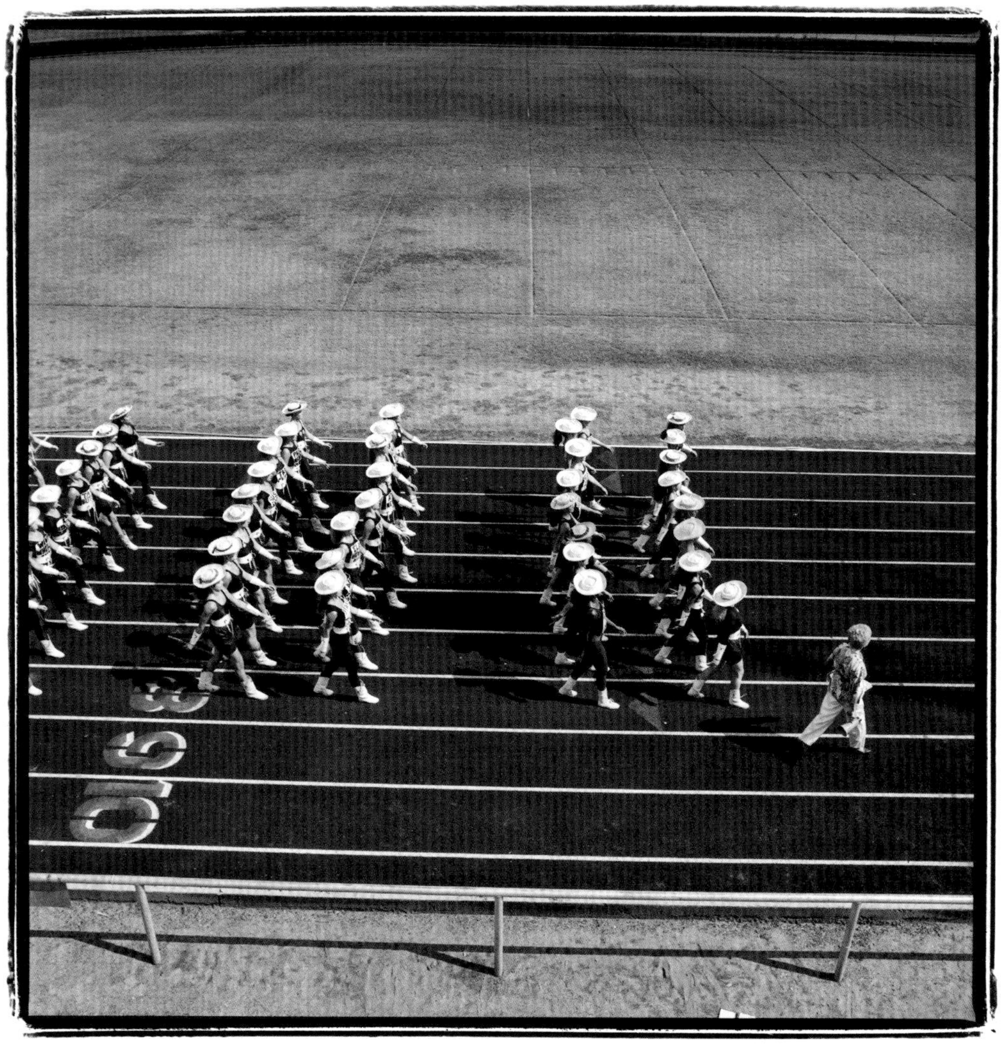

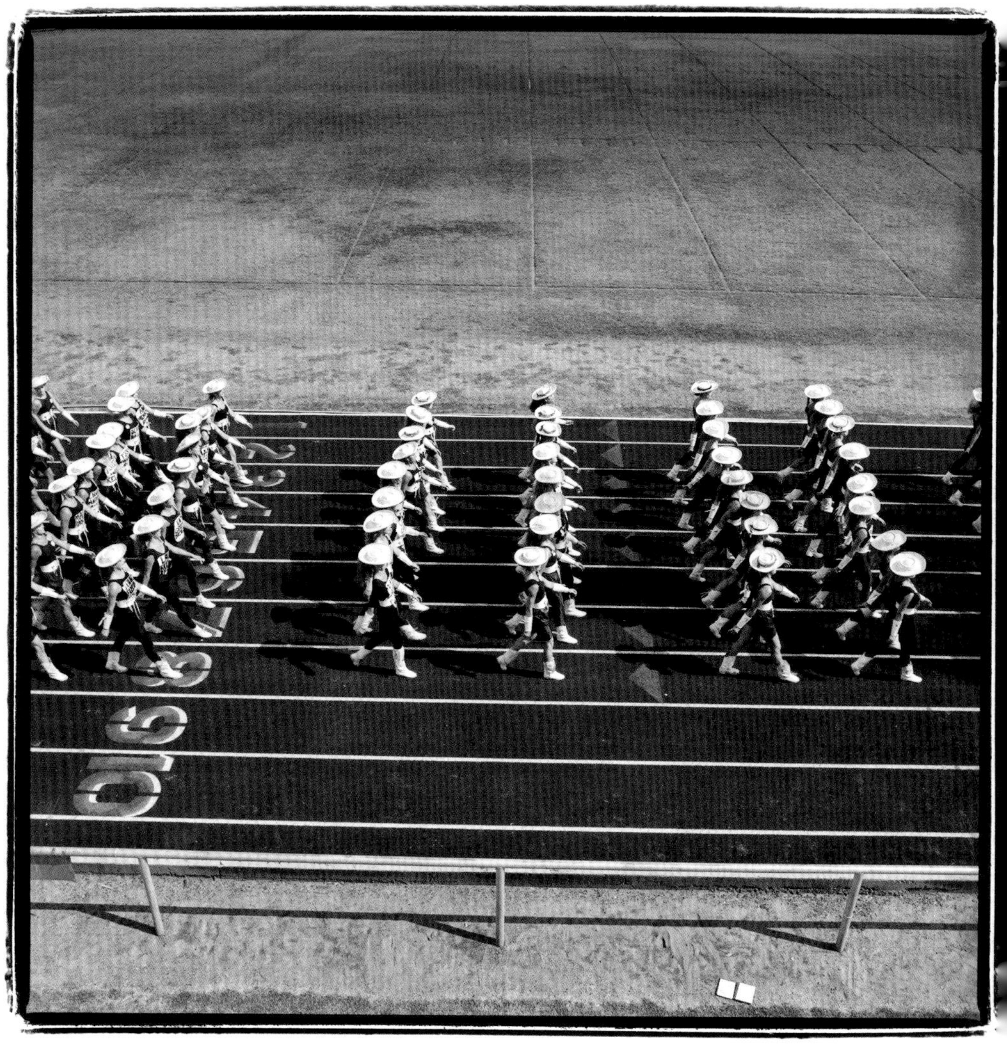

92–95 **TRACK QUAD I–IV** 1989

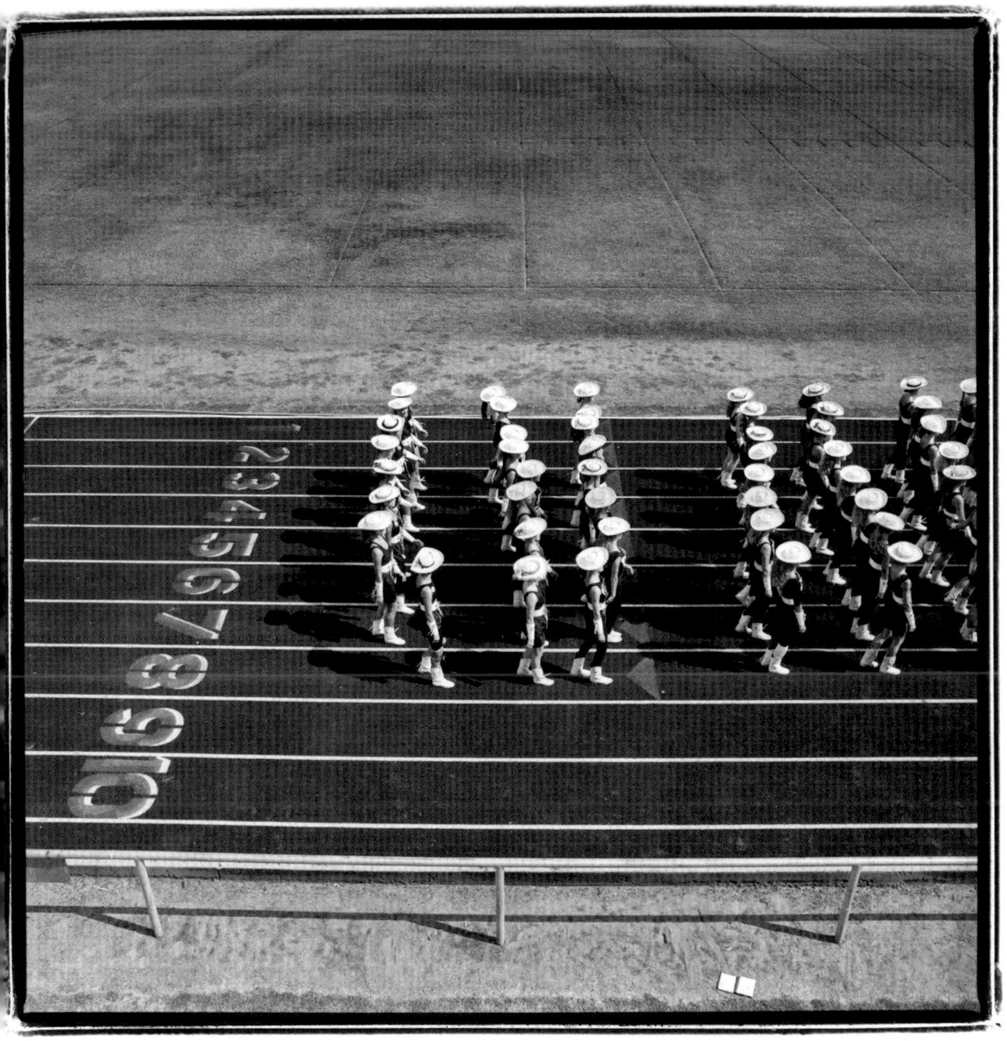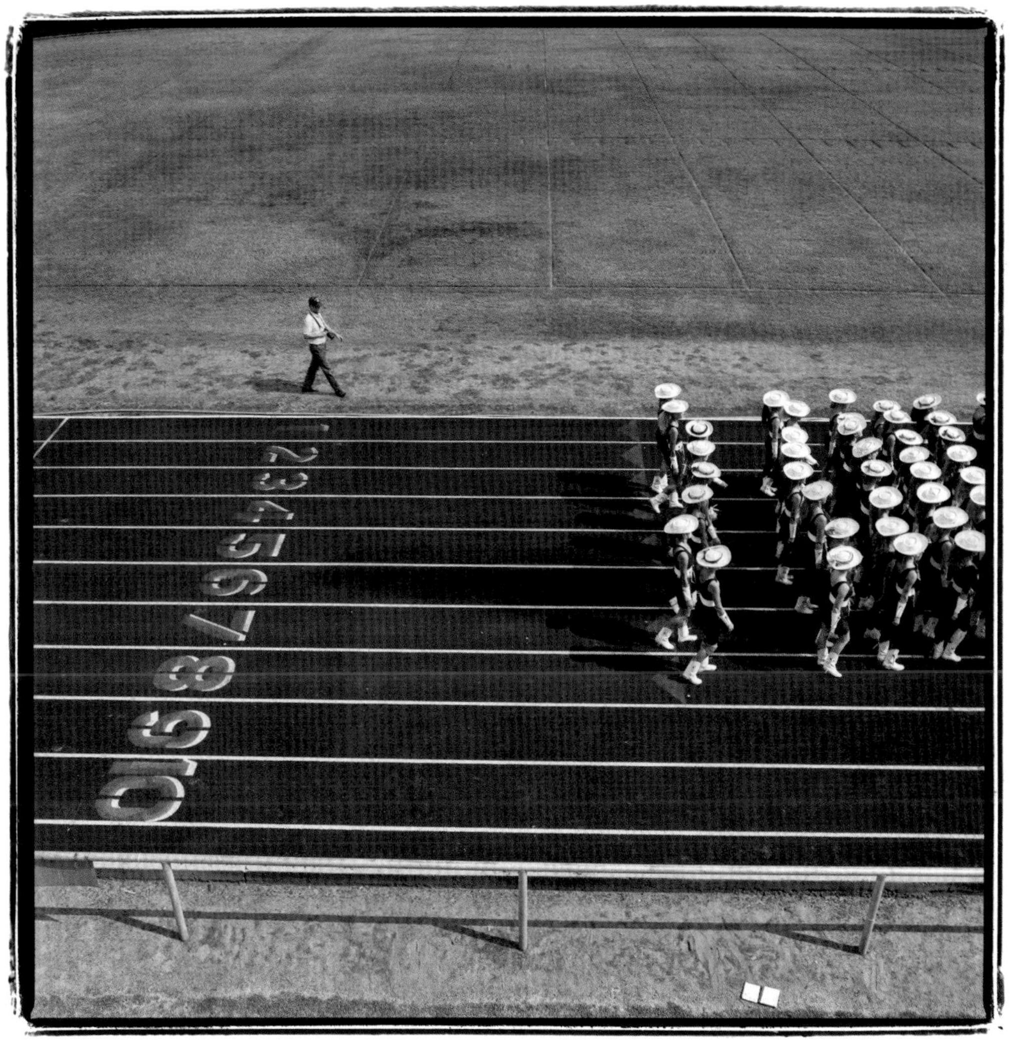

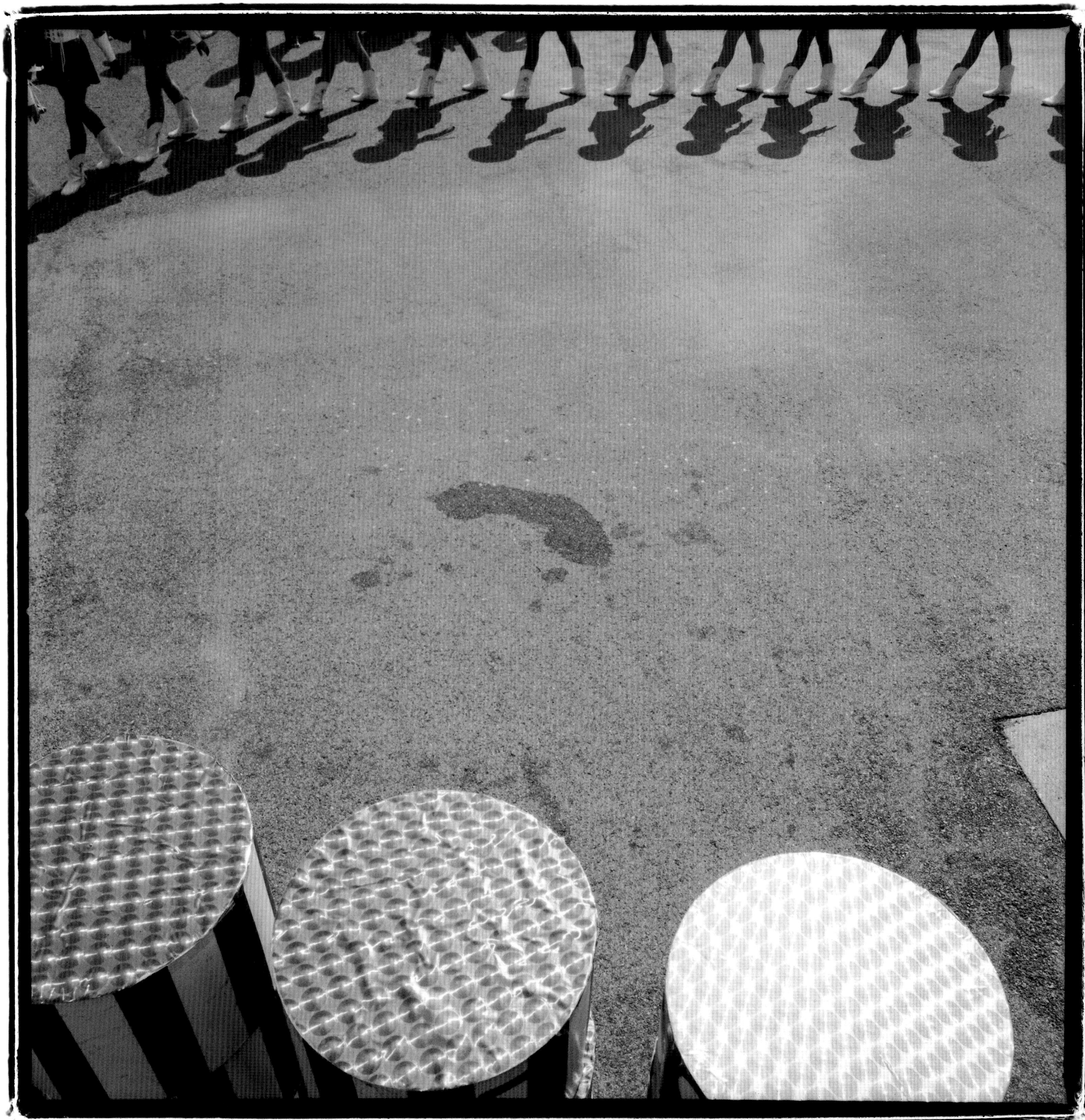

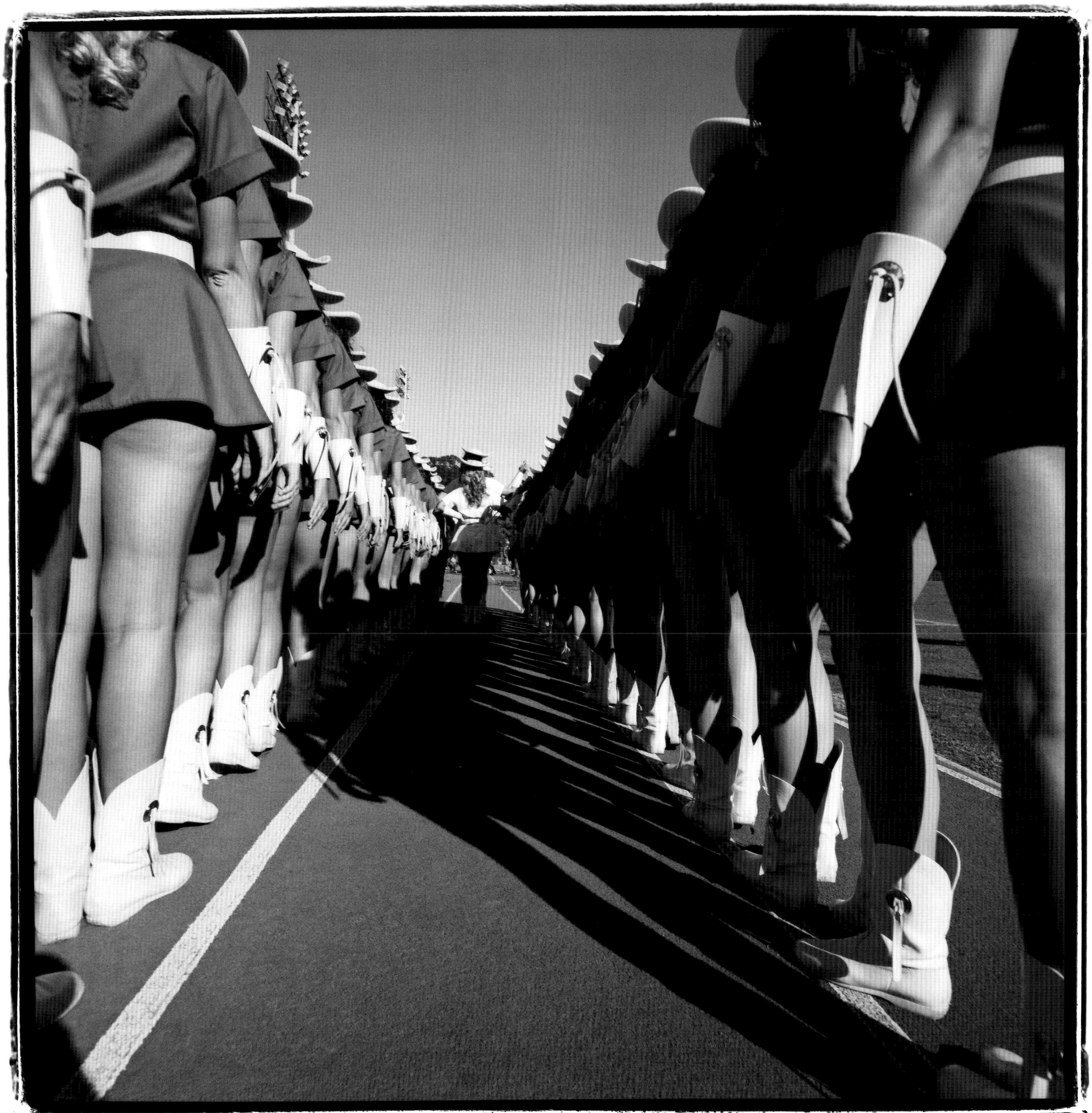

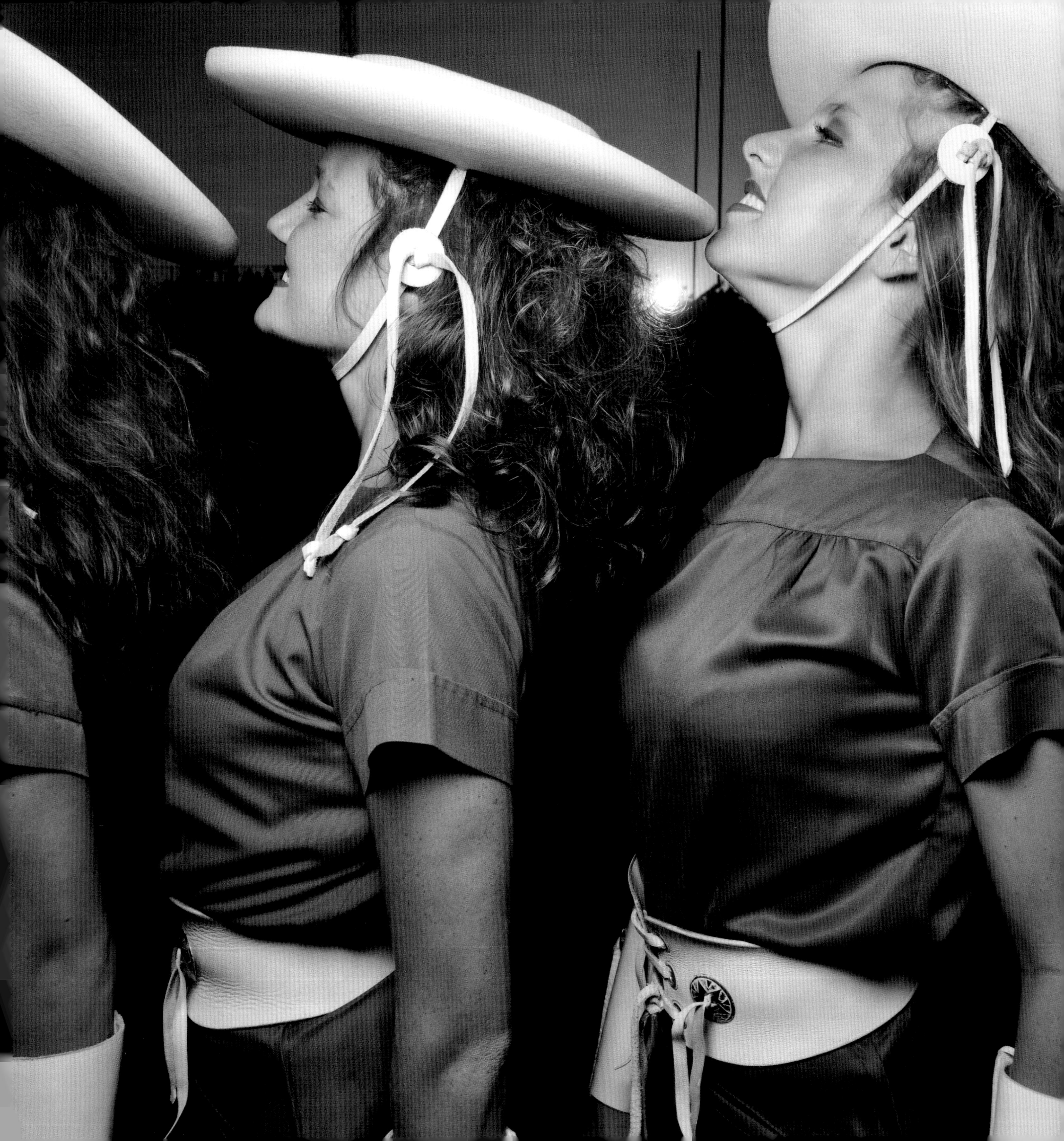

98 **SUNSET** 1995

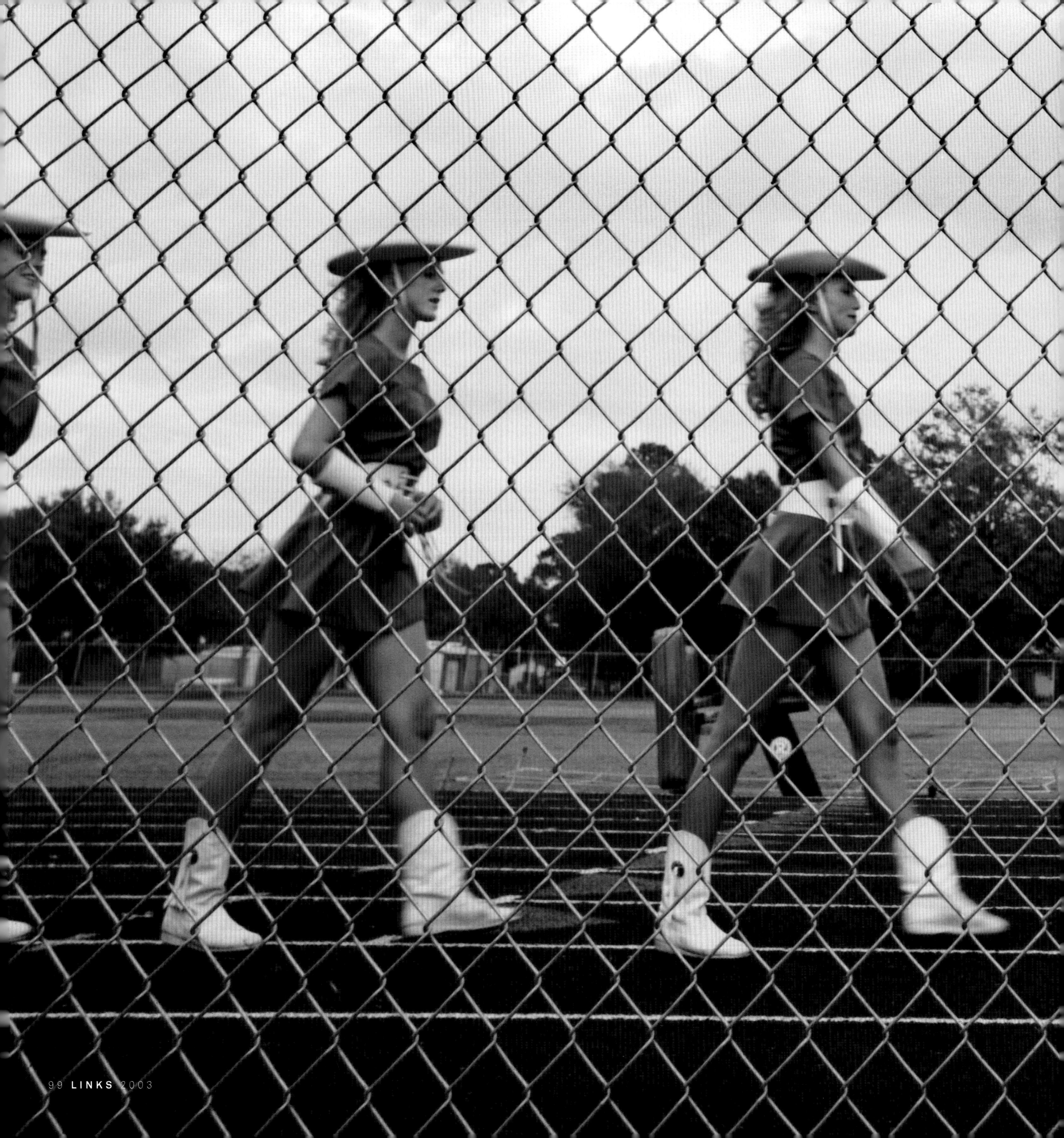

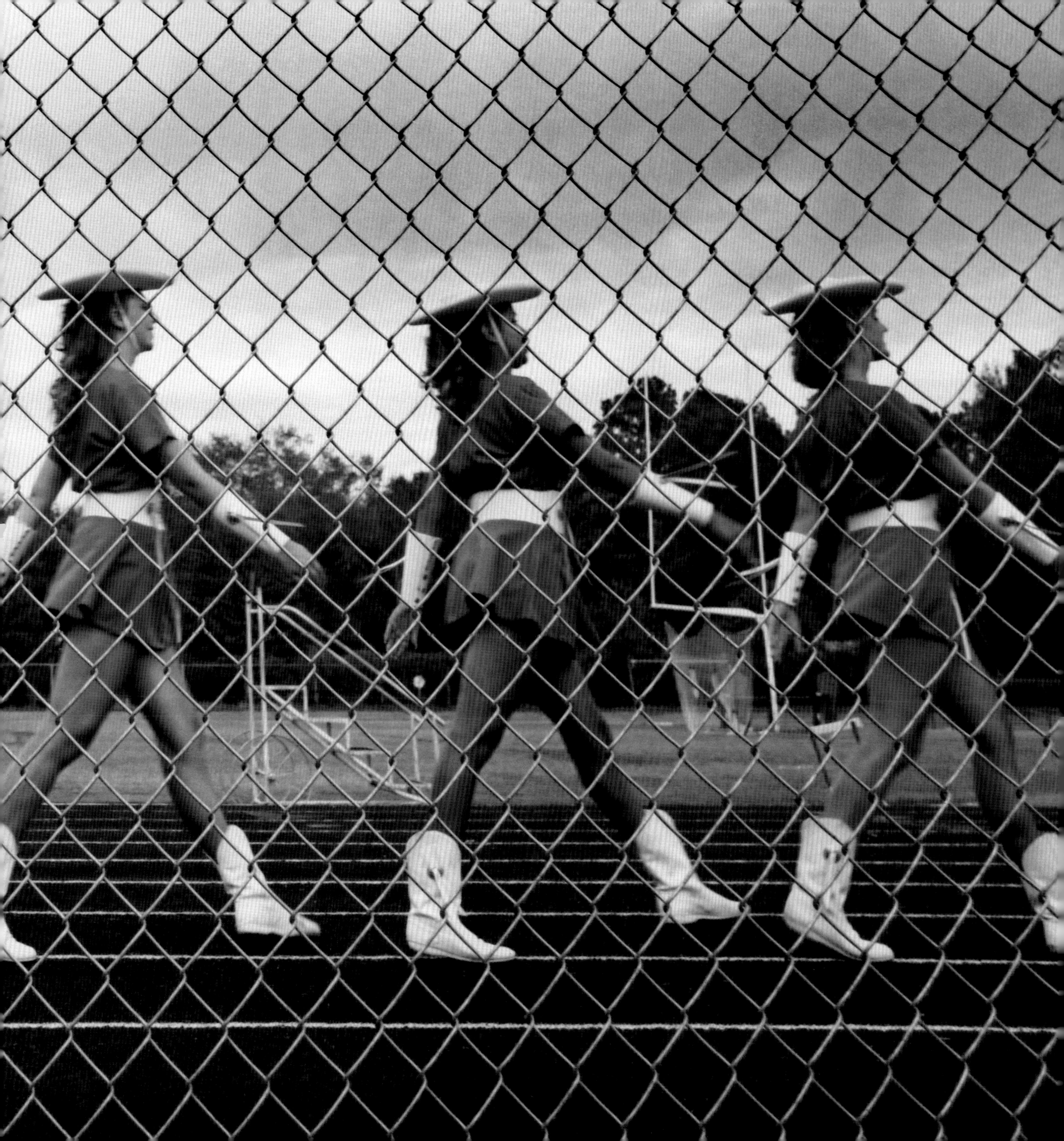

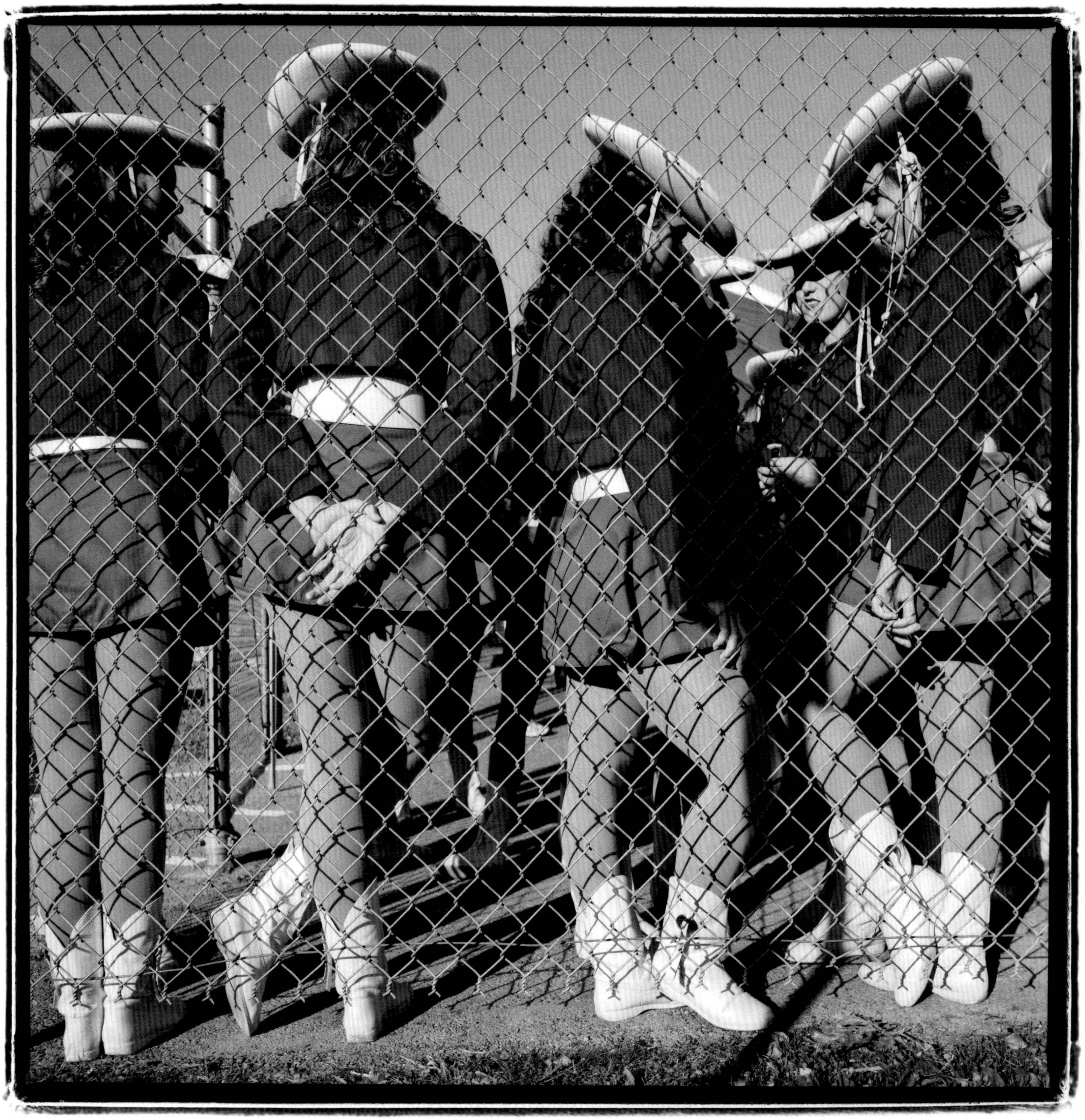

 FENCED RETTES 2006

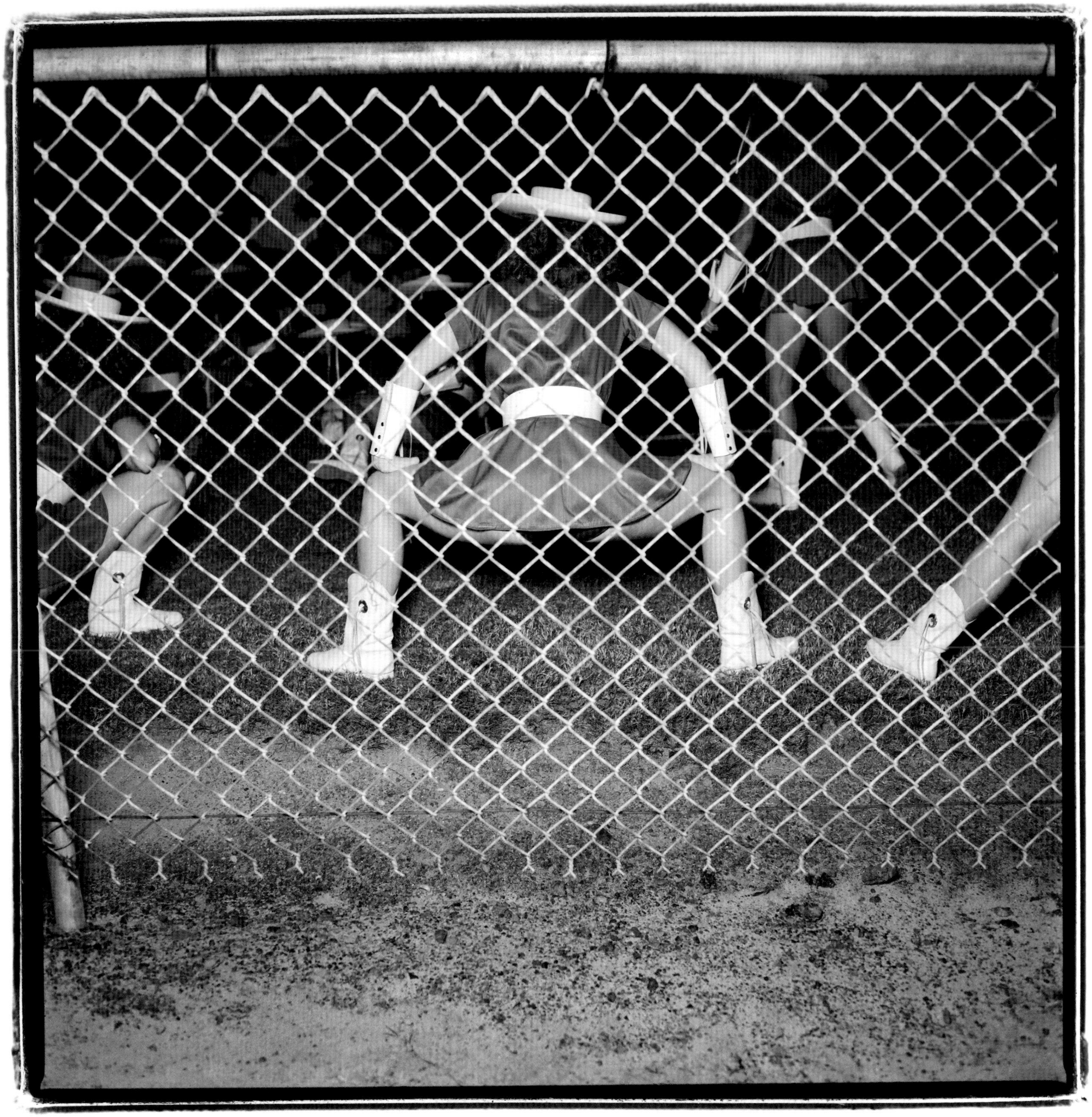

101 **CHAIN LINK I** 1989

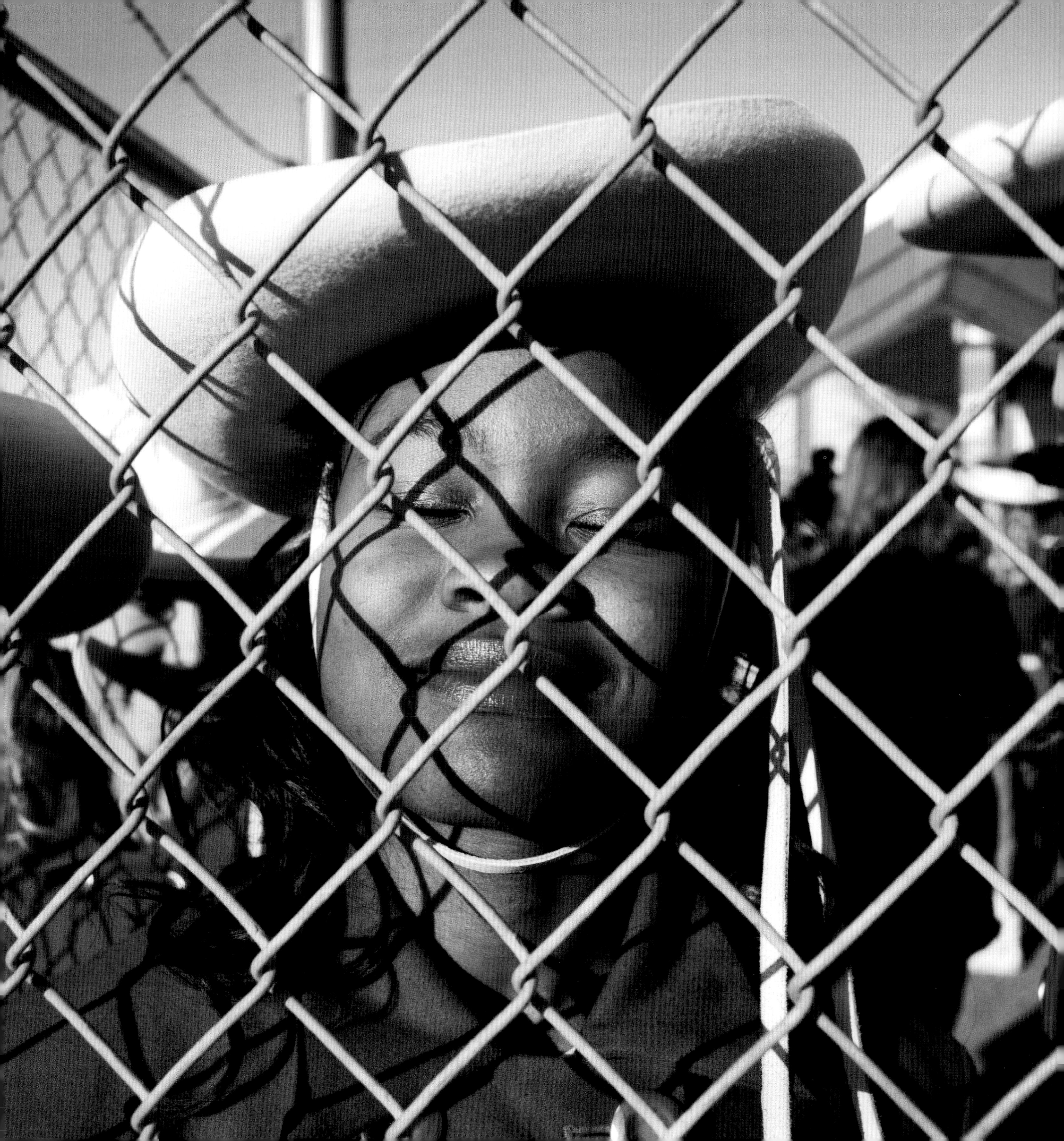

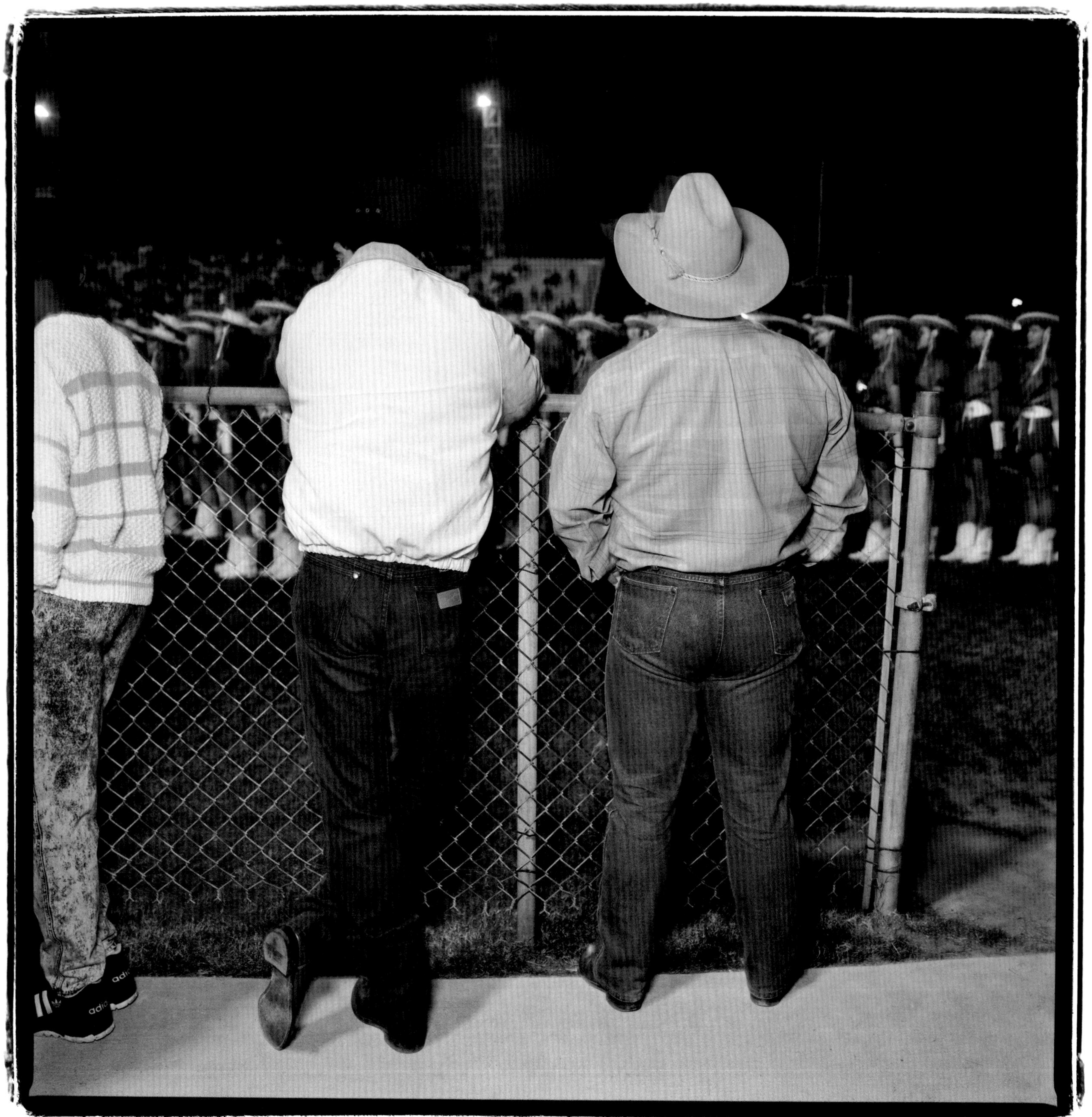

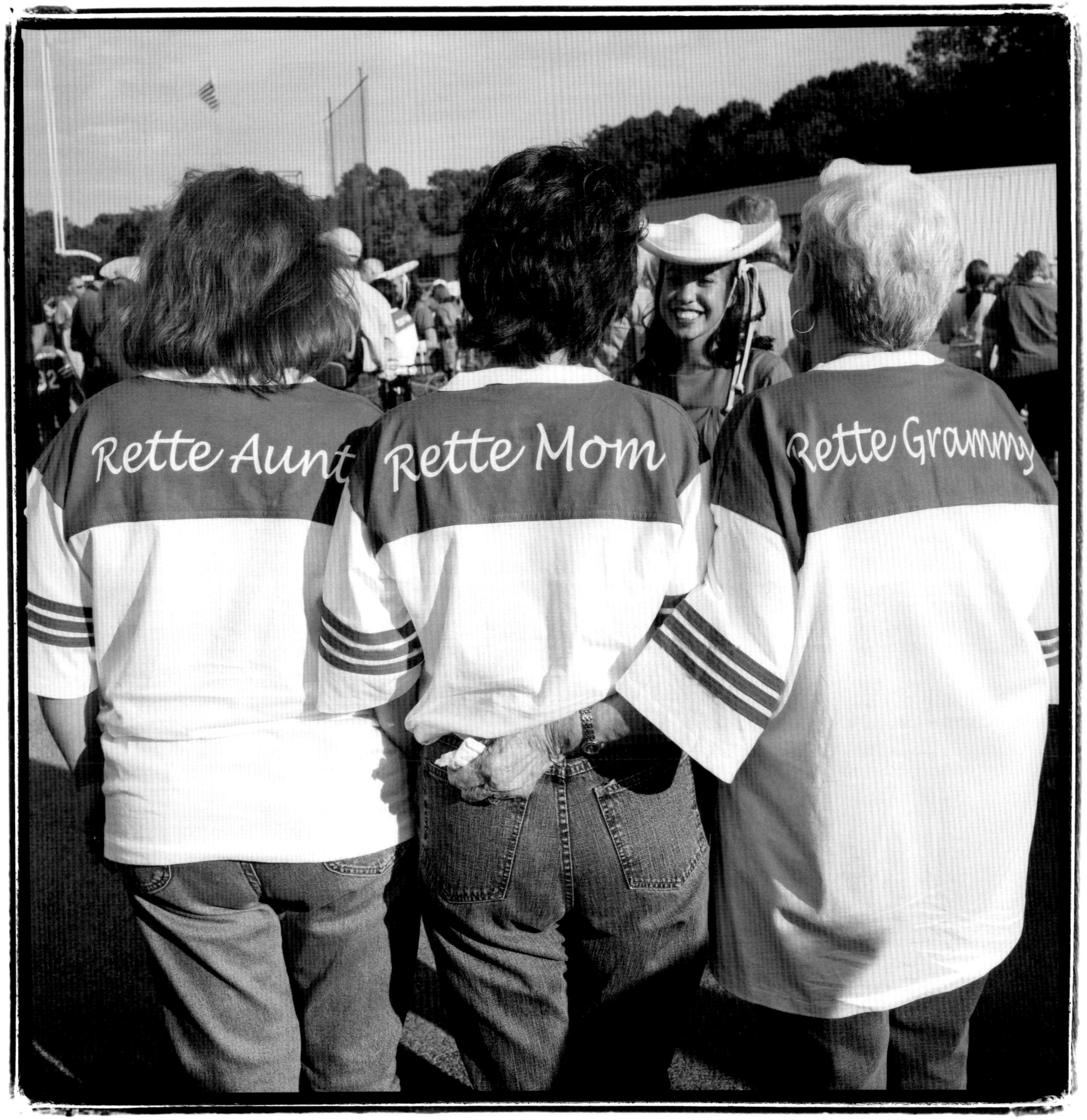

 RETTE AUNT, MOM, GRANDMOTHER 2006

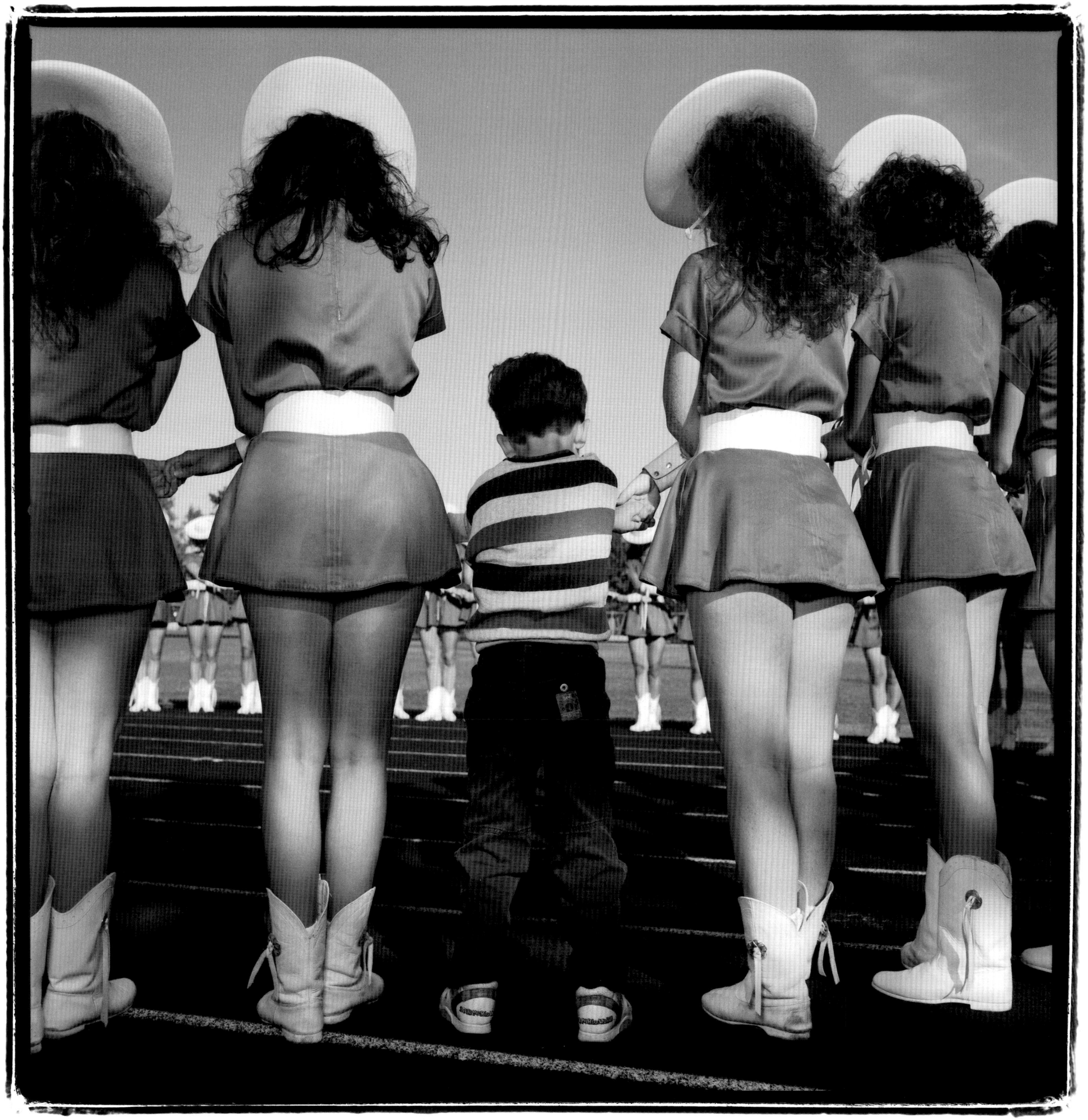

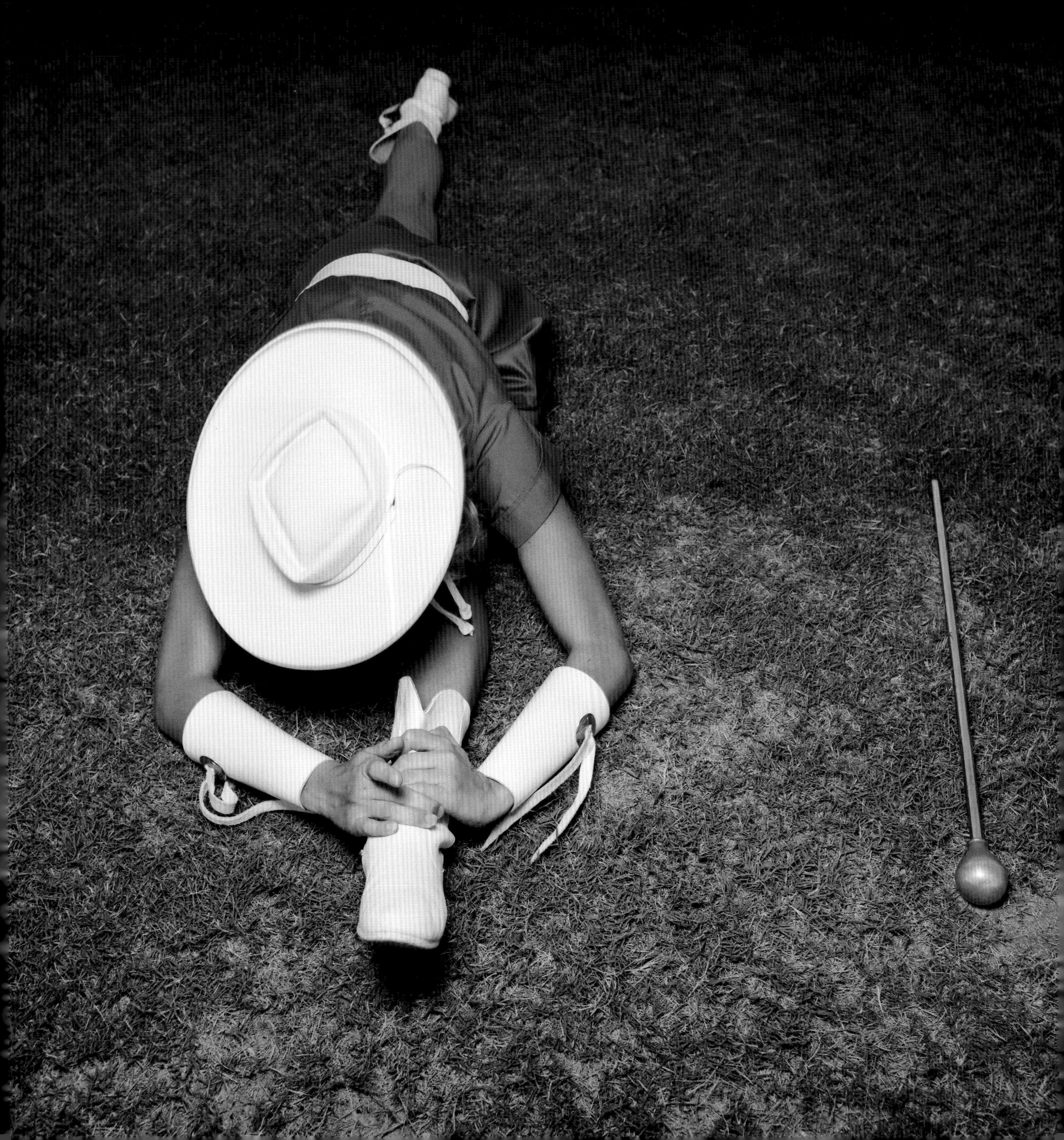

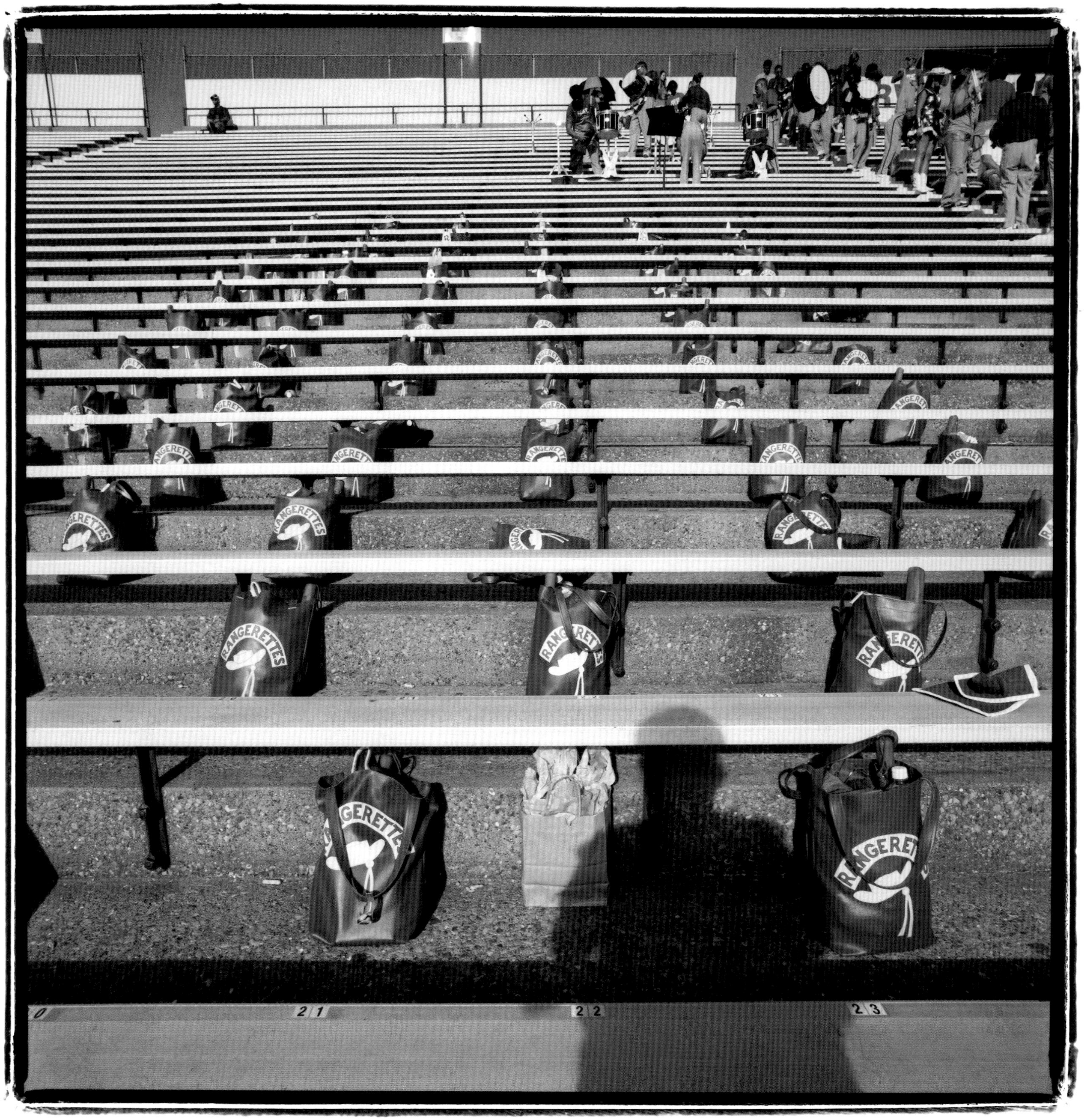

107 **RETTE STANDS II** 2006

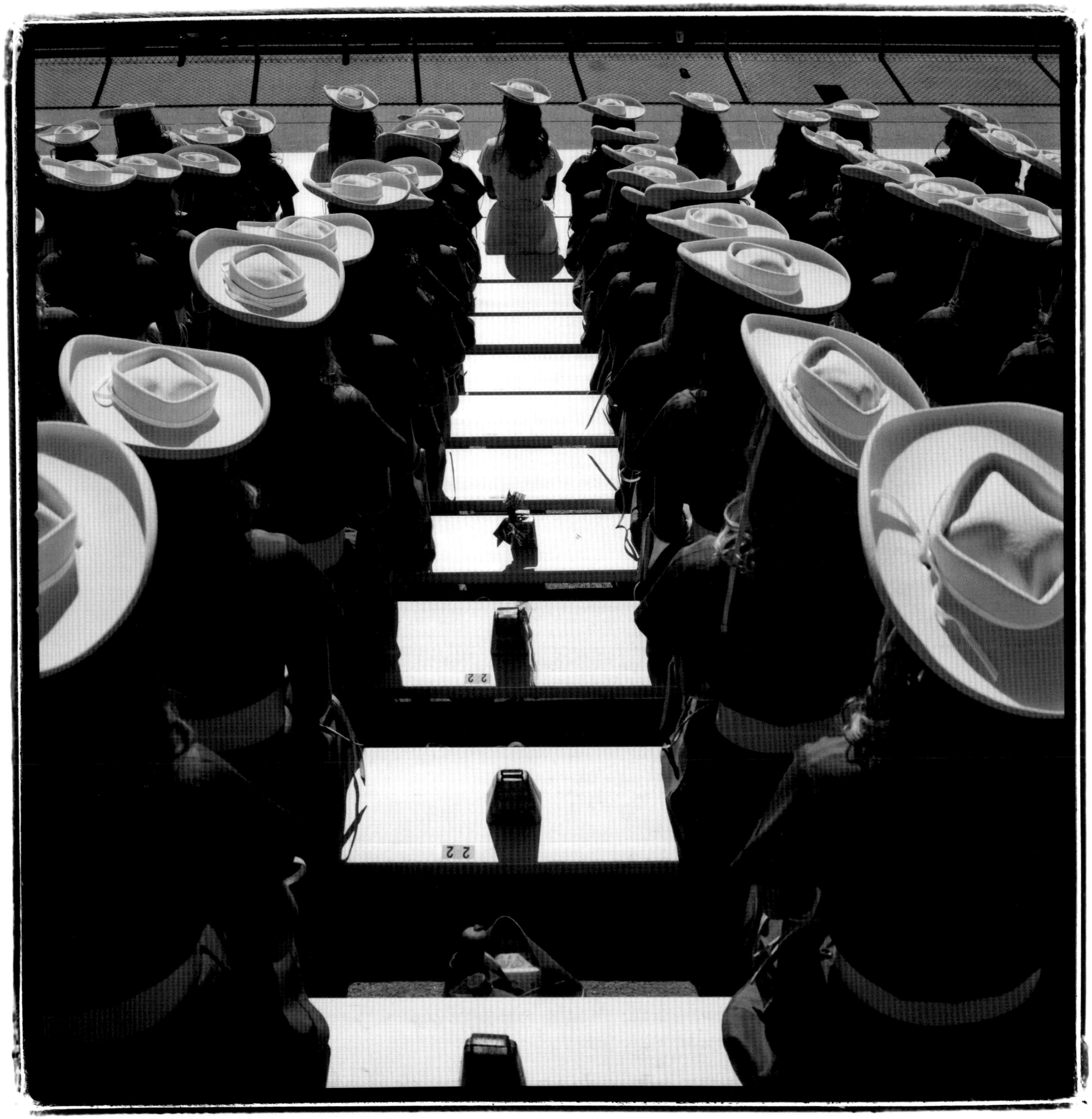

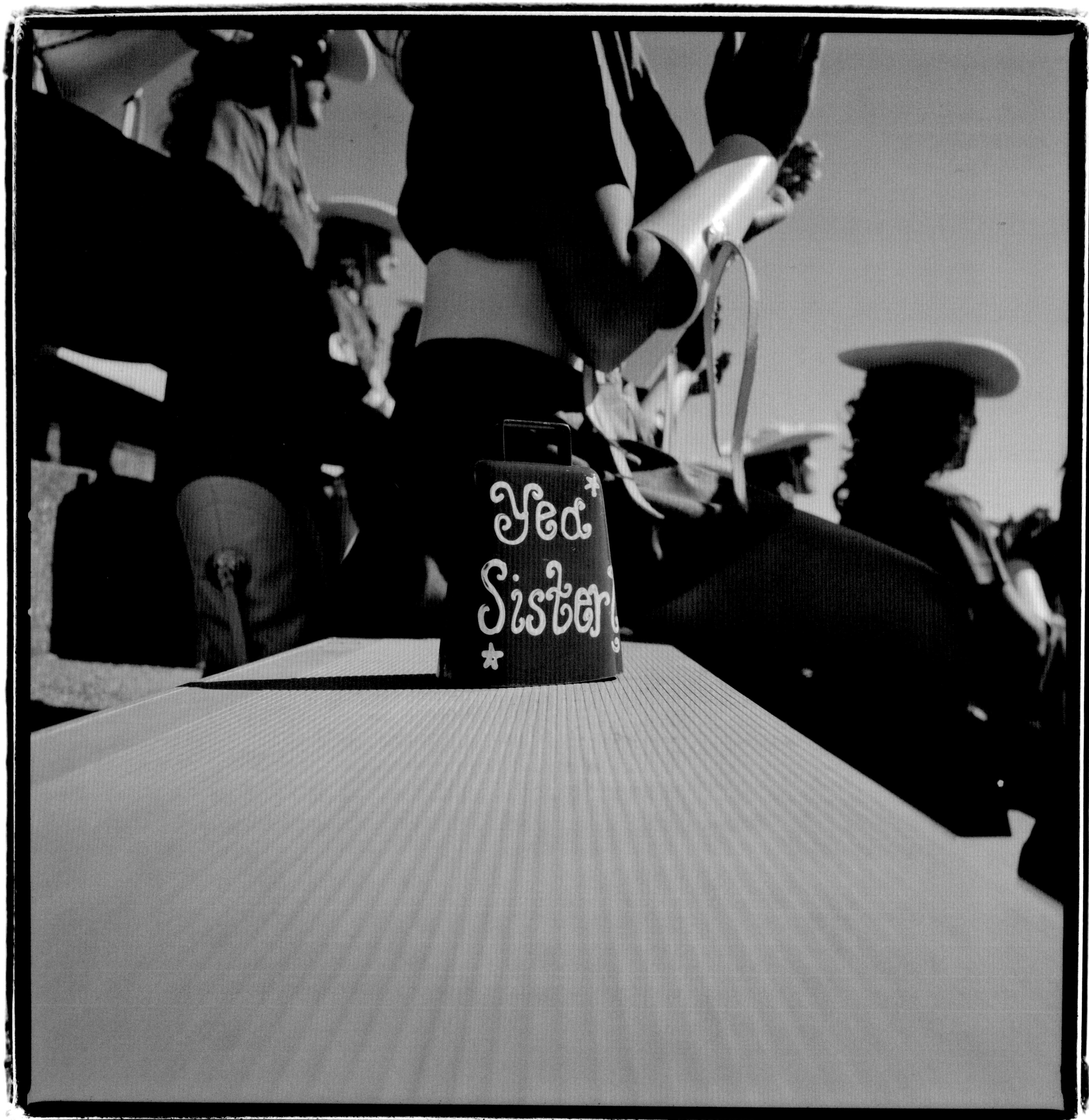
Yea Sister!

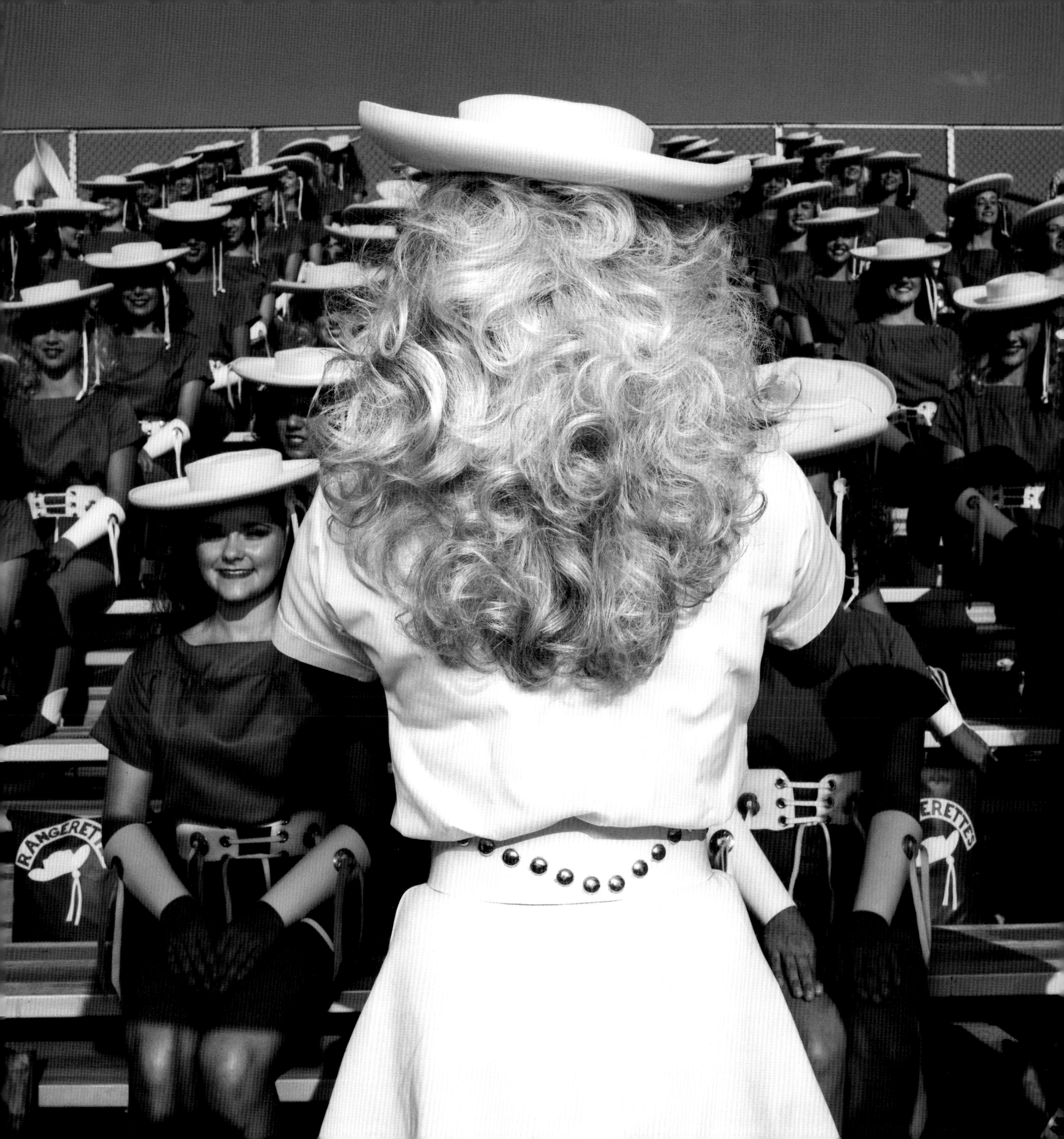
RANGERETTES

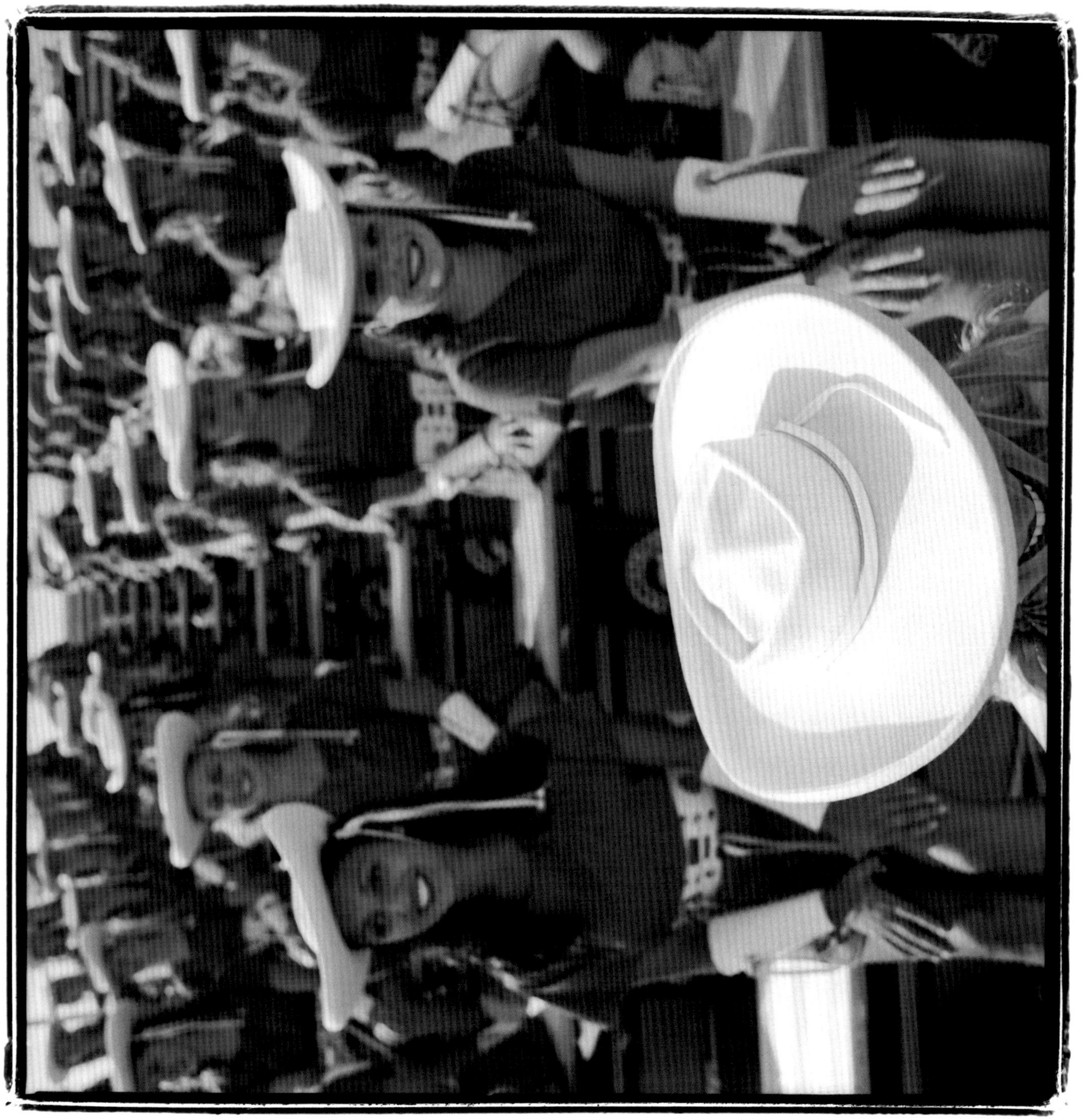

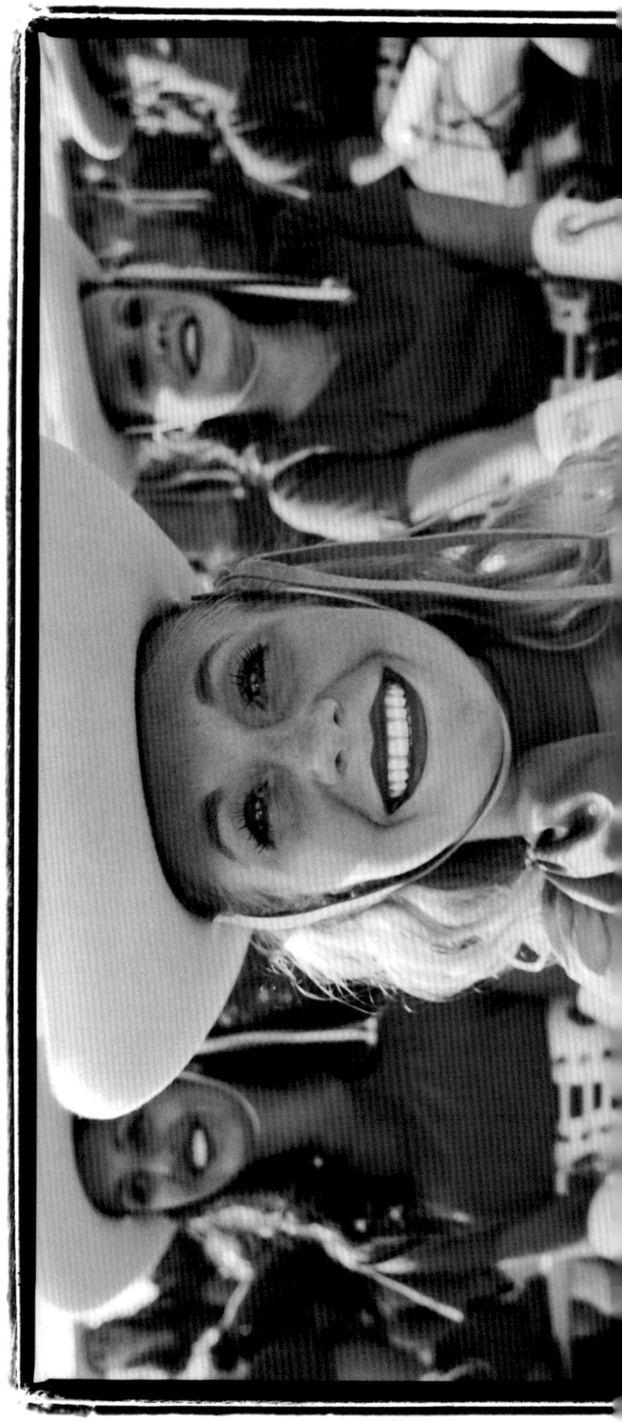

111–113 **OFFICER TRIPTYCH** 2003

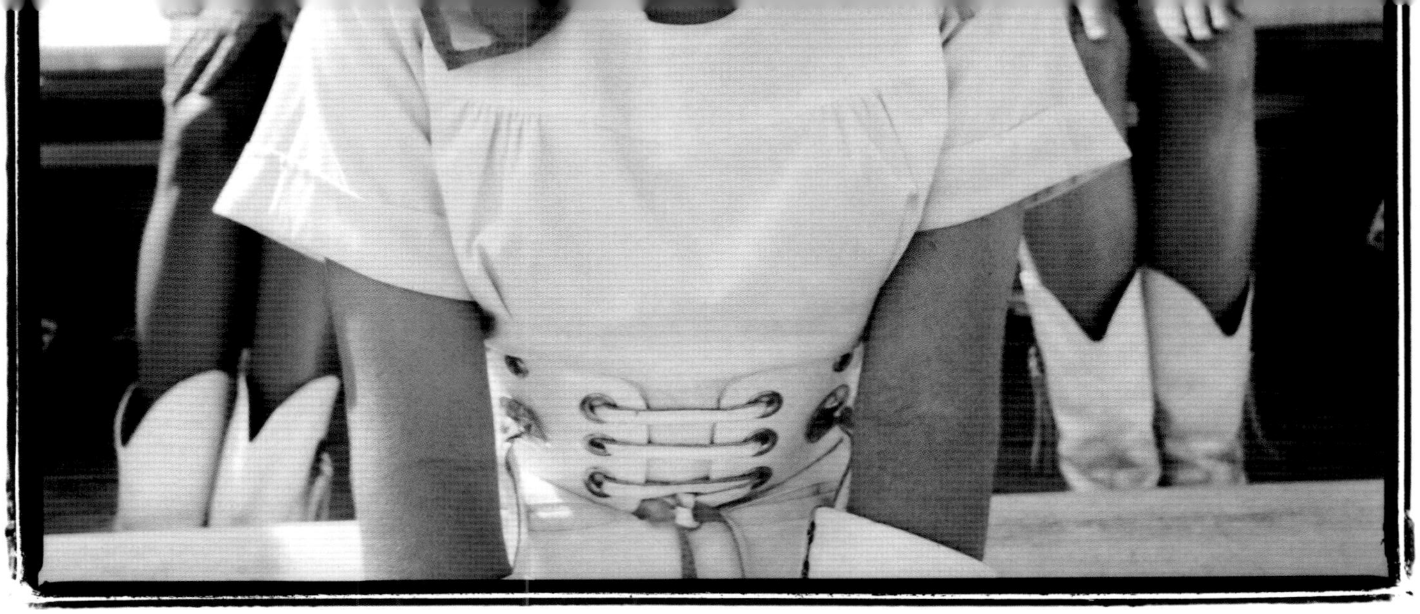

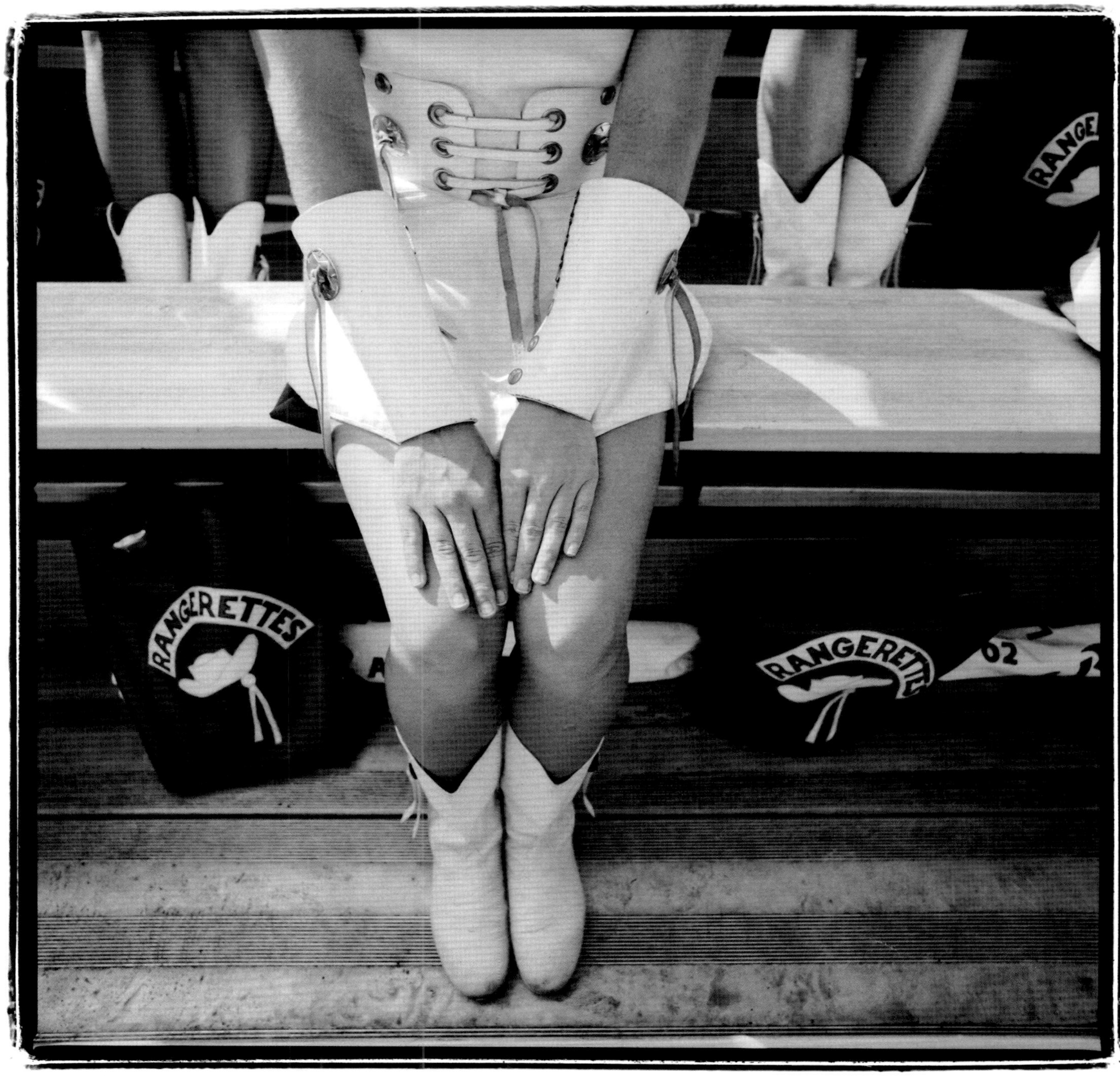
RANGERETTES
RANGERETTES

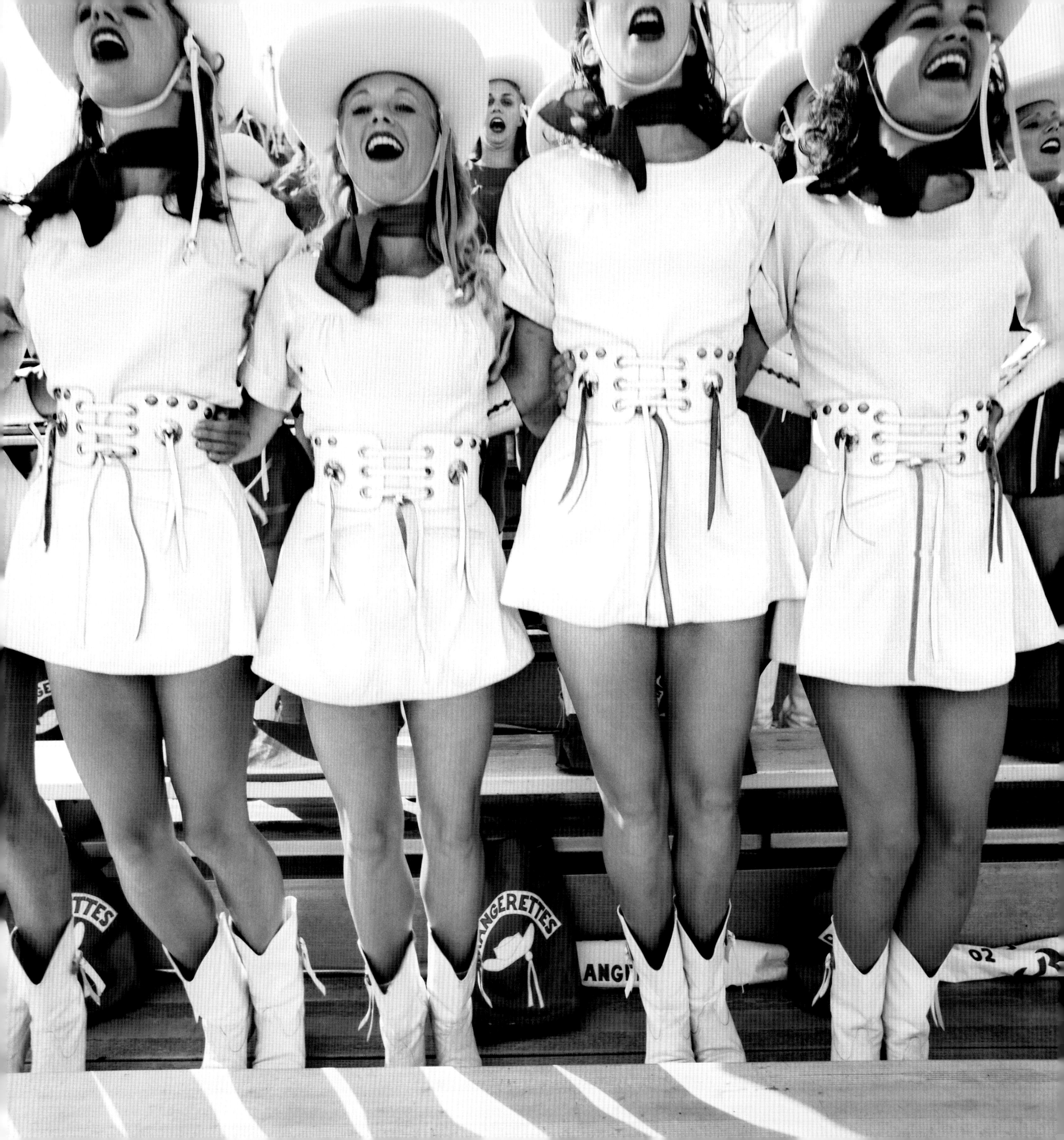

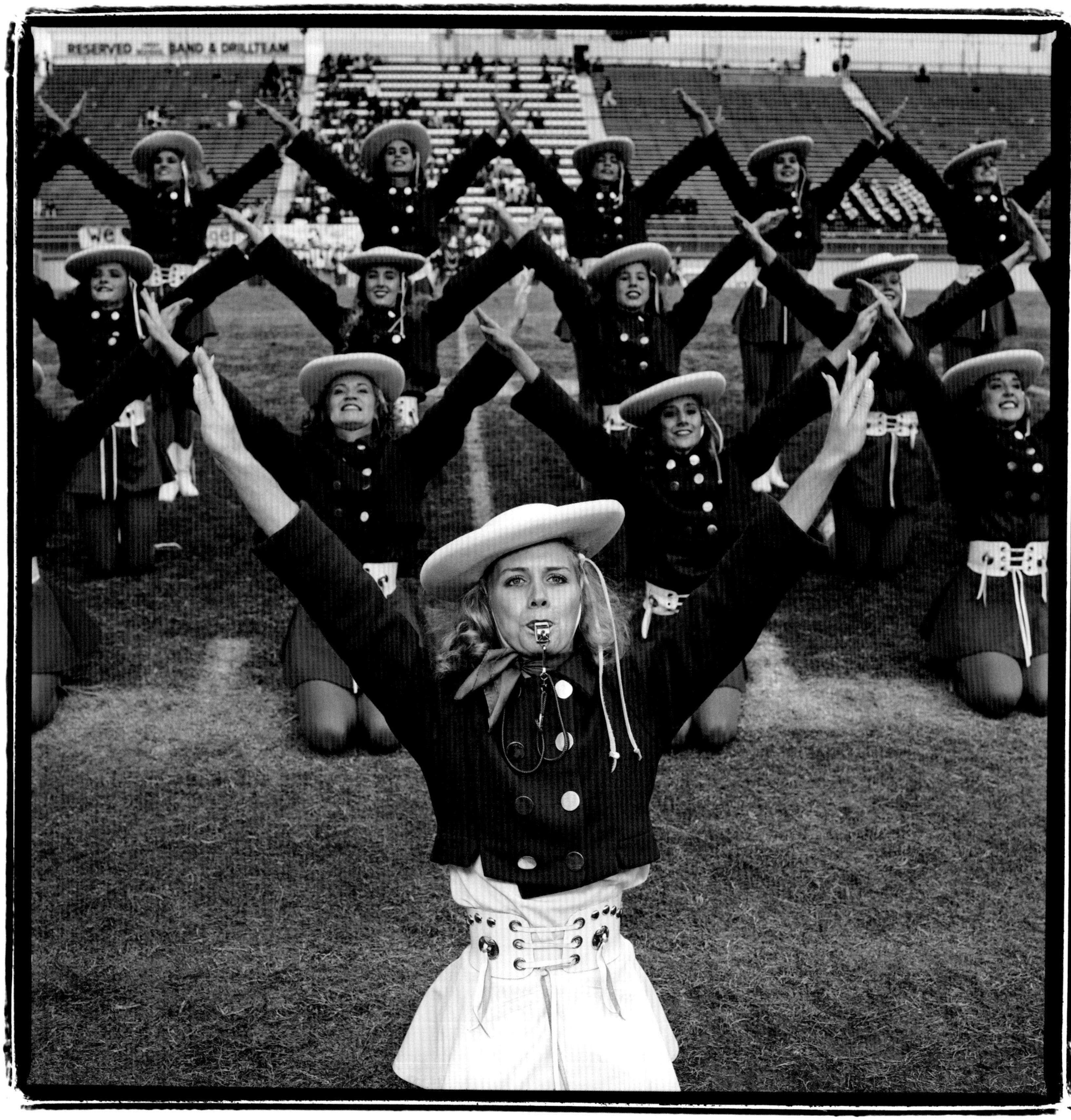

 LIEUTENANT 1989

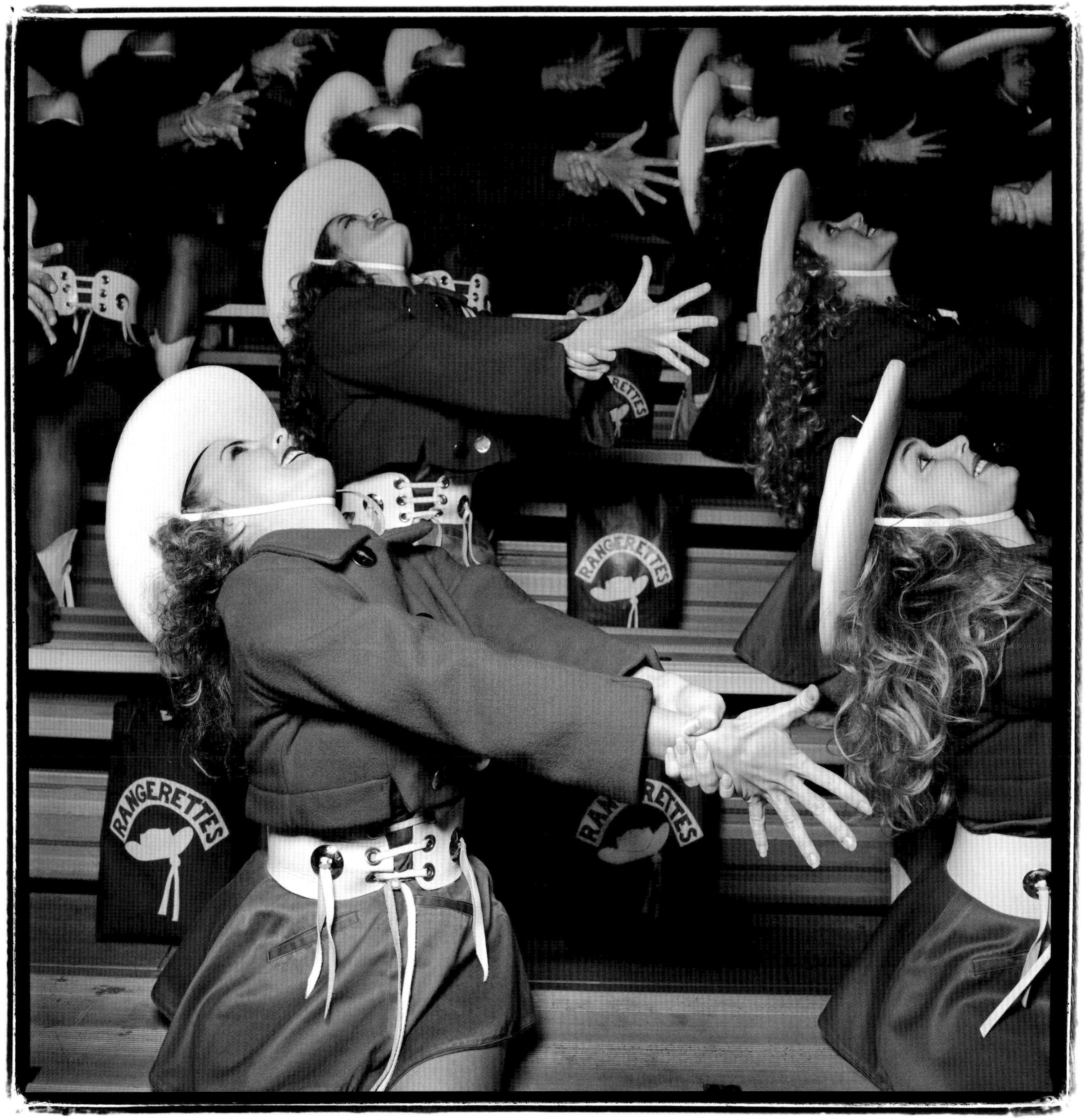

 STADIUM PERFORMANCE 1989

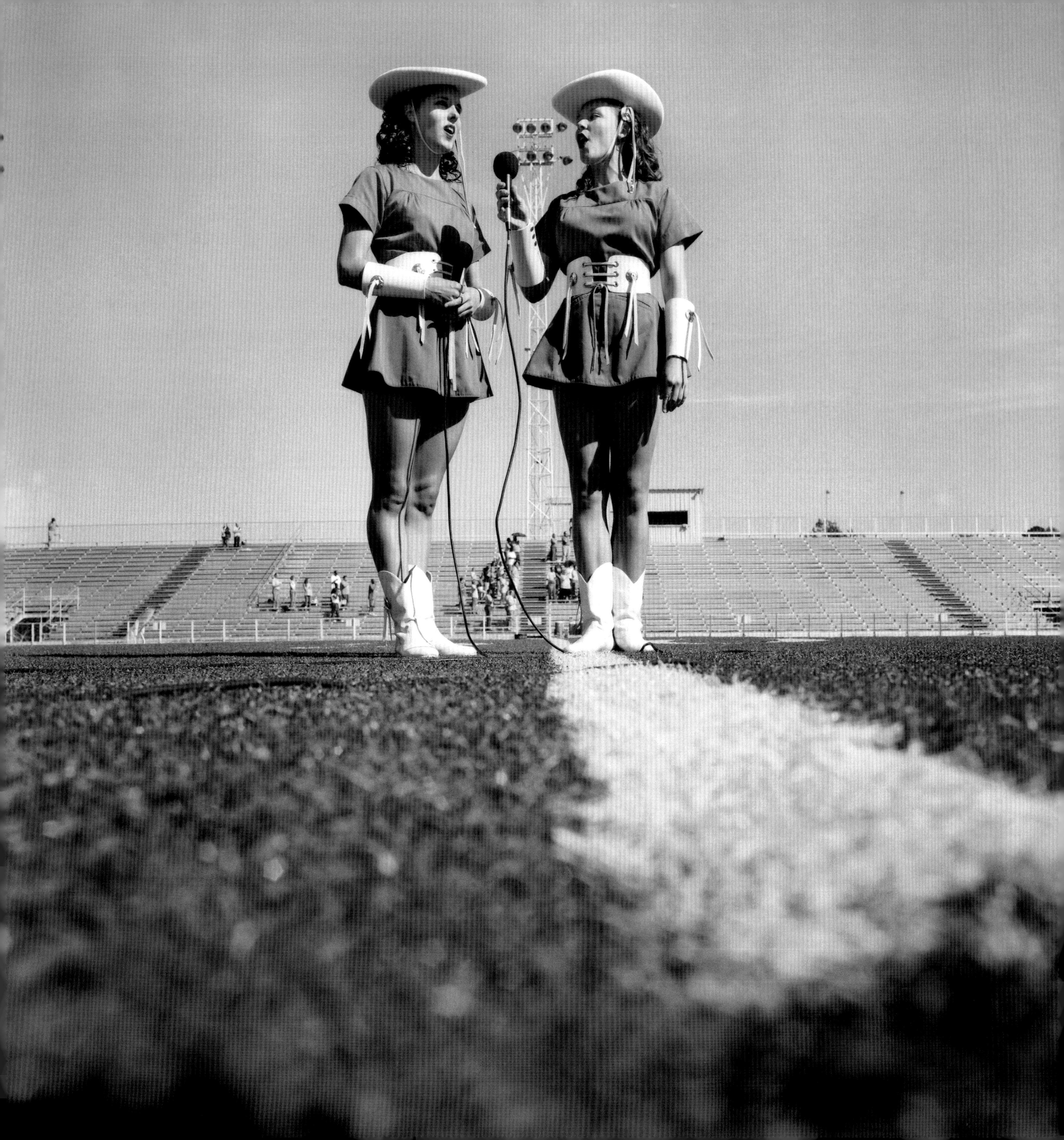

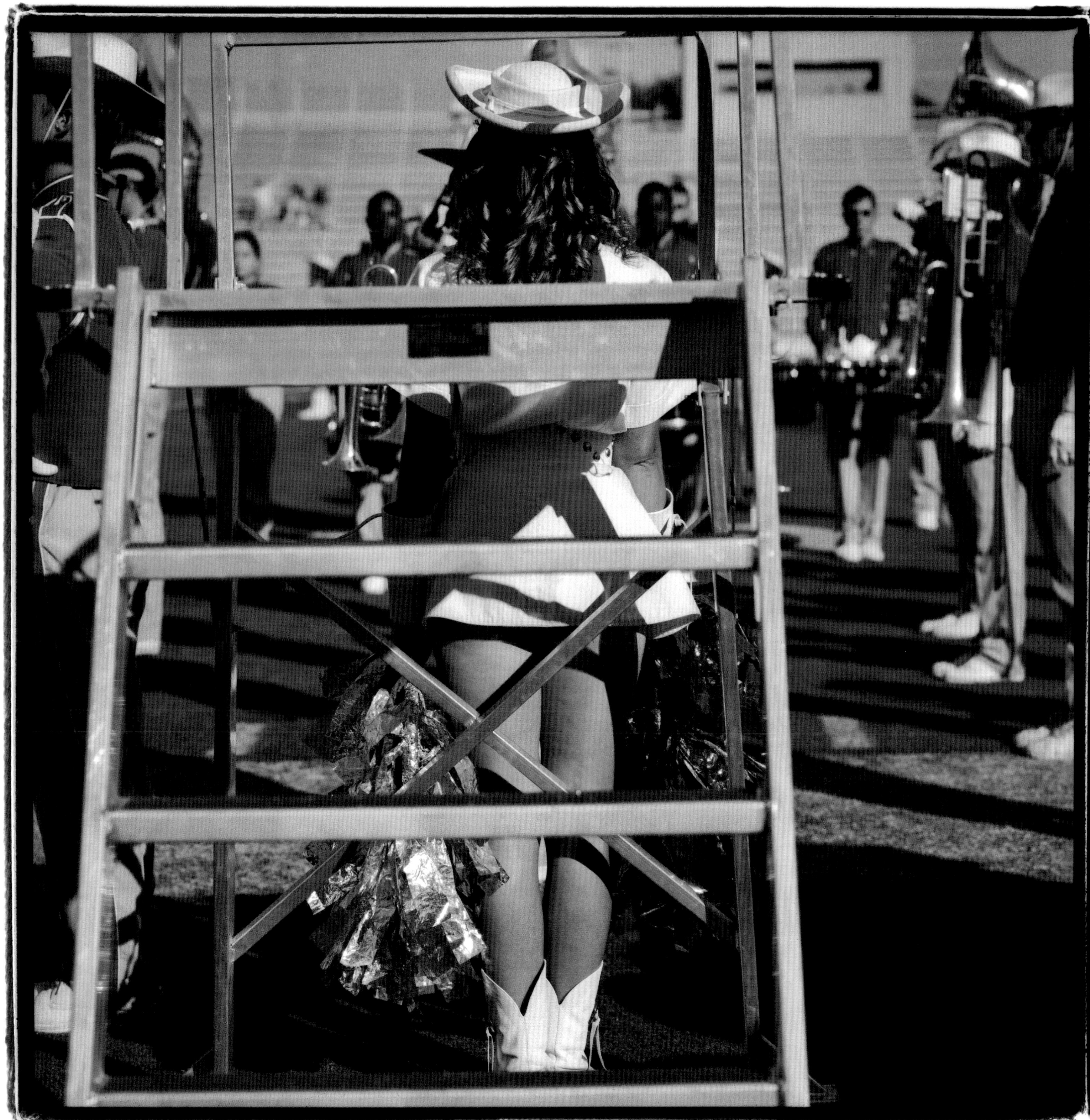

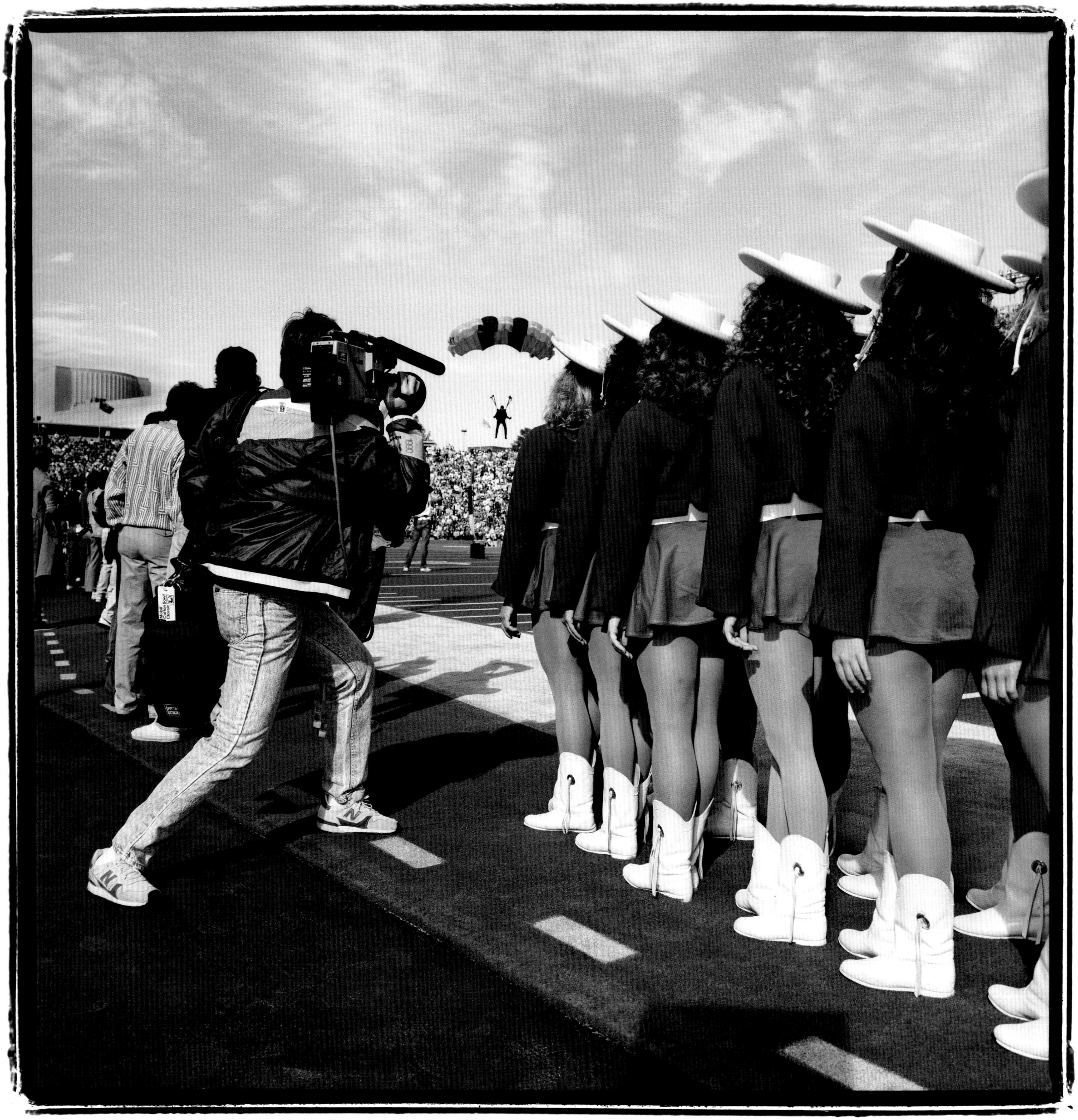

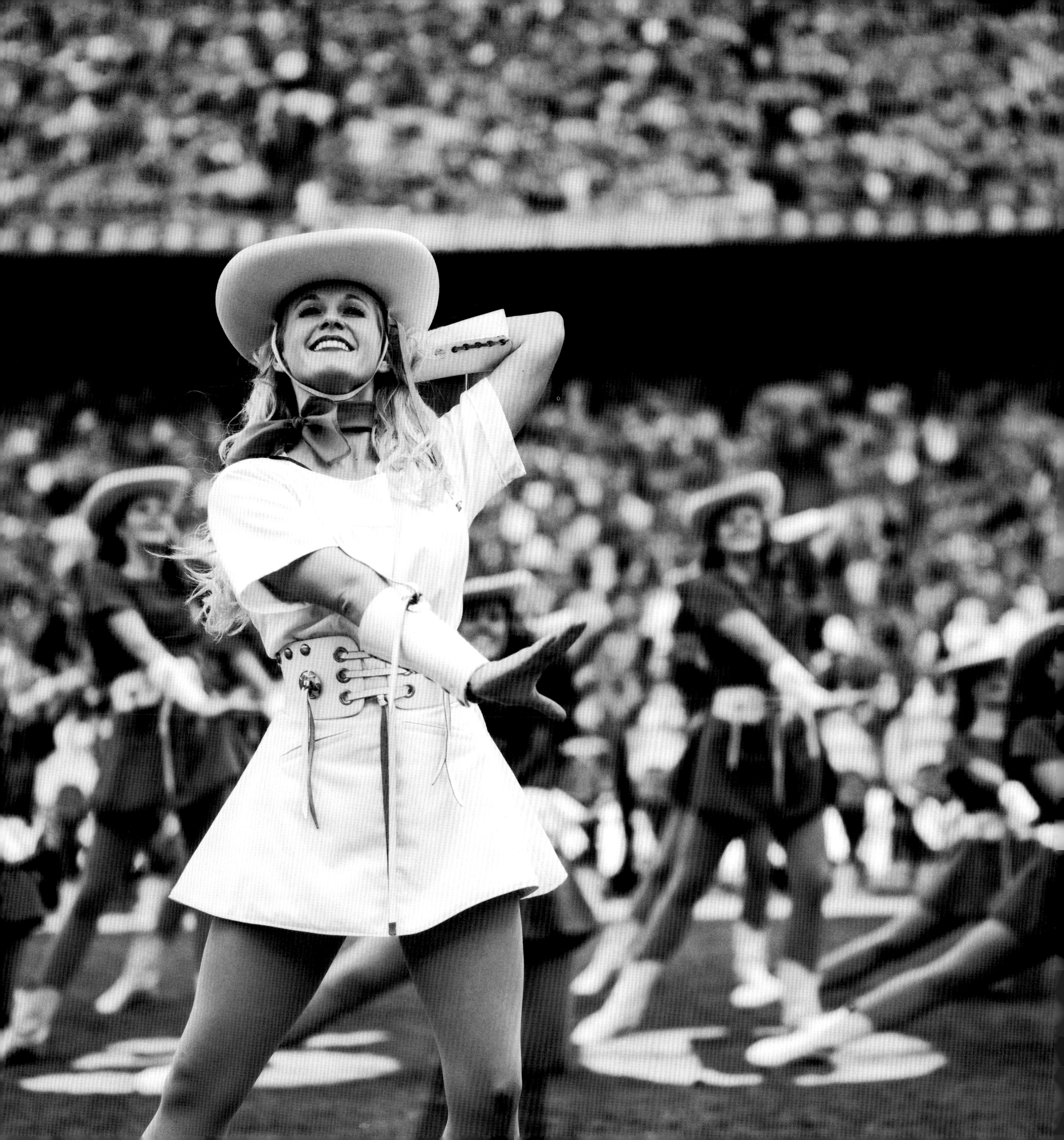

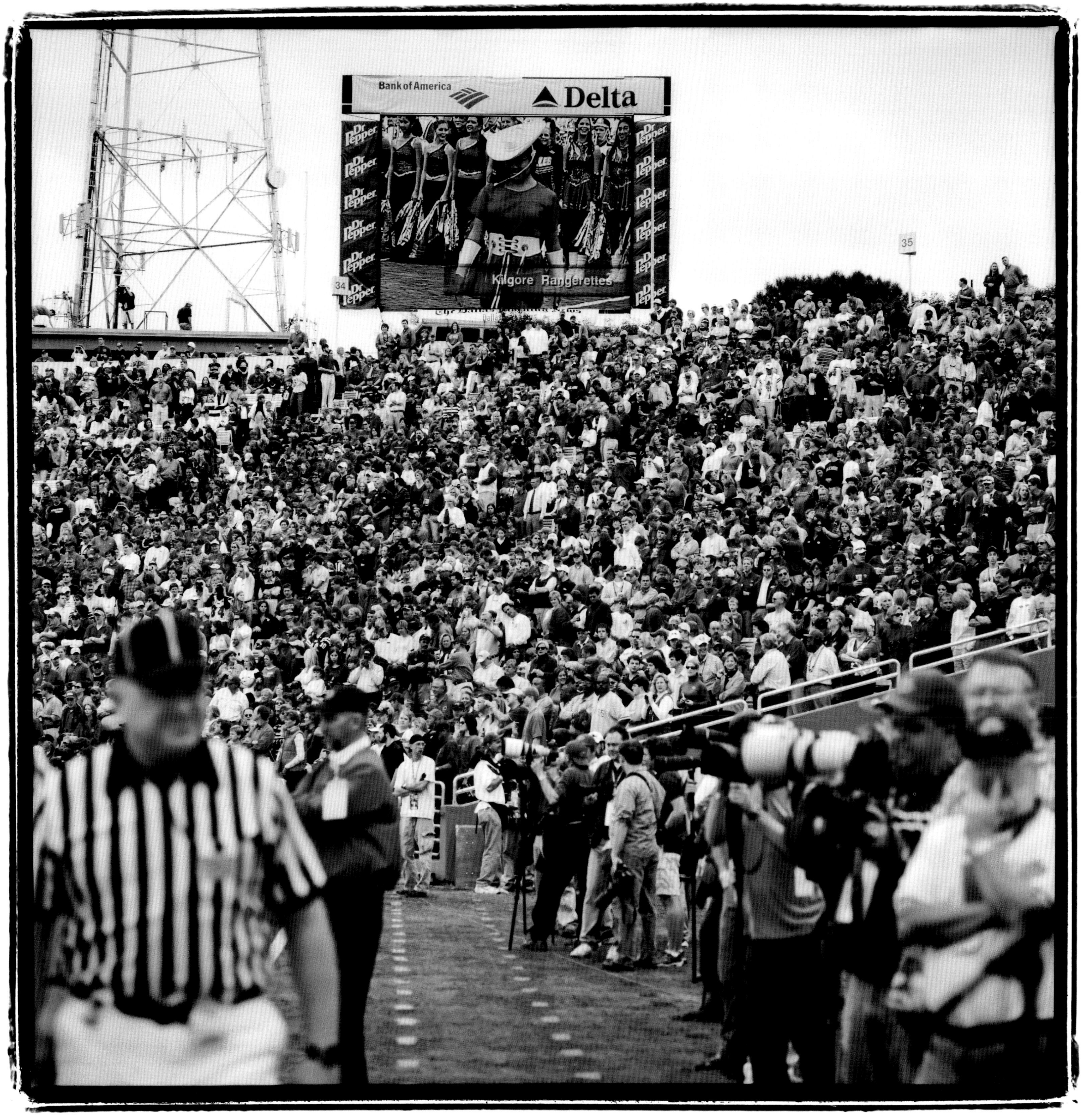
Bank of America
Delta
Dr Pepper
Kilgore Rangerettes
34
35

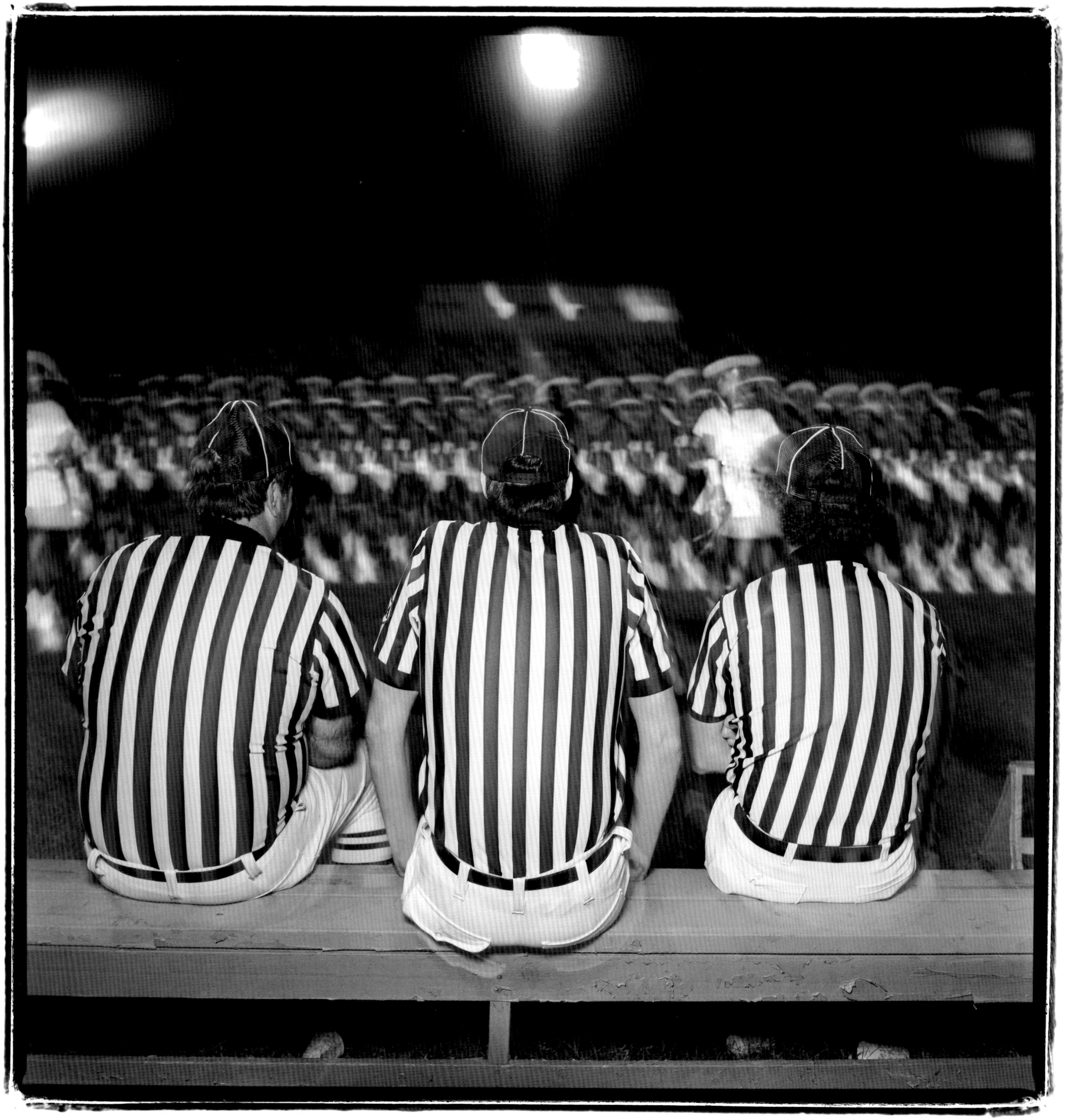

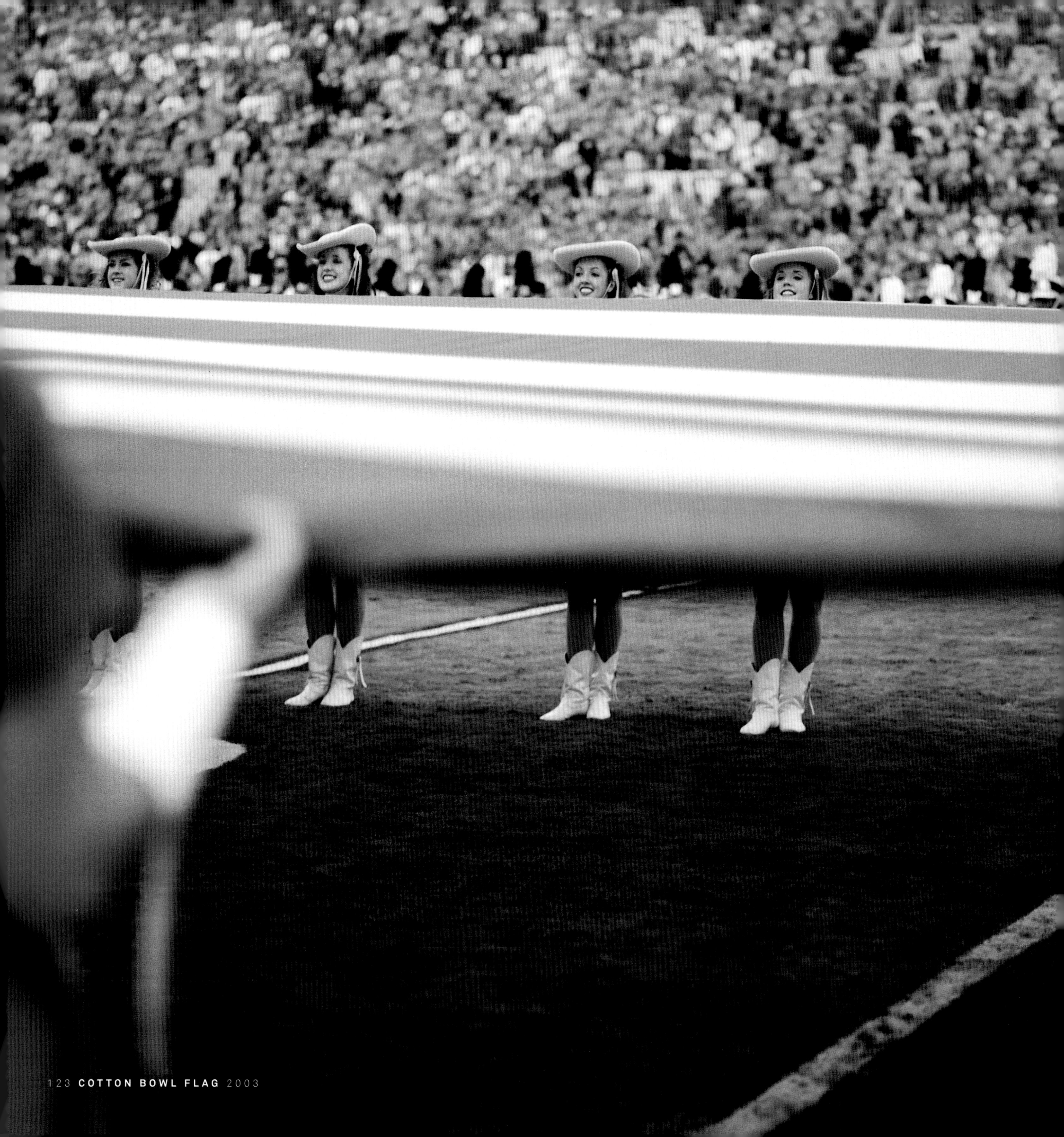

 COTTON BOWL FLAG 2003

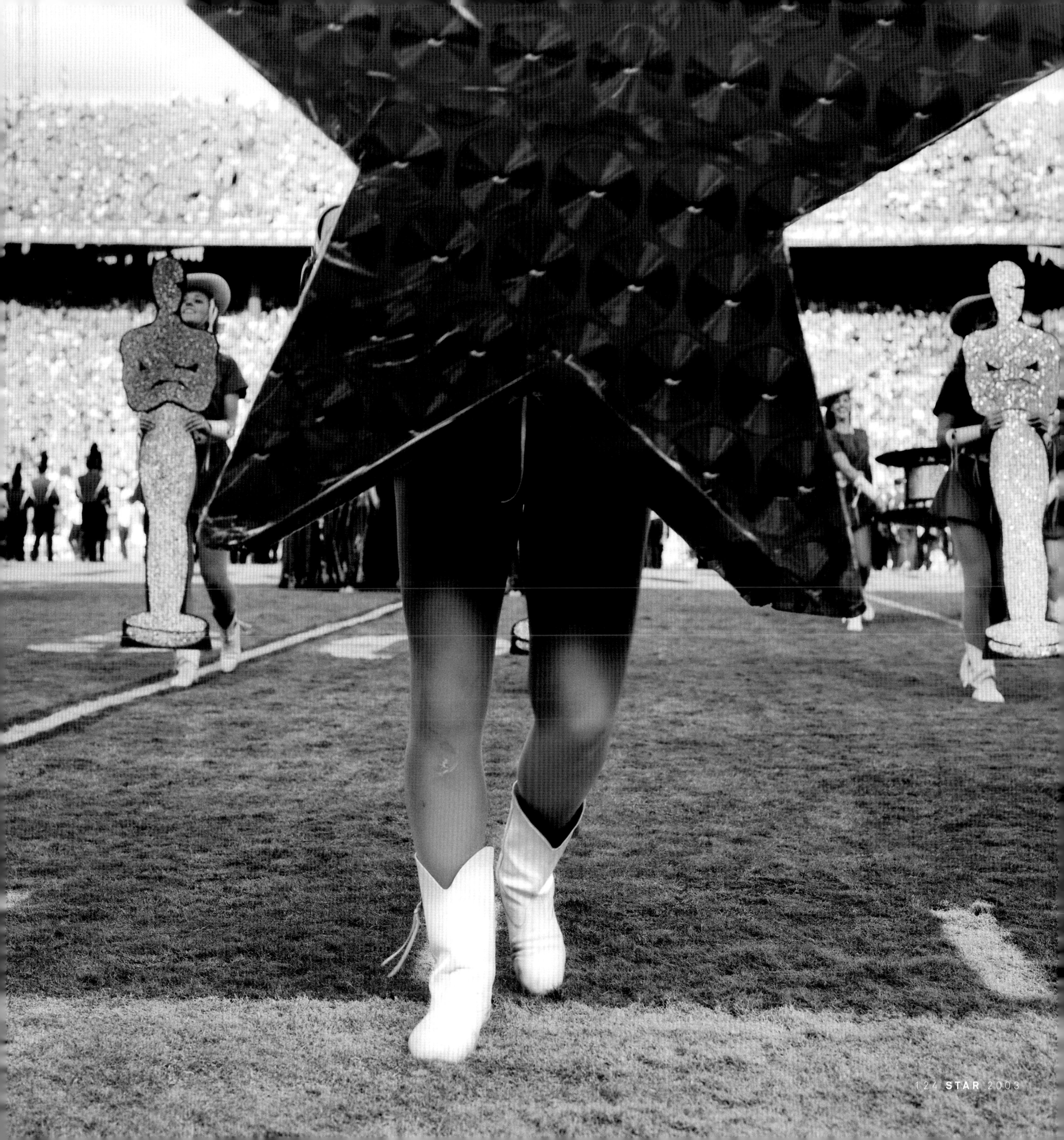

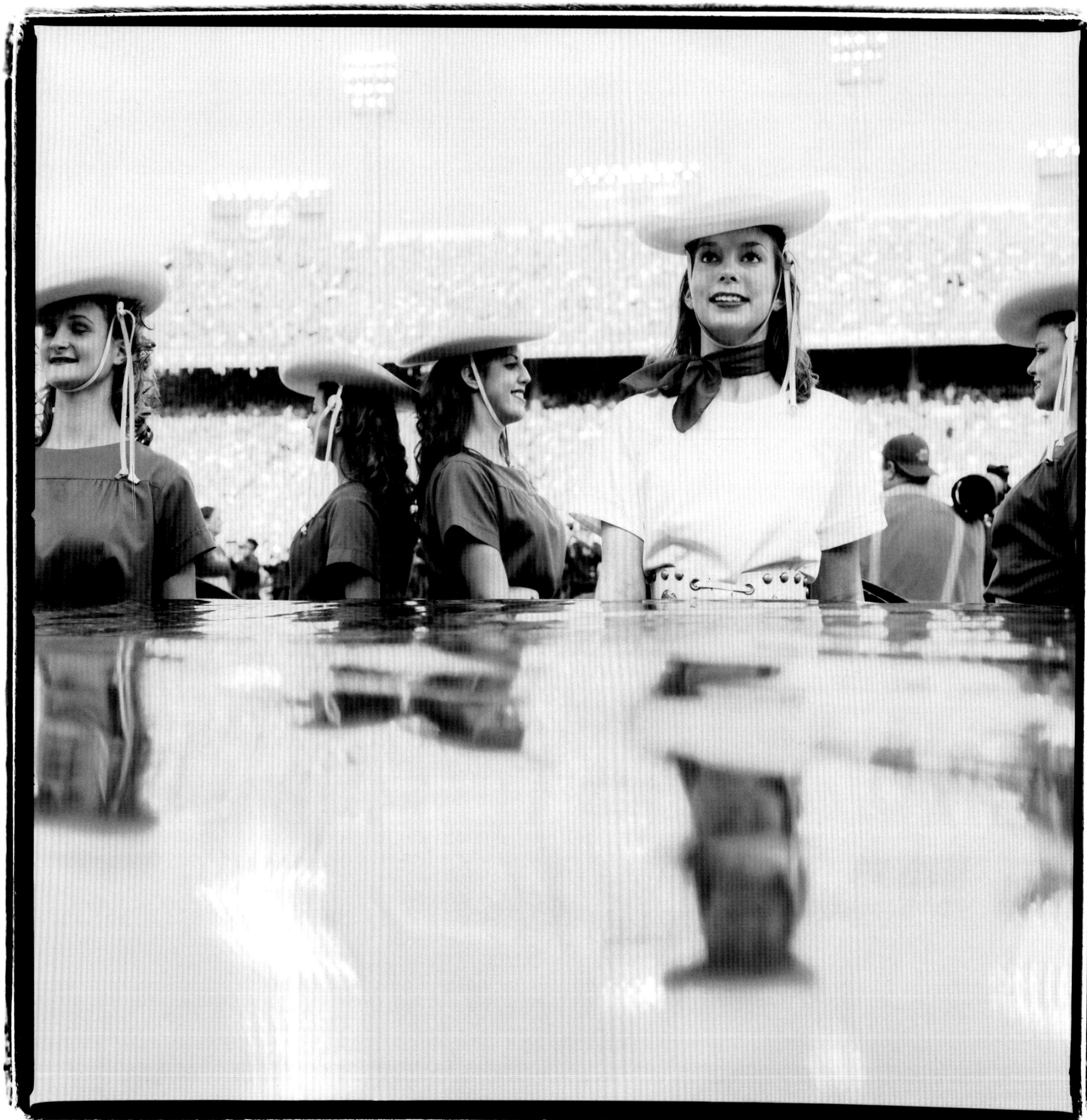

 COTTON BOWL REFLECTION 2004

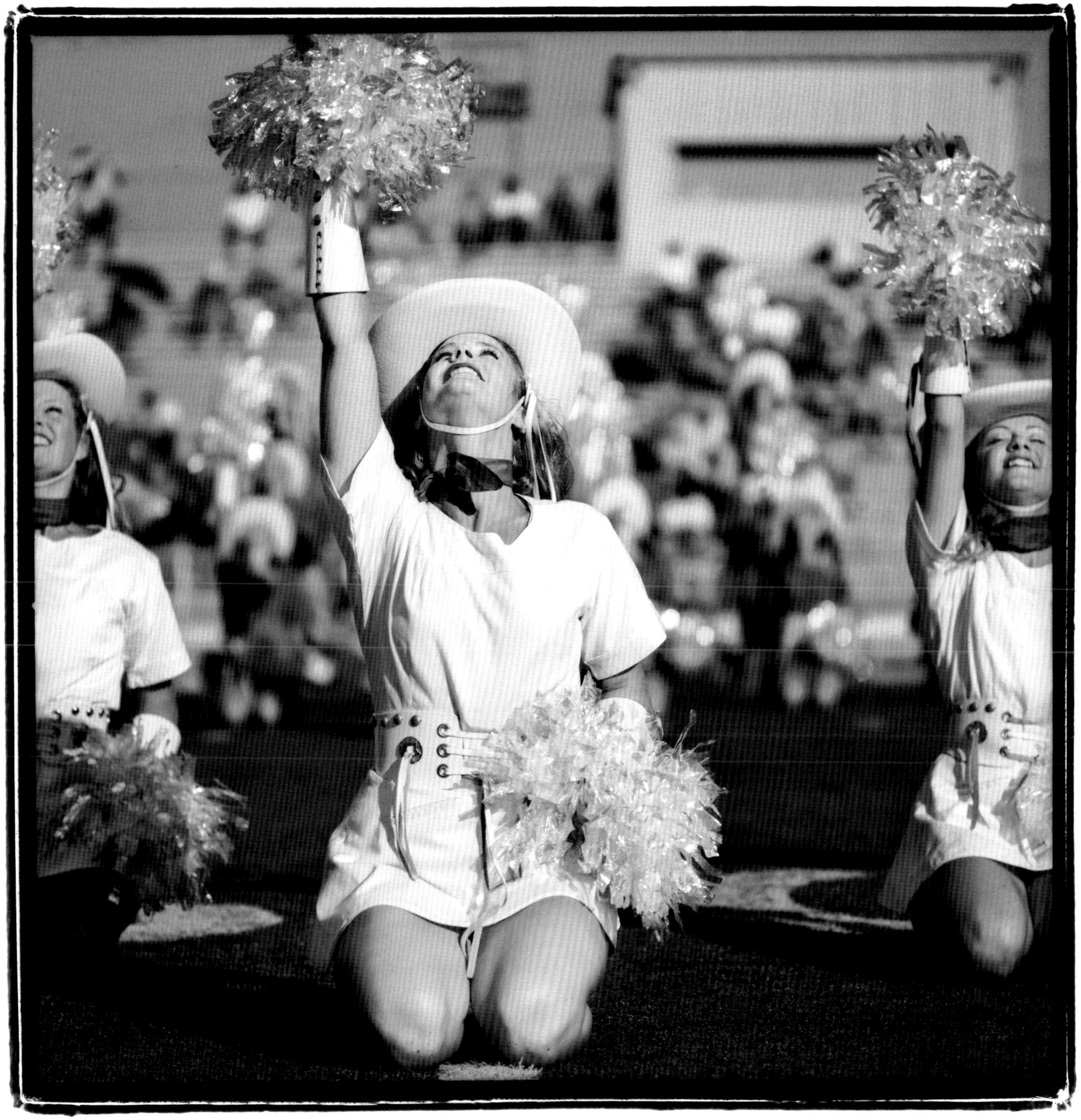

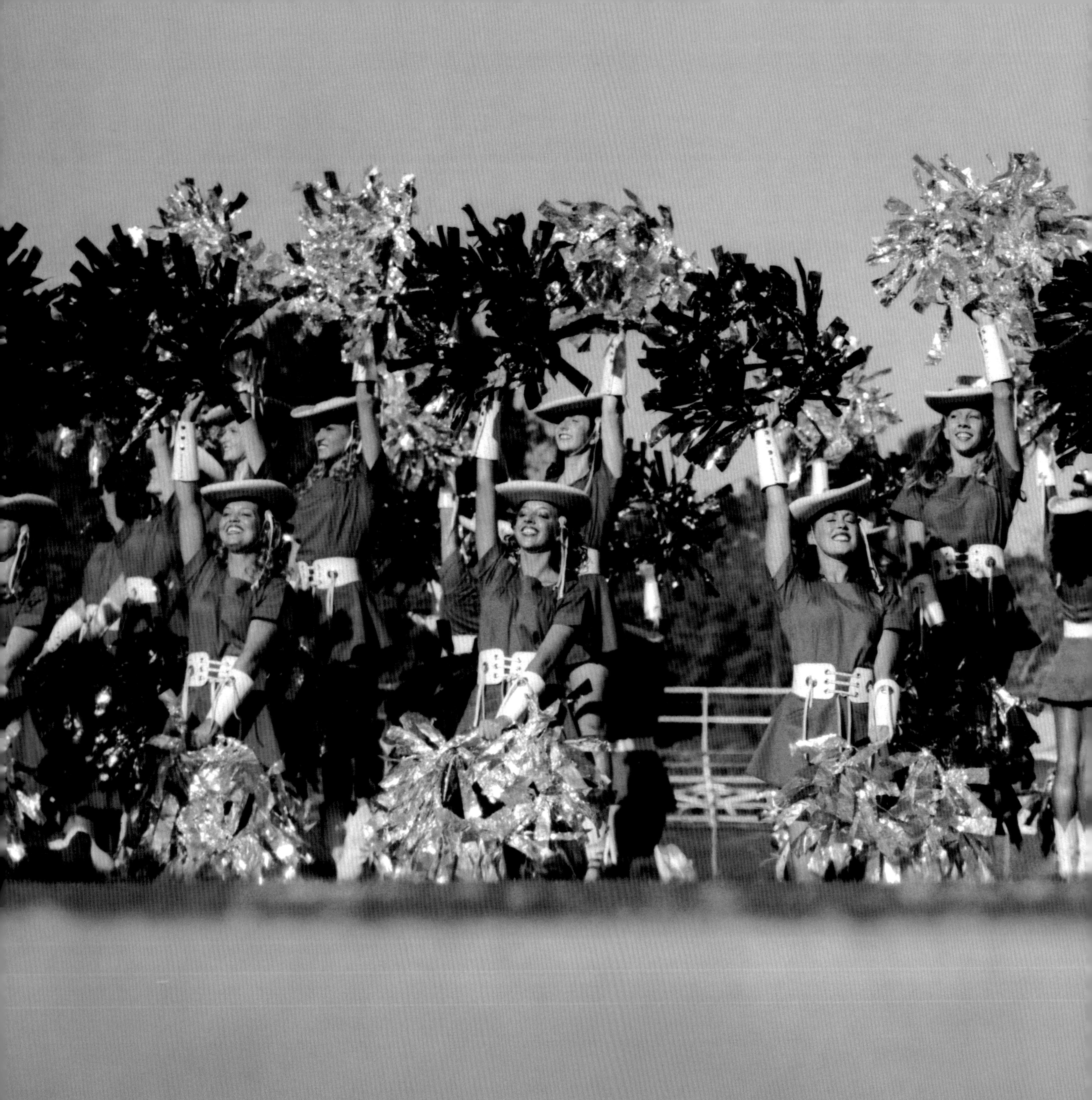

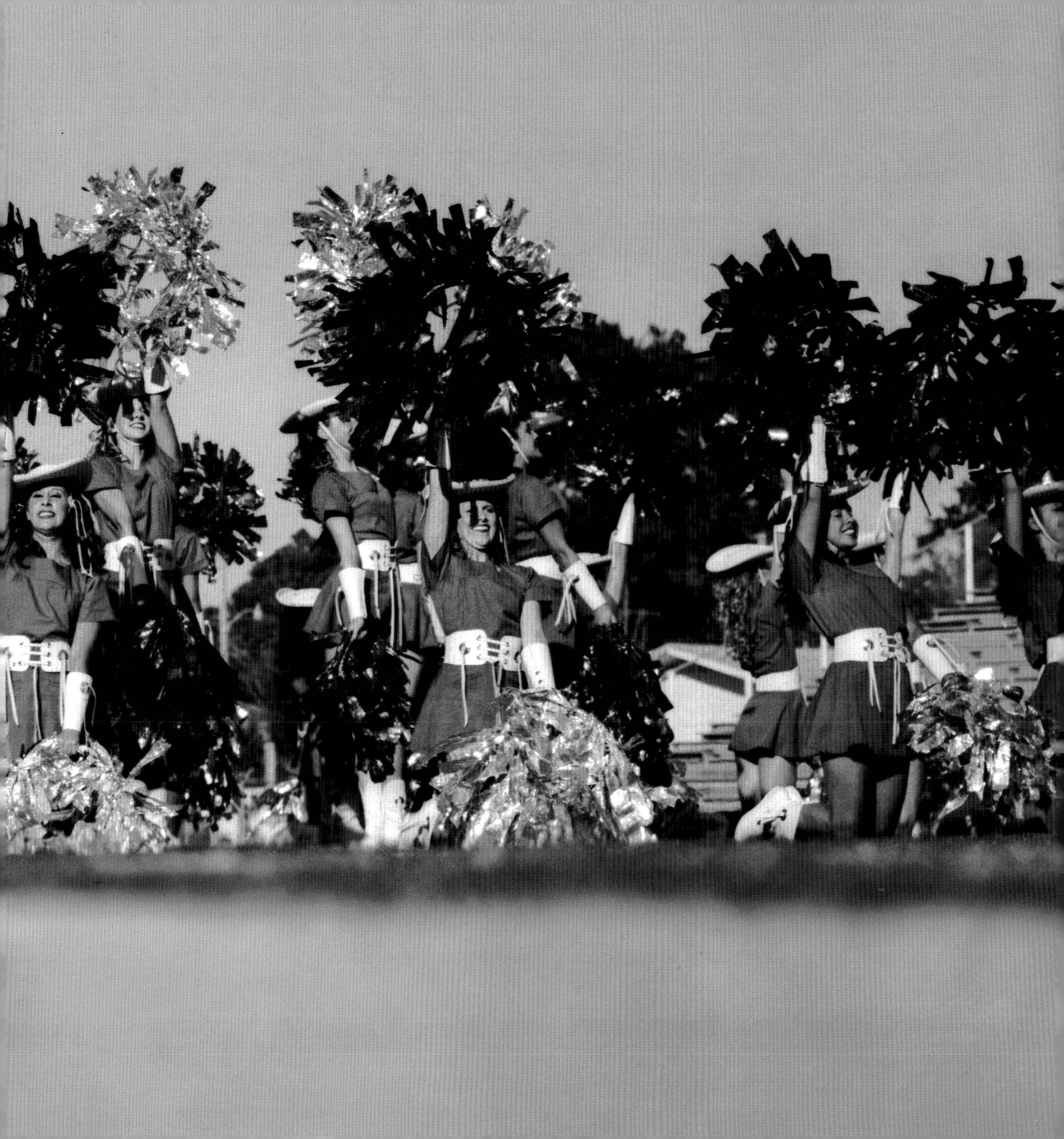

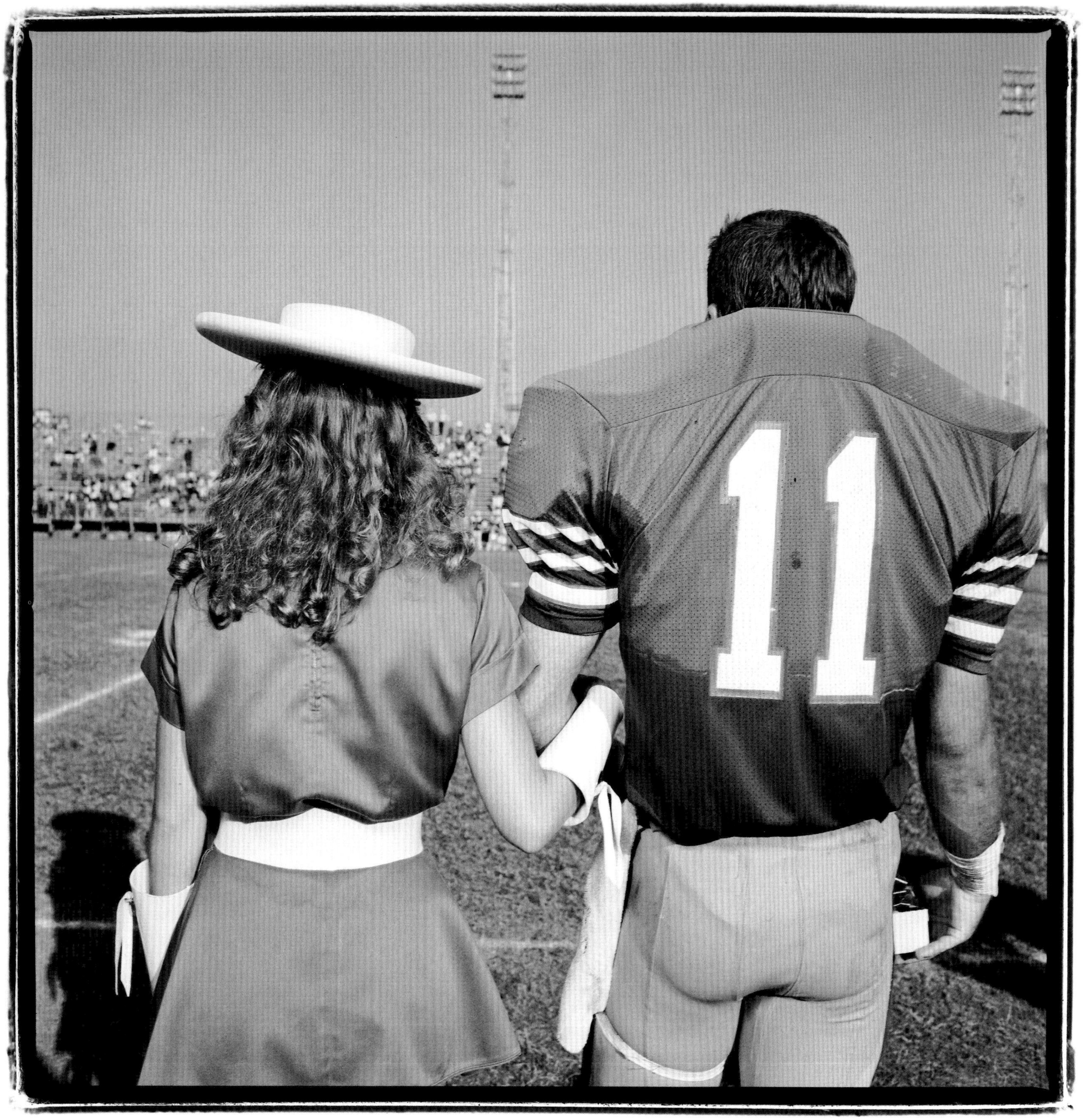

 HOMECOMING KING AND QUEEN I 1989

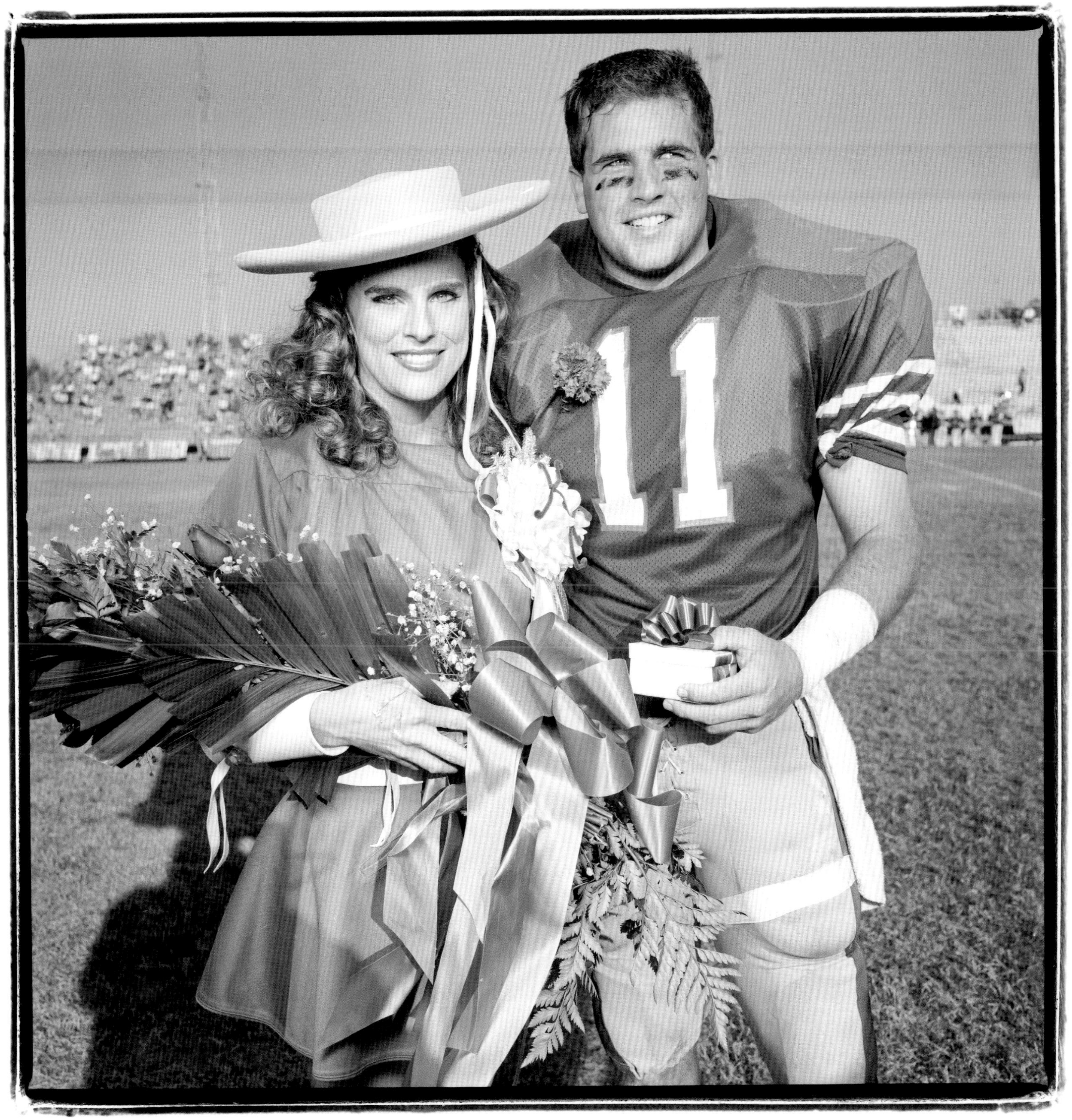

129 **HOMECOMING KING AND QUEEN II** 1989

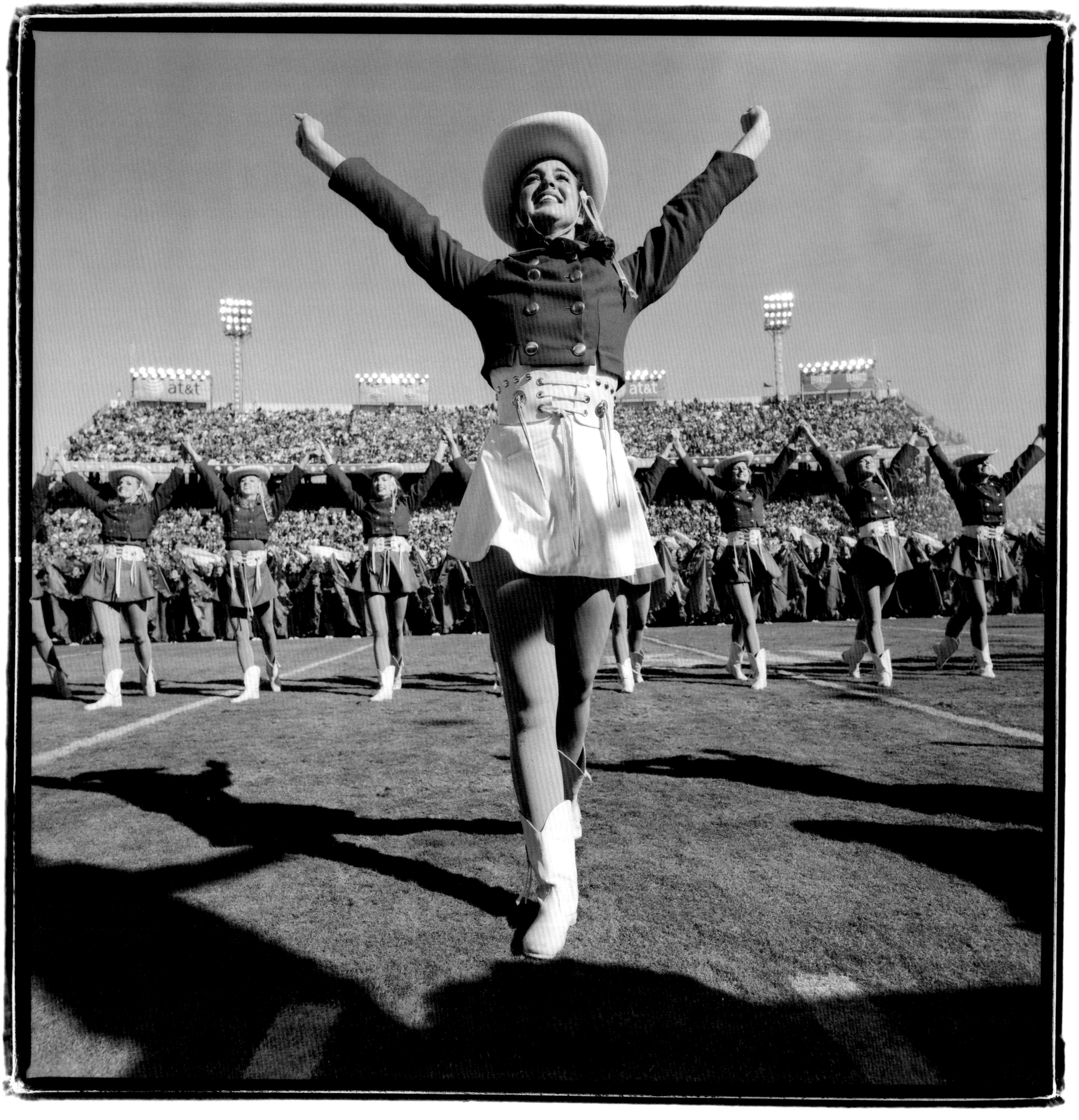
at&t
at&t

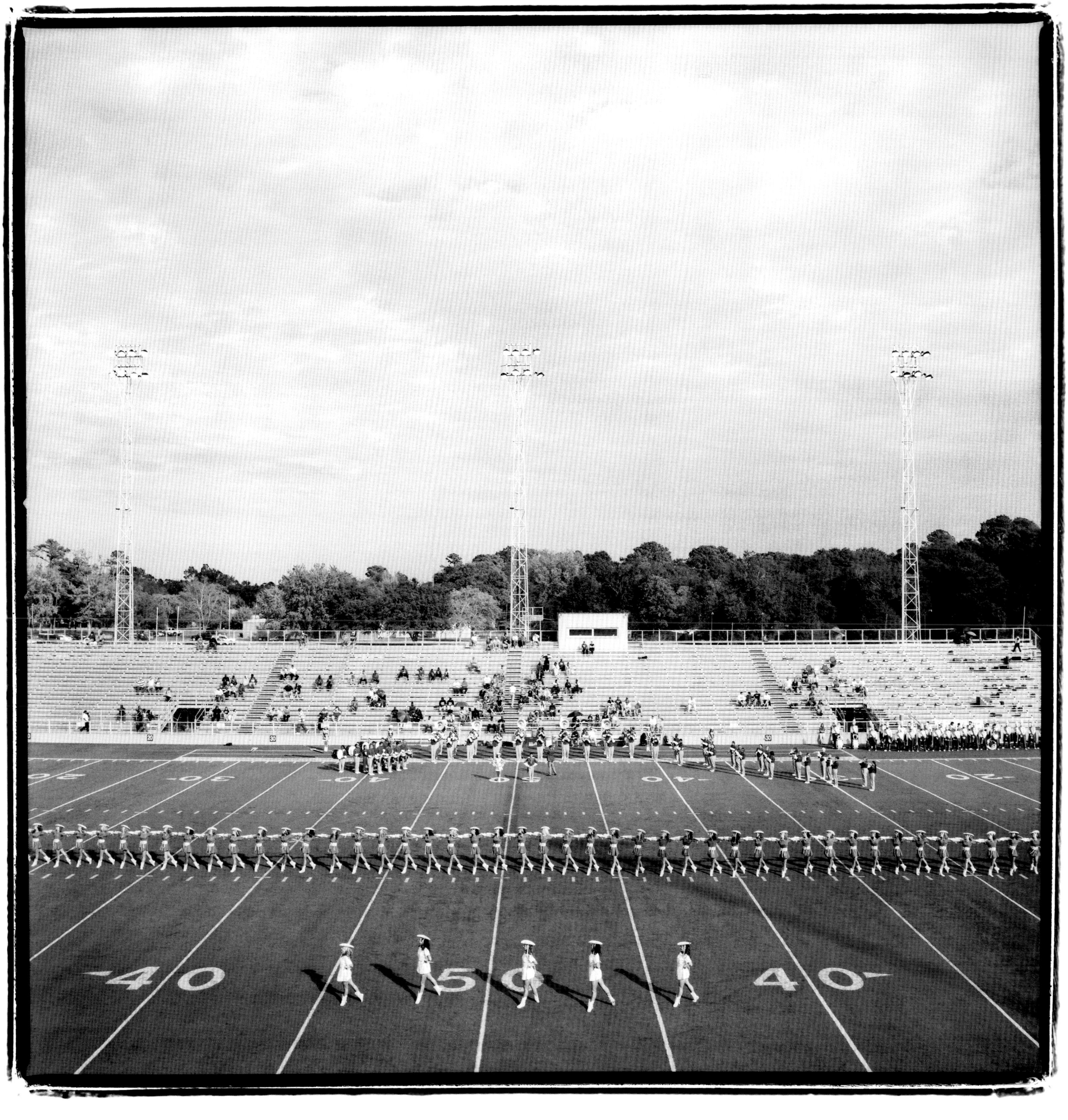

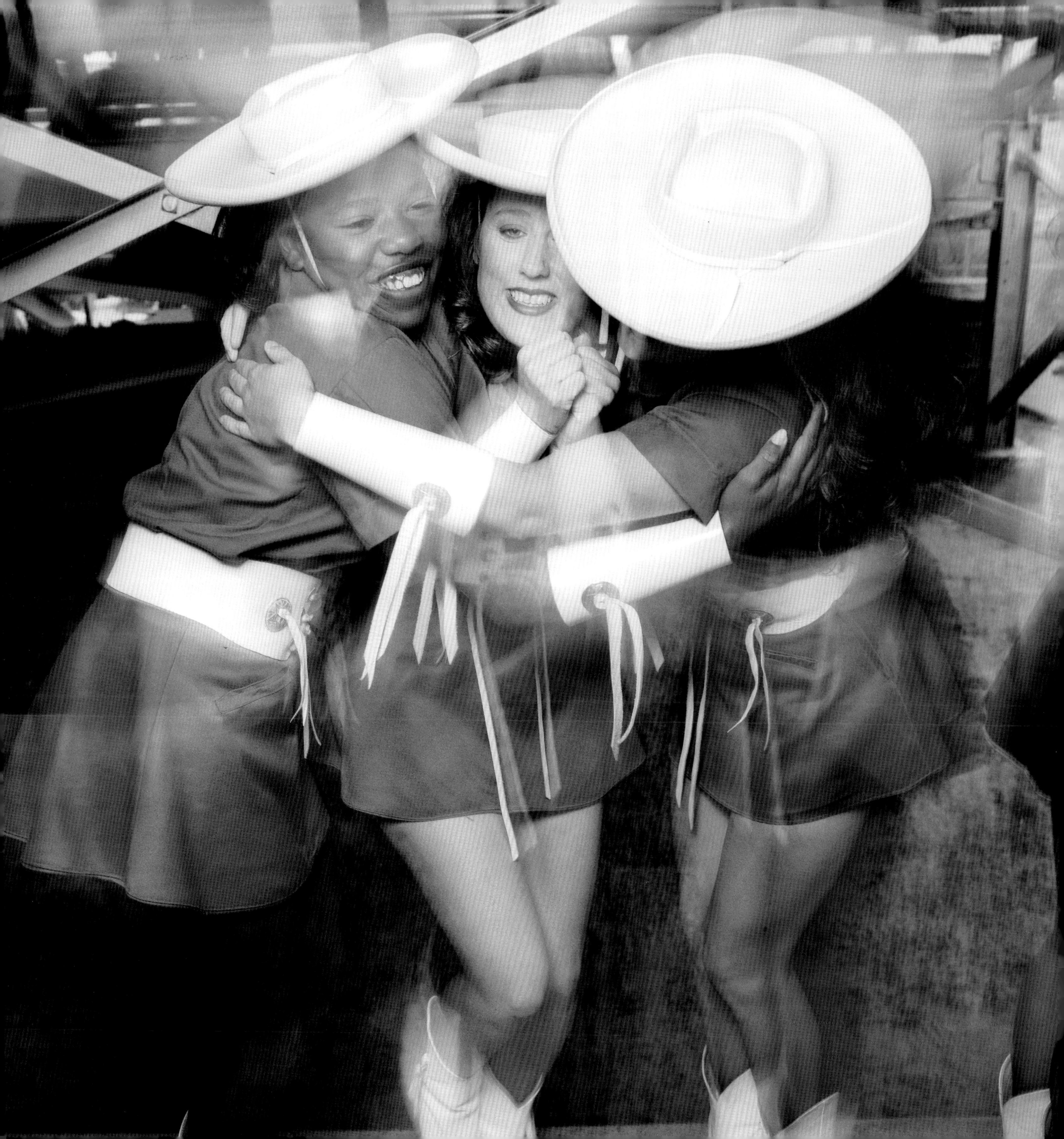

THE RANGERETTE PROJECT

O. RUFUS LOVETT

The path that led to my fascination with photographing the Rangerettes began decades ago, in the 1960s. It was in Alabama, as a boy, that I first saw a dance drill team, the Marching Ballerinas. My dad was the photographer at Jacksonville State University, and as he filmed the football games atop the press box, I had the best seat in the stadium for viewing the halftime performances. It wasn't until about a decade later, when I arrived in Texas to go to school, that I first heard of the Rangerettes. A friend's sister told me she was a "Wranglerette [a member of a drill team at a Houston high school], not to be confused with the famous Rangerettes."

A few years later, as a photography student, I was investigating Elliott Erwitt's photographic style and wit. In my research I saw a picture of him in Kilgore, Texas, with a group of Rangerettes. This was perhaps a sign (unrealized at the time), since I have now been a teacher at Kilgore College for thirty years. It was not long after joining Kilgore College that I found myself atop another press box at football games, filming for the coaching staff and watching the halftime performances of the Rangerettes. During this period, each semester I would share with my photography students *Beauty Knows No Pain* by Elliott Erwitt, a compelling black-and-white documentary that portrays the Rangerettes. I remember, on more than one occasion in my past, hearing graduate students who were studying sociology and psychology refer to this film about the Rangerettes, since it was used as a study in human behavior.

I spent about a decade filming these weekend small-town football extravaganzas, viewing Rangerette performances, and reviewing the Erwitt film, more times than I can remember. As a consequence I felt bound to project my photographic interest concerning the 'Rettes. I retired from making the game films to allow myself time on the field to take pictures. It was not by design, but by chance, that I began this project on the Rangerettes' fiftieth anniversary in 1989.

Precision, discipline, beauty, prestige, tradition—all are attributes that I have heard used to describe the Kilgore College Rangerettes, the nation's first dance drill team. A classic cultural icon, the Rangerettes, in all their beauty, pageantry, and patriotic red, white, and blue uniforms, have met with several United States presidents, have been featured in hundreds of publications including *Life, Newsweek, Esquire,* and *Texas Monthly*, and have performed coast to coast in the United States and in eight foreign countries. Yet none of these achievements is what drew me to photograph their public performances and rehearsals.

I am intrigued by the glamour of the Rangerettes' performances juxtaposed with the small-town atmosphere, football turf, metal bleachers, chain-link fences, and asphalt and concrete environment. Also interesting is the sense that my human subjects are not transformed into portraits of personalities, but rather into still-life images of place. Because the Rangerettes appear as an ensemble, a loss of personal identity often occurs; the individuals become depictions of shapes, patterns, and designs.

And finally, there is a certain timeless quality possessed by the Rangerettes—one that recalls the wonderment of my boyhood, and those many Saturday evenings with my dad atop the football stadium press box.

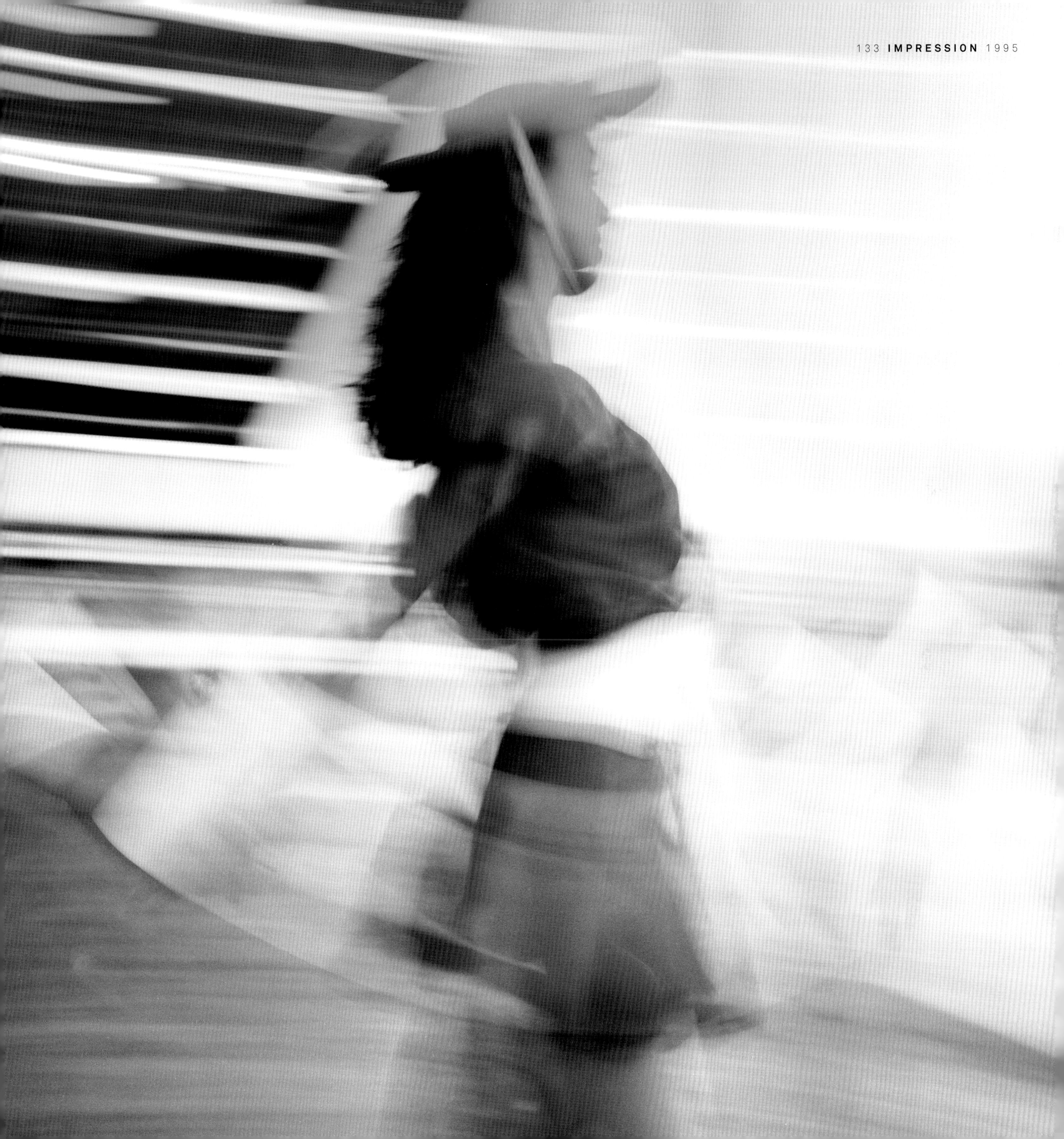

THE **PLATES**

ACKNOWLEDGMENTS

In the beginning, Gussie Nell Davis created the Kilgore College Rangerettes. Thank you, Miss Davis.

It is the second director of the Rangerettes, Deana Bolton Covin, to whom I owe gratitude for allowing me to travel with the Rangerettes when I began this photographic project in 1989. Thank you also to Dana Blair, the third director of the Rangerettes, and the assistant director and choreographer Shelley Wayne. It is with genuine sincerity that I acknowledge the decades of Kilgore College Rangerettes and the Rangerette Forevers as collaborators in this effort. It was their spirit, discipline, and kindness that sustained my energy to continue photographing the Rangerettes.

I wish to express my gratitude to all my friends in the photographic art community who have supported this work. It is my longtime friend, artist Gary Frields, whose encouragement meant so much at the inception of this project. Artists Mary McCleary and Robert Kinsel have offered thoughtful responses to the pictures since the project's beginnings; I will always be grateful for their input. Thank you to Clint Willour, whose interpretations and sense of humor are very much appreciated. Bill Wittliff's photographic work and his Southwestern and Mexican Photography collection are truly motivations to us all. And I thank my friend Gary Borders, who played a positive instrumental role in the first reproduction of this Rangerette project.

In 1990, it was DJ Stout who first published "Pauline," the high-kick picture, in *Texas Monthly*. DJ's distinctive vision respects the image in a way that endows the book design with an extraordinary quality. Thanks to DJ and Julie Savasky for the magnificent design of this book.

Anne Wilkes Tucker and Roy Flukinger were also among the first to recognize the importance of this series of photographs. I appreciate their years of support and encouragement. Thanks are also due to Anne for introducing me to Elliott Erwitt. I am tremendously honored to have Elliott's writing included in this publication. The foreword he wrote for this book reflects a sincere appreciation for the photographic subject and the importance of interpreting life as we discover it. His photographs and wit will always be an inspiration. Elliott Erwitt, I thank you.

Katy Vine's wonderful introduction that graces the pages of this book echoes her personal experience with the Rangerettes. Her exceptional, insightful writing is immensely appreciated.

Perhaps the circle of life for a teacher is complete when the teacher becomes the student of the student. Thank you to Scott C. Campbell for his loyalty as a friend and colleague. The digital technology that he so graciously shared enhanced the reproduction of this book.

It is with deep appreciation and affection that I extend thanks to Richard and Martha Rorschach for their thirty years of friendship and their kind generosity toward the production of this book. Also, I wish to express my gratitude to Clifton and Shirley Caldwell and the National Endowment for the Humanities for making this book possible.

I would like to pass along a sincere thank-you to all the staff at UT Press who helped produce this book. Cheers to you, Bill Bishel, Ellen McKie, Lynne Chapman, and Nancy Bryan. Finally, I extend particular appreciation to Dave Hamrick for his interest in photography, his confidence, and our shared sense of humor.

I will always be most grateful for the love and support of my family. Thank you, Frances, and thank you, Dad.